Raising Standards in Literacy

Edited by Ros Fisher, Greg Brooks and Maureen Lewis

ROUTLEDGE / FALMER
Taylor & Francis Group

London and New York

First published 2002
by RoutledgeFalmer
11 New Fetter Lane, London EC4P 4EE

Simultaneously published in the USA and Canada
by RoutledgeFalmer
29 West 35th Street, New York, NY 10001

RoutledgeFalmer is an imprint of the Taylor & Francis Group

© 2002 selection and editorial matter, Ros Fisher, Greg Brooks and
Maureen Lewis © individual chapters, the contributors

Typeset in Sabon by Taylor & Francis Books Ltd
Printed and bound in Great Britain by MPG Books Ltd, Bodmin

British Library Cataloguing in Publication Data
A catalogue record for this book is available from the British Library

Library of Congress Cataloging in Publication Data
A catalog record has been requested for this title

ISBN 0–415–26350–6 (hbk)
ISBN 0–415–26351–4 (pbk)

Raising Standards in Literacy

Raising Standards in Literacy represents the best of current thinking and research about literacy. The book is the outcome of a high-profile series of seminars on raising standards in literacy, and includes contributions from an impressive group of international researchers and policy makers. By offering a rich and unique mix of contemporary perspectives, this book provides an invaluable source of study into the latest research and developments in the teaching of literacy.

It includes sections on:

- how research into literacy teaching can inform new approaches found in England, the USA and Australia
- the issues involved in assessing progress in literacy and the validity of research claims made about standards of attainment
- the ways in which literacy education is developing in England, the USA and Australia.

The book celebrates the apparent success of current initiatives at the same time as raising questions about the feasibility and relevance of such initiatives to the literacy needs of the twenty-first century. It is essential reading for literacy co-ordinators and consultants and for all those undertaking further study or research in literacy education.

Ros Fisher is Reader in Literacy Education at Rolle School of Education, University of Plymouth.

Greg Brooks is a Professorial Research Fellow at the University of Sheffield.

Maureen Lewis is a Senior Lecturer in Language and Literacy at the University of Plymouth.

Language and Literacy in Action Series
Series Editor: David Wray

Contents

Illustrations

Figures

Tables

Contributors

Mary Bailey is Lecturer in English Education in the Centre for Literacy Studies at the University of Nottingham School of Education. Prior to taking up this post she researched cognitive processes in writing, before teaching English in secondary schools for ten years.

Roger Beard has taught in primary schools and a college of higher education and is now Reader in Literacy Education at the University of Leeds. In 1998 he was commissioned by the Department for Education and Employment to write the Review of Research and Other Related Evidence for the National Literacy Strategy.

Greg Brooks is at the School of Education, University of Sheffield. He has worked full-time in educational research for over twenty years, and directed many literacy-related projects and evaluations. His most recent report is *Progress in Adult Literacy: Do Learners Learn?* (G. Brooks *et al.*, London: Basic Skills Agency, 2001).

Victoria Carrington is a Lecturer in Education at the University of Queensland. Her research interests include sociology of literacy, Middle Years of Schooling, and globalisation theory.

Gillian Essex has taught in many settings, most recently as head teacher of a primary school. She is currently a Manager in the Learning and Teaching Innovation Division of the Department of Education, Employment and Training in Victoria. She co-ordinated the Early Literacy Research Project and is the co-author of a number of components of the Early Years Literacy Program.

Ros Fisher has taught in primary schools in the north-west of England and in the USA. She is now Reader in Literacy Education at Rolle School of Education at the University of Plymouth working with initial training students and teachers. She writes widely about the teaching of early literacy and is currently researching the development of teachers in the NLS. She has recently written *Inside the Literacy Hour* (Routledge 2002).

Eve Gregory is Professor of Language and Culture in Education, Goldsmiths College, University of London. Her books include *Making Sense of a New World: Learning to Read in a Second Language* (Sage 1996), *One Child, Many Worlds: Early Learning in Multicultural Communities* (Fulton and Teachers' College Press 1997) and *City Literacies: Learning to Read Across Generations and Cultures* (joint author, Ann Williams) (Routledge 2000).

Colin Harrison is Professor of Literacy Studies in Education at the University of Nottingham. He is a former President of the United Kingdom Reading Association. His main research interests are reading comprehension, curriculum evaluation and new technologies.

Elfrieda H. Hiebert is a professor in the School of Education at the University of Michigan. Hiebert has worked in the field of reading education for more than thirty years as a teacher and as a teacher educator and researcher. Her research on how instructional and assessment practices influence literacy acquisition, especially among low-income children, has been widely published and cited.

James V. Hoffman is Professor of Language and Literacy Studies at The University of Texas at Austin and is an affiliated scholar with CIERA (The Centre for the Improvement of Early Reading Achievement). His research interests are focused in the areas of beginning reading, texts and reading teacher preparation. Jim is Past President of the National Reading Conference and former editor of the *Reading Research Quarterly*. He currently serves as editor of *The Yearbook of the National Reading Conference*.

Sue Horner is the leader of the English, literacy and communications team at the Qualifications and Curriculum Authority in England. The Authority is responsible for the National Curriculum and its assessments, and for the regulation of public examinations. The English team focuses on provision in the English Language Arts for those from age 3 to adults.

Laura Huxford was appointed director of training of the National Literacy Strategy in 1998. Her teaching career spanned primary and special education and she spent ten years in teacher training.

Clare Kelly was an Assistant Director at the Centre for Language in Primary Education before she took up her present post as co-ordinator of Primary English courses at Goldsmiths. Her main areas of research and publication are early literacy, the teaching of reading and social and cultural literacy practices at home and school.

Maureen Lewis is a Senior Lecturer in Language and Literacy at the University of Plymouth. She is an experienced teacher and researcher and was co-director of the influential Nuffield *Extending Literacy*

Project. She has published widely on many aspects of literacy but is best known for her work on reading and writing non-fiction texts and the development of 'writing frames'. She has previously published *Extending Literacy: Children Reading and Writing Non-fiction* with Routledge.

Allan Luke teaches literacy education, sociology and policy studies at the University of Queensland, Australia. His work on language and literacy includes: *Literacy, Textbooks and Ideology* (Falmer 1988), *Towards a Critical Sociology of Reading Pedagogy* (Benjamins 1990), *The Social Construction of Literacy in the Classroom* (Macmillan 1994) and *Constructing Critical Literacies* (Hampton 1997). He recently completed the *'New Basics' Curriculum Reform, Literate Futures: The Queensland State Literacy Policy* and is currently Chief Advisor to the Minister of Education.

Jane Medwell is a former primary school teacher, currently Lecturer in Literacy Education at the University of Warwick. She has carried out a number of research projects into aspects of literacy education and has written numerous books and articles on topics ranging from the use of electronic books with young children, to classroom contexts for writing.

The National Commission on Excellence in Elementary Teacher Preparation for Reading Instruction is a Commission of the International Reading Association. The charge of the Commission is to conduct research on the impact of reading teacher education programmes on beginning teachers' reading instruction. The International Reading Association is a network of over 350,000 reading professionals who are members, institutions, councils and affiliates. The purpose of the Association is to improve reading instruction and reading achievement. **Cathy M. Roller** is Director of Research and Policy for the International Reading Association. Prior to 1998 when she assumed this post she was a reading teacher educator and researcher at the University of Iowa for 19 years.

Victoria Purcell-Gates is Professor of Literacy at Michigan State University. Her research covers literacy development across the ages and much of it is located in community literacy practice. She has taught struggling readers for over 30 years, serving as director at several university-based literacy clinics.

Bridie Raban is the Inaugural Mooroolbeek Chair of Early Childhood at the University of Melbourne, Australia, where she is also Director of the Early Education Research Unit. She is keenly interested in the literacy development of all children and currently trains the Reading Recovery tutors in Victoria and Tasmania, Australia.

Marian Sainsbury is a Deputy Head of the Department of Assessment and Measurement at the National Foundation for Educational Research. She is currently director of the projects developing the national tests in English at Key Stages 1 and 2 for England and Wales.

Ann Williams is a research fellow at Goldsmiths and Kings Colleges, University of London. Having worked as a language teacher in a variety of contexts, her research interests lie in literacy and the phonological and grammatical aspects of modern British English. She has carried out many funded projects and is the author, with Eve Gregory, of *City Literacies: Learning to Read across Generations and Cultures*.

David Wray taught in primary schools and is currently Professor of Literacy Education at the University of Warwick. He has published 40 books on aspects of literacy teaching and is best known for his work on the *Extending Literacy (EXEL) Project*, funded by the Nuffield Foundation, which was concerned with helping pupils at all levels read and write information texts effectively.

Series editor's preface

David Wray

There can be few areas of educational endeavour which have been more controversial than that of teaching literacy. Perhaps because, in an increasingly information-dense society, the ability to make sense of and to produce text is self-evidently crucial to success, even survival, literacy has assumed the major burden as a litmus test of 'educatedness'. With such a critical role in the process of becoming educated, it is inevitable that there will continue to be major debates about exactly what it means to be literate, and about how such a state might most effectively be brought about – that is, how literacy is taught. A proportion of the energy behind such debates has come from the diverse findings of research into processes and pedagogy. Yet much of the debate, especially in the popular media, has lacked a close reference to research findings and has focused instead on somewhat emotional reactions and prejudices.

Students of literacy and literacy education who want to move beyond the superficiality of mass media debates need access to reports and discussions of key research findings. There is plenty such material, yet it tends to suffer from two major problems. First, it can be rather difficult to locate as it has tended to be published in a diverse range of academic journals, papers and monographs. Secondly, research reports are usually written for an academic audience and make great demands on practitioners and others who wish to understand what the practical classroom implications are of what the research reports.

It is to address both these problems, but especially the latter, that this series has been developed. The books in the series deal with aspects of the teaching of literacy and language in a variety of educational settings. The main feature of all the contributing volumes is to provide a research-grounded background for teaching action in literacy and language. The books either, therefore, provide a review of existing research and theory in an area, or an account of original research, together with a clear résumé and/or set of suggestions as to how this background might influence the teaching of this area. The series acts, therefore, as a bridge between academic research books and practical teaching handbooks.

Raising Standards in Literacy

This is the third volume in the series and is the first edited collection. The chapters in this book originated, in the main, as presentations at a series of seminars organised by the editors, along with Colin Harrison, and sponsored by the Economic and Social Research Council. These seminars involved a number of researchers and educationalists from both the UK and the USA and focused on the somewhat vexed issue of standards in literacy and current strategies for raising these.

Raising literacy standards is, of course, the subject of intense debate and interest internationally. In the twenty-first century, no country with aspirations for economic and intellectual success can afford to take for granted increasing literacy in its population. Accordingly, most governments have instituted, or are about to institute, major changes in curricula, pedagogy and teacher preparation for literacy development in schools. These developments are under way now, and the pace of change promises only to accelerate.

One kind of voice which has not always had the impact it perhaps might have had on the nature of these changes in literacy curricula and pedagogies is that of the researcher, or academic. The present book attempts to redress this somewhat by presenting material written from a research perspective. It includes papers on teacher preparation, effective teaching of literacy, insights into reading comprehension and approaches to assessment, to mention just a few topics. It will find a ready readership not only among fellow researchers but also among teachers who wish to probe beyond received wisdoms in teaching literacy.

David Wray
University of Warwick
January 2002

Introduction

Ros Fisher, Greg Brooks and Maureen Lewis

This book arose out of an Economic and Social Research Council (UK) funded international research seminar series entitled 'Raising Standards in Literacy' that was held during 1999–2000. The issue of literacy standards has been a topic of heated debate for many years. Closely tied to this debate have always been concerns about whether different teaching methods and teaching styles impact upon the standards of literacy children achieve and how these standards can be measured. This is an international debate. Different paradigms of literacy teaching are under review worldwide.

The seminar group was set up at the same time as the National Literacy Strategy (NLS) was launched throughout England as a key UK government strategy to raise standards of literacy. There has never before been such a far-reaching government initiative to influence directly the teaching and learning of reading and writing. Many of the teaching methods and the organisational structure of the NLS are based on research and practice from other parts of the English-speaking world, but in 1998 they represented new ways of working for many teachers in the UK.

The seminar series aimed to gather together key researchers, policy makers and invited international experts in the field of literacy teaching in order to offer a forum for examining and laying open to scrutiny, within the academic community and beyond, the tacit and explicit assumptions which underpin the National Literacy Strategy. The seminar series was focused on both cognition and pedagogy. It aimed to encourage a debate that was necessary, but which had only just begun to take place at that time within the research community, in order to identify and make available for policy-makers, teachers and other academics an analysis of the current strategy and recommendations for development which draw upon the best of current international research.

Three seminars took place, each over two days, and were held at the University of Plymouth, Rolle School of Education (May 1999), National Foundation for Educational Research (November 1999) and the University of Nottingham (May 2000). Researchers from England and the United States met with policy makers from the English National Literacy Strategy, the Qualifications and Curriculum Authority (QCA) and the Office for Standards in Education (Ofsted) to discuss recent research and policy initiatives. This book contains most of the papers given at the seminars and all of these have been updated in 2001. In addition, the book contains two contributions from Australia that are also concerned with the question of literacy standards.

The book is set out in three sections. Part I, 'Research into the teaching of literacy', discusses how research about all aspects of the teaching of literacy can inform new approaches to be found in England, the USA and Australia. The collection of chapters offers both research reviews and descriptions of specific research studies.

Colin Harrison and Mary Bailey, both from the University of Nottingham, begin by offering research reviews that summarise evidence in answer to important questions related to literacy. In his chapter 'What does research tell us about how to develop comprehension?', Harrison argues that there has been an enormous amount of research activity in this area in the last decade or so and that a characteristic of this has been an emphasis on collaborative or interactive approaches to reading. He claims there is a consensus view emerging of how to develop reading comprehension, which is firmly based on research.

Mary Bailey considers 'What does research tell us about how we should be developing written composition?' from several research perspectives. From these differing perspectives she identifies pedagogical themes that are common to all but points out that within this consensus there are differing emphases on the role of explicit teaching and the teaching of metalanguage.

Following these overviews into two major aspects of literacy, Roger Beard of the University of Leeds argues that, because the National Literacy Strategy was based on research into what works, it was always likely to be successful in its stated aim of raising standards. He makes the point that it is the combination of research from the area of school effectiveness with research about effective literacy practices that is one of the distinct features of the creation of the strategy.

Following these three research overviews, David Wray and Jane Medwell of the University of Warwick offer us a report on a specific research project that was commissioned to enquire into the characteristics and practices of effective teachers of literacy. Their findings show that effective teachers do display common characteristics and literacy teaching practices. Although this study predates the introduction of the National Literacy Strategy (with its extensive in-service programme for all primary teachers), it offers us useful indications as to what it is teachers need to know and understand – not least of which is their finding that effective teachers of literacy have an extensive knowledge of texts.

Clare Kelly, Eve Gregory and Ann Williams, from the University of London Goldsmiths' College, move our focus from teachers and schools to

children and their community literacy practices. Their research
timely reminder that literacy practices are aspects not only of
also of power structures, and that school-sanctioned literacy i
a multiplicity of literacies which take place in peoples' lives. T
question of how far classroom-based literacy practices acknowledge
value children's community literacies. This theme is taken up in the
following two sections.

The final chapter of Part I describes an analysis of the words used in
basal readers (reading schemes) in the USA over the last few decades. Jim
Hoffman of the University of Texas suggests that these reflect the
prevailing ideology. He argues that, rather than reflecting the growing
consensus on how to teach reading (as reflected in Colin Harrison's
chapter), basal reading schemes in Texas have continued to reflect a divide
between literature-based texts to improve content and interest and texts
with increased decodability. This has led to a decrease in predictable text
features as well as a decrease in text quality.

Maureen Lewis from the University of Plymouth concludes Part I with a
reflection on its chapters. She argues that, with the major government
educational agencies in the UK, the USA and Australia increasingly
stressing the need for educational reform to be driven by research findings,
the kind of research and research reviews offered in this section give a
powerful rebuttal to claims that much educational research is irrelevant,
'pseudo-academic obfuscation' (Woodhead, 1998). The importance of
well-founded data is an issue that runs through the whole book, and is
explored in Part II through the theme of assessment.

The second section of the book, 'What counts as evidence?', looks at
the issues involved in assessing progress in literacy and considers the
validity of the research claims made about assessment of literacy, and
about whether standards are being raised.

Vicky Purcell-Gates of Michigan State University raises strong concerns
about the trend in the United States towards (back?) to simple definitions
of reading and the dangers she sees in this, especially the neglect of the
socio-cultural aspect.

Sue Horner of the Qualifications and Curriculum Authority for England
describes some of the complexity of the construct of reading underlying
the national tests for 7-, 11- and 14-year-olds in England.

Marian Sainsbury of the National Foundation for Educational Research
in England analyses the problems inherent in devising any half-decent
(valid and reliable) test, and gives detailed examples of processes involved
in doing so.

Greg Brooks, now at the University of Sheffield in England but previously for 20 years at the National Foundation for Educational Research,
presents a 'counting of the evidence' on whether standards are rising/being
raised in four spheres: the link between pre-school experience and early

literacy development, initial literacy learning, helping struggling readers and adult literacy. Apart from some aspects of initial teaching and learning, he finds the field underdeveloped.

Finally, Greg Brooks considers the issues raised in this section and suggests that the chapters represent a logical sequence – from deciding how literacy is to be defined, through the development of good instruments to measure it, and on to findings. He claims that the first two of these are in better shape than the third.

In Part III, 'Developing teacher practice', the ways in which the issue of raising standards of literacy is being addressed in England, the USA and parts of Australia are explored. The first two chapters in this section focus on issues related to raising standards in literacy in the USA: the first looks at initial teacher education and the second at state- and school-based initiatives. In both these chapters the diversity and different approaches current in the USA are discussed.

Elfrieda Hiebert from the University of Michigan reviews the predominant means by which American states and schools are addressing the drive to meet the literacy needs of the twenty-first century: reading textbooks and model programmes. She argues that none of the initiatives or mandates are supported by untainted research evidence and suggests that the two types of initiative should be considered together, and evidence as to their efficacy sought and attended to.

Cathy Roller, director of research and policy with the International Reading Association, reports on the work of the National Commission on Excellence in Elementary Teacher Preparation for Reading Instruction. She describes what appear to be effective in teacher education programmes in the USA.

The two chapters that follow consider the introduction of the National Literacy Strategy in England. This initiative (together with the National Numeracy Strategy) has been described by the international team from Ontario, Canada under Michael Fullan as 'among the most ambitious large-scale educational reform strategies in the world and, without question ... among the most explicit and comprehensive in their attention to what is required for successful implementation' (Earl *et al.*, 2000: 1).

Laura Huxford, deputy director of the National Literacy Strategy in England, reviews the introduction of the NLS and explains the supporting programmes that have underpinned its implementation. She argues strongly that the strategy is successful in raising standards despite early claims that it was over-ambitious.

Maureen Lewis and Ros Fisher from the University of Plymouth consider how the NLS has impacted on individual classrooms. From a small sample of classrooms in the first two years of the strategy, they argue that whereas some considerable changes have been made in the organisation of literacy teaching, change in pedagogy is not so well established in all classrooms.

Australia, like the United States, adopts different approaches according to individual state or school policy. However, the literacy block that is widely used in this country shares many features of literacy programmes elsewhere.

Bridie Raban from the University of Melbourne and Gillian Essex, manager in the Learning and Teaching Innovation Division of the Department of Education, Employment and Training in Victoria, describe the Victoria Early Years Literacy Programme. This programme, with its two-hour literacy block, has many similarities to the National Literacy Strategy, but also many differences. The authors claim that large gains in reading achievement have been achieved, and that the programme has 'raised the status of teachers as professionals'.

On the other hand, Allan Luke and Victoria Carrington from the University of Queensland describe an initiative that rejects current pre-packaged literacy programmes that stand alone in favour of adopting, they claim, an over-simplistic and reductionist view of literacy. They argue that current ways of literacy teaching are based on anachronistic views of literacy and a deficit model of children and teaching, and suggest that literacy learning should be based within broader curriculum and cultural contexts.

Conclusions

The varied themes and issues that are picked up and explored in this book indicate many agreements and some differences in the three countries represented here. The recognition that there is a need to educate children for the literacy demands of the twenty-first century is undisputed, whether seen as resulting from previous low standards or as a concern to improve on existing practice. There is a sense that we need to learn from each other – both from research and from policy initiatives in other parts of the world. Differences lie in the extent to which raising standards is seen as an issue with many possible solutions and the freedom to choose different solutions, or an issue with a single externally prescribed approach. And, allied to this, is the extent to which the local context can be trusted to implement and evaluate its own solutions. Underlying all sections of the book is a plea for education to recognise the diverse and rich backgrounds of the pupils whose needs are the focus of our endeavour.

A striking difference that arises from these chapters is the extent to which writing is seen as an integral part of literacy. Writing is foregrounded in nearly all the chapters written by English authors, whereas the terms 'reading' and 'literacy' seem to be used almost synonymously by Australian and American authors. It was interesting to discover that when results from writing assessments were requested for the Victoria Early Years Literacy Programme, none were readily available.

Although each chapter can be read separately, in its entirety the book provides a snapshot of the state of play in literacy research and reform from three continents. It also presents a picture of academics and policy makers engaging in debate in an endeavour to ensure that children learn to use and enjoy the possibilities that literacy offers in the twenty-first century.

References

Earl, L., Fullan, M., Leithwood, K. and Watson, N. (2000) *Watching and Learning: First Annual Report of OISE/UT Evaluation of the Implementation of the National Literacy and Numeracy Strategies*, Ontario Institute for Studies in Education, University of Toronto, January 2000.

Woodhead, C. (1998) 'Academia gone to seed', *New Statesman* 11 (20 March): 51.

Part I

Research into the teaching of literacy

1 What does research tell us about how to develop comprehension?

Colin Harrison

Introduction

It is easy to make the assumption that we know about reading comprehension. It's the part of reading that's beyond word recognition, it's about understanding what we read, and it develops gradually and 'naturally', as a reader becomes more fluent, and more experienced, and more confident. This is the common sense view, but I want to challenge it and to suggest that reading comprehension does not develop 'naturally', that it can be helpful to consider separately the development of reading fluency and the development of reading comprehension and that, broadly speaking, current research suggests that reading comprehension is harder to get at, harder to develop, and even more complex than we had realised.

In advancing this argument, I want to give attention to four questions:

• What do we know about comprehension?
• What do we know about how people learn to improve their comprehension?
• What do publishers, the National Curriculum and the National Literacy Strategy (NLS) in England have to say about developing comprehension?
• In the light of the answers to the first three questions, what should we be doing to develop comprehension?

What do we know about comprehension?

If we want to begin at the beginning, it's never wrong to begin with definitions, and the dictionary. But in the case of comprehension, we hit a difficulty. Definitions of the word *comprehension* are sometimes vague and mostly problematic, one way or another. The *Oxford English Dictionary* (*OED*) has:

> the action of comprehending; the action or fact of comprehending with the mind; understanding. The ability to understand a passage of text and answer questions on it, as at school or psychological exercise.

The first part of this definition is circular, and even the reference to a synonym, *understanding*, does not carry us very far forward. The second part of the definition is tautological: *comprehension* is what a comprehension test tests. Similarly, *Chambers Dictionary* defines *comprehension* as the *power of the mind to understand*, and then goes on to define to *understand* as to *comprehend*. *Webster's Collegiate Dictionary* gives *the act or action of grasping with the intellect: understanding*, and then works hard to avoid circularity in its definitions of *understand*, putting an emphasis on the very different ways the verb is used in context, but finally noting that the words *comprehension* and *understanding* are often used interchangeably.

The International Reading Association's (IRA) *Dictionary of Reading* (1982, subsequently revised) takes us further and gives:

> the process of getting meaning of a communication, as in a personal letter, speech, sign language; the knowledge or understanding that is the result of such a process.

This is a fuller definition, and while it gives more exemplars, it also turns primarily on our interpretation of the word *understanding*. The IRA dictionary does, however, give much fuller definitions of *reading*: definitions which are complex, and which include not only comprehension, but also notions of *behavioural adaptation* in the light of what is read. The IRA dictionary defines *reading comprehension* just as fully, and its multiple definitions include:

- understanding what is read
- understanding in relation to a presumed hierarchy of comprehension processes
- interpreting
- evaluating
- reacting in a creative, intuitive way.

The IRA dictionary definition of reading comprehension (Harris and Hodges, 1981) also quotes two definitions from authoritative sources, researchers who conducted classical studies in the field:

> Comprehension involves the recovery and interpretation of the abstract deep structural relations underlying sentences (Bransford and Johnson)

> Comprehension is a process of integrating new sentences with antecedent information in extrasentential structures (P. Thorndyke).

We can discern two strands within these approaches to definition:

- Definitions which talk about the *products* of reading
- Definitions which attempt to get at the *processes* of reading.

It is not easy to get at the processes that underpin reading comprehension, but it is much easier to get at the products, or at least some of them, and so it is understandable that some definitions should define comprehension in relation to test data, since such definitions are at least based on evidence and practice rather than theories. However, I want to argue that we can't develop comprehension unless we have a deeper understanding of what it is about, and to do this we have to consider the processes.

Both definitions of the IRA *Dictionary of Reading* say helpful and illuminating things about the processes. Bransford and Johnson's definition emphasises the fact that comprehension is not simply about vocabulary, and it's not about surface meaning. It is about getting under the surface and gaining some understanding of the relationships between the structural elements – whether these are words, concepts or propositions. Thorndyke's definition takes the theme of processing and integrating chunks of information two stages further. It first emphasises the importance within comprehension of the reader's integration of new information with that which has gone before (we could characterise this as creating internal cohesion); at the same time, the reader is also relating new information encountered in a text to their own model of the world, and these are the extrasentential structures to which Thorndyke's definition refers. (We could characterise this as creating external cohesion.) Taken together, these two definitions go a long way towards clarifying for us how challenging, complex and individual are the processes of comprehension.

Historically, debates about the nature of reading comprehension have been something of a battleground, and these debates have been particularly vociferous around the theme of the supposed sub-skills of reading comprehension. The basic issue has been a twofold one: first to identify the sub-skills of comprehension, and second to establish whether or not they form some sort of hierarchy. Such debates flourished in the post-war period, and we might have forgotten them by now were it not that their legacy has been so enduring, and this legacy has taken the form of reading comprehension exercises based on such models.

With hindsight, it is reasonable to ask why on earth generations of schoolchildren have been required to spend time doing comprehension exercises. After all, we don't have children doing sentence composing exercises to improve their writing, or oral presentation exercises to improve their speaking. Why should readers spend time doing comprehension exercises? One possible answer might be in order to prepare for high-stakes tests involving a similar instrument, but, in reality, most teachers who give comprehension exercises do so with the expectation that doing them is worthwhile in its own right, and that some general improvement in reading might be the result. Unfortunately, this expectation may be little more than an assumption based on teachers' custom and practice, and the research evidence to support it is weak. There has been a good deal of research into the presumed hierarchy of comprehension processes, mostly based on a series of factor-analytical studies conducted in the period 1945–80 (see, for example Davis, 1944; Lunzer, Waite and Dolan, 1979). Many of these studies were essentially attempts to enlist support for what we may call a prescription model of comprehension skills development.

In the prescription model, the student takes a comprehension test, and is given a score on each of the sub-skill areas. The teacher then decides in which of the supposed sub-skills the reader is deficient, and then gives additional skills practice in the form of comprehension exercises focused on the individual sub-skills, until the reader's deficiency is remedied. The following is an example of the type of sub-skills list used in these studies:

- Vocabulary
- Literal comprehension
- Inferential comprehension
- Locating the main idea
- Evaluation.

However, this approach is flawed in a number of ways. First, it only works if the skills are indeed in some sense independent – but the consensus view from the research studies is that they aren't. Certainly the tasks, and therefore the products of different 'sub-skill' areas, look different, but this does not mean that the cognitive processes involved are different. The different 'sub-skill' scales tend to correlate with each other very highly, with correlations in the range 0.6–0.7. This suggests that the supposed sub-skills are essentially measuring the same thing. Second, the prescription approach only works if giving students comprehension exercises is effective in developing reading comprehension, and here again the research evidence is problematic. The Effective Use of Reading Project (Lunzer and Gardner, 1979), in a landmark study of comprehension development, found that students doing comprehension exercises actually did very little reading. Children who were focused on a reading comprehension task actually spent less than 5 per cent of their time reading, but used 65 per cent of their time in writing. In other words, the skill that was being practised was answering comprehension questions in writing, rather than reading. So even if reading comprehension scores went up, this could be attributable to a practice effect in writing comprehension test answers, rather than in improving the construct of reading itself.

An even greater problem, from a pedagogical viewpoint, is that comprehension exercises provided little or no feedback from which students might learn how to improve. This was felt by the Effective Use of Reading team to be crucial, since without feedback students might have improved in terms of fluency, but were much less likely to improve in terms of comprehension.

The argument here is supported by a quite extensive but little-known study by Bloomer (1966), an American researcher into cloze procedure. In the early days, cloze procedure was thought to hold a great deal of promise as a reading development activity. After all, the reasoning goes, it is impossible to fill in the gaps in a cloze exercise without undertaking some processing at a fairly deep level. Consider the following sentence, and the cognitive challenge of filling in the missing word:

> The boy and girl, ——————————— and wife now, father and mother, lived in a three-room apartment under a dentist's office.
> (from *Distance*, a short story by Raymond Carver)

Adults who are asked to fill in the missing word all report the same thing: it is completely impossible to predict the missing word simply on the basis of the first four words of the sentence. If they are given the remainder of the sentence, however, three things happen. First they rapidly deduce that the missing word is *husband*, working from the symmetry with *boy and girl*, and the familiar collocation of *husband and wife*. But then, they go on and read the rest of the sentence, and realise that things may not be so simple. Why does the author say *now*? Are there two people or six living in the apartment? There is a further round of reprocessing, before they decide that the answer is that two people who have known each other since childhood, and who are now married with a child or children, live in the apartment.

The fact that the task of filling in the gaps in a text can involve such deep processing led (and still leads) teachers to feel that cloze might be very useful for promoting reading development. What Bloomer did was to test this intuition empirically. He gave junior high school students weeks of practice in doing cloze exercises and then tested their reading levels against those of a control group. The result was disappointing – the students who had spent weeks doing cloze exercises, and, one hoped, had been processing texts deeply in order to do so, had not improved. However, with hindsight, one can see why this might have happened. What the students had been doing were what Bloomer called 'non-overt-reinforced' cloze exercises. In other words, the students did not receive any reinforcement, any feedback, on their answers, whether those answers were correct or incorrect. In fact, in structural terms, what the students had been doing for many weeks were a series of reading tests – tests which confirmed the level of their reading ability, but which did nothing to improve that level. From a pedagogical point of view, non-overt-reinforced cloze exercises were a flop. But if this is the case for cloze, are comprehension exercises any different? The answer again is no. Unless there is feedback on the basis of which the reader may learn how to become a more skilled or more thoughtful reader, comprehension exercises, on which teachers have relied for decades to play their part in reading development, may be a more or less complete waste of time.

What do we know about how people develop their comprehension?

During the last twenty years of the twentieth century there was an enormous amount of activity in the psychology of reading, so let us turn to some recent accounts of where recent research has taken us. First, let us admit that it is not easy to gain a coherent impression of the work that has been done in researching the complexities of reading comprehension. Walter Kintsch, who has made one of the most ambitious attempts to produce a coherent account of reading comprehension processes (Kintsch, 1998), begins his book by saying that psychologists have not been successful at researching complex cognitive processes in a coherent and integrated manner. Michael Pressley, who has conducted some of the most thoughtful and detailed classroom-based studies of reading comprehension yet attempted, noted that research into reading comprehension has been either naturalistic (focusing on comprehension strategies as they are made manifest in the classroom), or skill-based (and conducted in what is in effect a laboratory setting, which ignores a reader's own strategies). As a result, research into comprehension has been fragmented and unintegrated (Pressley, 2000: 546).

There is, however, general agreement among reading researchers that we currently have consensus in our understanding of word recognition processes, and their importance in reading comprehension. The Interactive-Compensatory model of reading comprehension (Stanovich, 1980) has remained widely accepted and largely unchallenged. What the model asserts is in principle very straightforward. Stanovich argued that, in reading, the brain needs to devote processing power to two tasks which are carried out in parallel: word recognition and comprehension. Certainly the two processes are not wholly independent, but the point is that the brain acts like a central processing unit, co-ordinating information from various sources, and in reading, as in all processing, the CPU has a finite capacity. What this means for reading is simple – the more processing capacity that is needed to decode words, the less there is available for comprehension. What a good reader needs to have, therefore, are rapid, automatic, context-free word recognition strategies. Of course, word recognition is speeded up by context effects, but the good reader is not reliant upon these context effects for word recognition. (Gough, 1984; Isakson and Miller, 1976) The implication here is that it is good for a reader to develop fluency – the ability to recognise words rapidly. This will improve comprehension, though only indirectly – by freeing-up processing capacity.

The other word-level activity for which there is good research support, though it has been an area somewhat neglected in recent years in the UK, has been work on improving vocabulary. This was an area which flourished in the English Coursebook era of the sixties and seventies, but which tended to die out as grammar exercises became less prominent. What is worth emphasising in this context are two points: first, the fact that improving vocabulary does improve comprehension, and second, that this can be done directly, but that it is best done through encouraging wide reading (Sternberg, 1987).

Some of the most important research into reading processes over the past twenty years has been on schema knowledge (Anderson, 1994), since this has deepened considerably our understanding of how readers learn from texts, particularly information texts. A schema is a kind of conceptual framework with slots into which subject-specific detail is posted as the reader builds up understanding. Schema theory predicts that readers gradually acquire a variety of schemata for text processing and storage, and therefore that having a rich repertoire of schemata is enormously valuable. But for a reader, possessing schemata is not in itself enough – the text type must be recognised and the appropriate schema activated if the reader is to make use of it for processing and storage; however, this may not always happen, either because the reader fails to pick up the text signals, or because the author has written an 'inconsiderate' text – that is, one which does not declare its own structure, or which is confusingly organised. An example of an inconsiderate structure might be an information book on diamonds that was organised purely using a sequential 'list' structure of points. A list structure is the default structure for an information text: in an information book it can be the text book equivalent of a shopping list that has been randomly reordered, with all the products which are normally found together separated, and with the organising structure of a sequential pathway through the supermarket abandoned. In our imaginary book on diamonds, there might be a series of two-page spreads, the first on famous jewels, then one on industrial diamonds, followed by a chapter on the diamond merchants of Amsterdam, then one on diamond mining in South Africa and another on famous thefts of diamonds. 'Inconsiderate' texts present tremendous challenges for the reader, and that challenge is even greater for the weak reader, since good readers can often supply a schema where the author neglected to offer one, but the weaker reader finds this too difficult, and might fail to learn from the text. Marshall and Glock (1978–9) carried out the seminal experimental study of this phenomenon, and later, making the point even more powerfully, Kintsch (1988) reported an interaction effect between reading ability and the capacity to deal with less coherent texts: low-knowledge readers profited from reading fully coherent texts, while high-knowledge readers learned better from less coherent text, presumably because for the latter group the less coherent text encouraged more active text processing.

This makes perfect sense: we learn more if we recognise the knowledge structure of incoming information, but we also learn more if that new knowledge is built upon firm semantic and epistemological foundations in the form of some prior knowledge. For a thorough review of the research on the relationship between prior knowledge and text comprehension, see the paper by Dochy, Segers and Buehl (1999) in the *Review of Educational*

Research. These authors do not doubt that there is a potentially powerful relationship between the two, but caution that if flawed methods are used for assessing the prior knowledge (or indeed the gains in knowledge), then the results can be not only inconclusive, they can be downright contradictory.

Two researchers who have consistently tried to amalgamate research-based theory and practice in the field of reading comprehension are Michael Pressley and Peter Afflerbach (1995). Their work has attempted to bring together aspects of reading development research which have often been investigated in fragmented or unco-ordinated ways, and to present the results in formats which are helpful for teachers. Pressley and Afflerbach emphasise that mature readers flexibly use a variety of processes as they read texts, and their list of strategies provides a useful checklist for teachers who might be considering how to structure a reading development curriculum:

- Being aware of purpose
- Reading selectively
- Revising hypotheses
- Revising prior knowledge
- Deducing meaning of unfamiliar words
- Marking texts or taking notes
- Planning how to make use of what they are learning.

(Pressley and Afflerbach, 1995)

In a more recent publication, Pressley (2000) takes his analysis further, and offers an eight-element list of approaches to reading development, and particularly comprehension development, which represent an up-to-date synthesis of all the major strands of research-derived strategies for improving reading. There isn't room in this chapter to cite all the evidence upon which Pressley builds his case, but I tend to share his view that we are not so much lacking research evidence in this area as we are collectively lacking the imagination to perceive that for too long reading comprehension instruction has been based on myth and custom rather than evidence. Pressley's list is of pedagogic strategies to improve comprehension as follows:

- Teach decoding, with an emphasis on morphology
- Drill students on sight words
- Teach the use of context cues and monitoring meaning
- Teach vocabulary
- Encourage extensive reading
- Encourage students to ask their own 'Why?' questions of a text
- Teach self-regulated comprehension strategies, for example:

- Prior knowledge activation
- Question generation
- Construction of mental images during reading
- Summarisation
- Analyse into story grammar components
- Encourage reciprocal teaching
- Teacher modelling of strategies plus scaffolding for student independence
- Encourage transactional strategies instruction.

It is interesting and instructive to compare this list with that quoted earlier as an example of the sort generated by the reading comprehension sub-skills debate. *Vocabulary* is present in both, but a much more subtle variety of approaches to word-level work is present in Pressley's more recent list, and this is indeed supported by current research – for example, the important study on the development of children's understanding of morphology and relationship with reading achievement conducted by Nunes and Bryant (2000). Instead of emphasising literal versus inferential comprehension (many commentators today would suggest that there is no such thing as reading without some form of inference generation), Pressley puts an emphasis on a number of ways in which the student's comprehension might be enhanced through engagement with the text. These approaches could be classified as primarily cognitive and social, but another equally helpful distinction might be active (for example, rehearsing prior knowledge, generating mental images, activating knowledge about text structure) and interactive (for example, asking 'why' questions, engaging in reciprocal teaching, working with the teacher to develop comprehension, and making use of transactional strategies instruction, which is an approach based on readers exploring texts with their peers and their teachers).

This emphasis on collaborative or interactive approaches to reading comprehension has been a characteristic of research in the field over the past ten years and has its theoretical roots in the critical literacy field, on the one hand (see, for example, Gee, 2001), and in neo-Vygotskian analysis, on the other (see, for example, Dodson, 2000). These sociocultural perspectives on reading comprehension seem likely to become even more dominant in the coming years for, as Jerome Bruner (2000) has reminded us, the very concept of a *text* is a representation of a way of knowing which recognises and respects otherness, and which cannot exist independently of its cultural identity.

These, then, are the recommendations from research that relate to the development of reading comprehension. Let us turn briefly to the issue of how publishers and (in England) the group who write the National Curriculum for English are envisioning the field, and the extent to which these are in harmony with the results from research.

What do publishers, the National Curriculum and the NLS have to say about developing comprehension?

In 2000, the American publisher Scott Foresman (Scott Foresman Reading, 2000) brought out a new basal. Some sections from the teacher's manual seem remarkably familiar, and could have been written twenty years ago. There was, for example, an emphasis on:

- Key comprehension skills taught and retaught;
- Main idea, supporting details, summarising, drawing conclusions, sequence, fact and opinion, cause and effect, classify, compare and contrast, making judgements, predicting, text structure.

But in the USA a reading scheme could not hit its market unless it included curriculum content that sounded familiar to American teachers; it is worth reading further as, in fact, the basal has a very strong research emphasis, and recommends teaching approaches which include Pressley's strategies as well as more traditional comprehension exercises. The manual argues, for example, that the teacher should be developing vocabulary with group work as well as individual work, and that the students will be more likely to improve their reading comprehension if they activate prior knowledge, if they engage in pre-reading class discussion, and if they engage in post-reading personal response. Scott Foresman, in common with all the other major basal publishers in the USA, places heavy emphasis on research, and reinforces this with background papers aimed at teachers and written by major figures in the field who have aligned themselves with their programme, and who had input into its design.

Scholastic would be a good example of an independent US publisher with a long-standing interest in developing students' study skills, and this company also has a research-informed position: Cathy Collins Block (2000), in a background paper for teachers, emphasises the importance of modelling strategic thinking, having practice in meaningful contexts, and in the teacher offering differentiated instruction. These emphases lead to the following recommended approaches:

- Developing strategic reading
- Avoiding prescriptive and depersonalised lessons
- Readers setting and monitoring their own purposes
- Readers being directly encouraged to understand themselves and their world
- Teacher modelling of strategies
- Teacher modelling how to set purposes
- Students spending more time reading fewer texts more deeply
- Teacher modelling and encouraging self-monitoring in reading
- Students working on cognitive, emotional and literary responses.

This is a fairly comprehensive list, and it is worth comparing it with the English National Curriculum (DfE, 1995), which put an initial emphasis on effective communication, but also stressed from the outset that English should enable students to become 'enthusiastic, responsive and knowledgeable readers'. There was also an emphasis on:

- Reading accurately, fluently and with understanding
- Understanding and responding
- Analysing and evaluating a wide range of texts.

The revised English National Curriculum (DfEE, 2000) also puts an emphasis on reading for meaning. Its goals are that children should be able:

(a) to extract meaning beyond the literal, explaining how the choice of language and style affects implied and explicit meanings;
(b) to analyse and discuss alternative interpretations, ambiguity and allusion;
(c) how ideas, values and emotions are explored and portrayed;
(d) to identify the perspectives offered on individuals, community and society;
(e) to consider how meanings are changed when texts are adapted to different media;
(f) read and appreciate the scope and richness of complete novels, plays and poems.

The goals listed above do, in my view, encompass many of the perspectives for developing comprehension that have emerged from current research. The emphasis on alternative interpretations and on sociocultural contexts for understanding are timely, and in the case of media studies somewhat ahead of most American reading curricula.

In England, the National Literacy Strategy offers an in-service and curriculum support framework for classroom teachers which will help to promote the achievement of the goals of the National Curriculum. At Key Stage 3, for example (ages 12–14), progress towards students achieving the goals is supported by an in-service programme (DfEE, 2001) which emphasises the following:

- Word level
  - Spelling
  - Spelling strategies
  - Vocabulary

- Sentence level
  - Sentence construction and punctuation
  - Paragraphing and cohesion

- Stylistic conventions
- Standard English

- Text level
  - Reading
  - Research and study skills
  - Reading for meaning
  - Understanding the author's craft
  - Study of literary texts

- Writing
  - Plan, draft and present
  - Imagine, explore, entertain
  - Inform, explain, describe
  - Persuade, argue, advise
  - Analyse, review, comment

- Speaking and listening
  - Speaking
  - Listening
  - Group discussion and interaction
  - Drama.

The Strategy is fairly prescriptive (in the sense that it offers detailed guidance for English departments on how to implement these objectives) and it is also atomistic, in that in order to support the teaching to the objectives, English departments in secondary schools have been given eight ring-bound folders containing over 1,500 pages of 'recommended' material published by the government and carefully linked to the overall aims of the programme. The government is determined to support pupils who are not achieving their full potential at the point at which they transfer to secondary school, and therefore more than three-quarters of this material is devoted to 'Literacy Progress Units' whose goal is to enable children to catch up with their peers.

However, it should also be noted that at Key Stage 3, a crucial part of the Strategy is the emphasis on a whole department's flexible use of elements from the Literacy Hour, which includes a central emphasis on interactive and highly participatory whole-class work, with pupil investigations and teacher modelling of strategies, followed by small-group work to scaffold, practice and embed the new learning. This is not easy to achieve, but the goals are precisely those recommended by Pressley (2000) of having teacher scaffolding followed by practice in developing student autonomy.

Conclusion

There are clear signs in these American reading approaches, and in the English National Literacy Strategy, that a consensus view is emerging of how to develop reading comprehension, and that view is firmly based on research. The key new emphases which have surfaced over the past decade have been (a) a clearer understanding of the skills which readers need to have automatised; (b) a strong emphasis on the sociocultural nature of reading, and the fact that reading is not simply active, but interactive, and located in a cultural and social context; and (c) emphasis on the crucial role of the teacher – in modelling and scaffolding children's entry into texts, but then gradually withdrawing, as the children develop confidence in their own ability to engage with the author and with each other in building meaning.

References

Anderson, R.C. (1994) 'The role of reader's schema in comprehension, learning and memory', in R.B. and M.R. Ruddell (eds) *Theoretical Models and Processes of Reading*, 4th edn (pp. 469–82), Newark, DE: International Reading Association.

Bloomer, R.H. (1966) *Non-overt Reinforced Cloze Procedure*, USOE Cooperative Research Project 2245, University of Connecticut.

Block, Cathy Collins (2000) 'How can we assist all students to comprehend well?', *Scholastic Literacy Research Papers*, New York: Scholastic.

Bruner, J. (2000) 'Reading for possible worlds', *National Reading Conference Yearbook 49*, Chicago: NRC. 31–40.

Davis F.B. (1944) 'Fundamental factors of comprehension in reading', *Psychometrica*, 9, 185–97.

Department for Education (DfE) (1995) *English in the National Curriculum*, London: DfE.

Department for Education and Employment (DfEE) (2000) *English in the National Curriculum*, London: DfEE.

—— (2001) *Key Stage 3 National Strategy. Framework for Teaching English: Years 7, 8 and 9*, London: DfEE.

Dochy, F., Segers, M. and Buehl, M. M. (1999) 'The relation between assessment practices and outcomes of studies: the case of research on prior knowledge', *Review of Educational Research* 69(2): 145–86.

Dodson, M.M. (2000) 'Monologic and dialogic conversations: how pre-service teachers socially construct knowledge through oral and computer mediated classroom discourse', *National Reading Conference Yearbook 49* (pp. 137–52), Chicago: NRC.

Gee, J.P. (2001) *Social Linguistics and Literacies: Ideologies in Discourses*, London: Falmer.

Gough, P.B. (1984) 'Word recognition', in P.D. Pearson, R. Barr, M. Kamil and P. Mosenthal (eds) *Handbook of Reading Research* (pp. 225–54), New York: Longman.

Harris, T.L. and Hodges, R.E. (eds) (1981) *A Dictionary of Reading and Related Terms*, Newark, DE: International Reading Association.

Isakson, R.L. and Miller, J.W. (1976) 'Sensitivity to syntactic and semantic cues in good and poor comprehenders', *Journal of Educational Psychology* 68: 787–92.

Kintsch, W. (1988) 'The role of knowledge in discourse comprehension: a construction-integration model', *Psychological Review* 85: 363–94.

Kintsch, W. (1998) *Comprehension: A Paradigm for Cognition*, Cambridge: Cambridge University Press.

Lunzer, E.A. and Gardner, W.K. (eds) (1979) *The Effective Use of Reading*, London: Heinemann.

Lunzer, E.A., Waite, M. and Dolan, T. (1979) 'Comprehension and comprehension tests', in E.A. Lunzer and W.K. Gardner (eds) *The Effective Use of Reading* (pp. 37–71), London: Heinemann.

Marshall, N. and Glock, M.D. (1978–9) 'Comprehension of connected discourse: a study into the relationships between the structure of text and information recalled', *Reading Research Quarterly*, 14(1): 10–56.

Nunes, T. and Bryant, P. (2000) 'The development of children's understanding of morphemes', paper presented at United Kingdom Reading Association annual conference, Oxford, July 2000.

Pressley, M. (2000) 'What should comprehension instruction be the instruction of?', in M. Kamil, P. Mosenthal, D. Pearson and R. Barr (eds) *Handbooks of Reading Research*, Vol. 3 (pp. 545–61), Hillsdale, NJ: Lawrence Erlbaum.

Pressley, M. and Afflerbach, P. (1995) *Verbal Protocols of Reading: The Nature of Constructively Responsive Reading*, Hillsdale, NJ: Lawrence Erlbaum.

Scott Foresman Reading (2000) *Teacher's Resource Package, Grade 6. Scott Foresman Reading 2000*, Glenview, IL: Scott Foresman.

Stanovich, K.E. (1980) 'Towards an interactive-compensatory model of individual differences in the development of reading fluency', *Reading Research Quarterly* 14(1): 32–71.

Sternberg, R.J. (1987) 'Most vocabulary is learned from context', in M.G. McKeown and M.E. Curtis (eds) *The Nature of Vocabulary Acquisition* (pp. 89–105), Hillsdale, NJ: Lawrence Erlbaum.

2 What does research tell us about how we should be developing written composition?

Mary Bailey

Introduction

What does research say about how we should be developing written composition? It is worth considering why this question is asked and who is, or perhaps should be, interested in its answer. In the context of a drive to raise standards in literacy, and when standards of achievement in writing are of particular concern – national test results in writing lag behind those in reading for eleven year olds in the United Kingdom – there is an awareness that we need to be more informed about the implications of research for practice. Where there is a national policy for the teaching of literacy, including unprecedented attention to the teaching of writing, one might reasonably expect that policy to exemplify, if not to explicate, the link between research and practice. However, this chapter will argue that there are two areas in which this link is fragile: first, that there is a gap (in the United Kingdom, at least) between what writing research suggests should be done and what national policy advocates; and, second, that there is a gap between what policy advocates, and how this is being interpreted in the classroom. There are also areas of debate in the connections between research, policy and practice in the teaching of reading, and, of course, there is an intrinsic relationship between reading and writing, but it is arguable that both policy makers and classroom teachers tend to be less clear about the research basis for developing writing than they are for developing reading.

This is not to imply that there should be a simple, unidirectional link from research to policy to practice. There are different influences at play: the best research takes into account real contexts and practical implications; policy should be determined by both good quality research and good practice (which, if properly evaluated, is also research); policy affects what research findings are promoted and what research is conducted, in that policy makers – at national government level – influence the allocation of some sources of research funding.

This chapter argues that for standards of achievement in writing to be raised we need to make the research basis for national literacy initiatives more explicit, and to question policy where it is not supported by research. We need to ensure that more teachers are confident in their understanding of children's writing development and the rationale for effective pedagogy.

The National Literacy Strategy in England: policy and practice

The implementation of the National Literacy Strategy in England can be used as an illustration of how the research–policy–practice link can be disrupted, despite the best intentions of those who drafted it. There have been significant changes in policy and practice in the teaching of literacy in the United Kingdom: more structured approaches to the teaching of writing and grammar are being introduced, including more direct teaching of whole classes. The aim of this critique is not to discredit the National Literacy Strategy, which is focusing much-needed attention on the development of writing, but to argue that some of the problems encountered with its implementation might be alleviated by making more explicit links to research.

Let us take a brief look, first, at the fragile link between research and policy. The two latest versions of *English in the National Curriculum* (DfE, 1995; DfEE, 1999) have specified the content of writing teaching – what should be taught – and, to some extent, how it should be taught, particularly with respect to the model of drafting and the key genres to be taught. Recent publications supplementing the National Curriculum have included further guidance, aimed at the secondary-aged sector, on improving writing (QCA, 1999a) and on the teaching of grammar in context (QCA, 1999b), both of which were informed by research, as well as the report of the Qualifications and Curriculum Agency Technical Accuracy Project (QCA, 1999c), which analysed the linguistic features of writing for GCSE examinations. With respect to writing, the current National Curriculum represents an example of policy refined through practice and relatively well grounded in research, albeit implicitly. However, the National Curriculum has not been charged with providing a detailed specification for the teaching of writing.

The introduction of *The National Literacy Strategy* (DfEE, 1998), for primary schools, and the *KS3 Strategy Framework for English* (DfEE, 2001a), for secondary schools, signifies a new political agenda in specifying exactly how writing should be taught. In these 'frameworks for teaching', learning objectives are presented at word, sentence and text level, allocated to different school years (and school terms, in the primary framework). This creates clearly delineated stages of progression out of the more general programmes of study in the National Curriculum, which were originally intended to guide teaching over a two to four-year period (depending on the Key Stage). The other strand to the National Literacy Strategy is the promotion of particular pedagogies, which move from demonstration and supported work into independent work within a daily structure. In the primary sector, this daily structure is known as the Literacy Hour. In the standards debate, the main area in which there seem to be anxieties is that of language structure and there has thus been more focus on the word and sentence levels recently, most notably in the National Literacy Strategy publication *Grammar for Writing* (DfEE, 2000). The National Literacy Strategy was under-theorised in its original form, although much of it draws implicitly on research. The NLS model of writing composition is influenced by the EXEL teaching model (Wray and Lewis, 1997), which is derived from the authors' own extensive research and clearly informed by the Australian genre school (for example, see Cope and Kalantzis, 1993) and by the neo-Vygotskian concept of scaffolding (Bruner, 1985; Maybin, Mercer and Stierer, 1992). One can also trace the influences of composition studies (notably Bereiter and Scardamalia, 1987) in the modelling and interventions of shared and guided writing.

There are other areas of the National Literacy Strategy which, in my view, are not so strongly supported by research and which are potentially confusing. For example, a 'searchlights model', which has little connection to research on reading, is proposed as a metaphor for the reading process (DfEE, 1998: 4). There is not space in this chapter for a full critique, but the main problem is that the 'model' is not a model: it provides a useful list of some of the factors that influence understanding (phonic, grammatical, contextual and visual) but it does not show how these are interrelated; it could be taken as suggesting an atomistic sub-skill view of reading; it does not indicate the nature of the relationship between visual representation and meaning; and it makes no reference to the social or intentional environment within which any act of reading occurs. More worryingly, it is also suggested that, by simply reversing the searchlights model, we have a useful metaphor for the writing process. The searchlights model is still referred to in recent publications such as *The National Literacy Strategy: Developing Early Writing* (DfEE, 2001b), which is otherwise full of sensible advice and suggestions for classroom activities.

Hilton (2001) challenges Beard's (2000a) claims that the approach to teaching writing in the National Literacy Strategy is supported by research, particularly for primary-school-age pupils. She argues that there are a number of flaws in the proposition that the teaching of 'basics', though direct instruction in discrete elements of grammar, and decontextualized shared and guided writing, will lead to a rise in the standard of children's writing. It should be clear from these examples that it might be difficult for teachers to discriminate between those areas of the National Literacy Strategy that are supported by research and those that are not.

The need for more explicit identification of supporting research has been recognised by the architects of the National Literacy Strategy who have commissioned post-hoc research reviews to make public the research basis of the strategies (Beard, 2000a, for primary; Harrison, in preparation, for Key Stage 3). However, these have been criticised. Hilton (2001) points out that Beard (2000a) devalues the National Curriculum model of teaching writing by interpreting this as a 'simple process' model when it is (rightly, in my view) described by Hilton as representing 'a hard-won victory for educationists who had maintained steadily over several years that children, like all writers, learn to write most effectively through deploying a series of complex recursive stages as the work progresses'. This 'recursive stages' model was substantially supported by composition research carried out with secondary level and undergraduate level writers, as well as 'expert' adult writers (Flower and Hayes, 1981, 1984; Hayes and Flower, 1980; Bereiter and Scardamalia, 1987). It is arguable that the National Literacy Strategy model is the more 'simple' model of writing pedagogy. To interpret the recursive stages model as a 'simple process' is to make the same mistake that teachers do if they teach drafting in an ineffective way. Teachers are just as, if not more, likely to teach the National Literacy Strategy simplistically, as a 'simple toolkit' model. Teachers will only teach writing effectively within the National Literacy Strategy if this is informed by, and orientated within, an understanding of the complexities of composition processes. It is also important not to elide 'process pedagogy' with 'process models' of composition – there are important differences. Hilton also disputes Beard's categorisation of 'shared writing' as an 'environmental' approach claiming that it is really more like Hillocks' (1995) less successful category of 'presentational' writing.

Turning to the link between policy and practice and how this can become fragile in certain circumstances, we can see how the interpretation of the National Literacy Strategy in schools and classrooms can, in some cases, lead to a further breakdown between policy and practice, and thus make the link between research and practice even more tenuous. Frater (2000) found, as a result of survey work in 32 primary schools in 1999/2000, that there was a tendency for teachers under pressure to interpret the National Literacy Strategy at a literal level, as a set of discrete and arbitrary activities. This 'anxious literalism' means that the National Literacy Strategy has had the unintended effect of leading to 'the discrete teaching of language skills and concepts' and 'the diminution, by such discrete work, of written composition'. This echoes the current widespread concern among classroom teachers that there is not enough time for extended and creative composition within the National Literacy Strategy. Frater found that in the less effective of the 32 schools, where achievement in writing had made least progress:

> the practice of written composition has been given such time as remains after concepts and skills, handled discretely, have been delivered. It can be added that the more discretely skills and knowledge

about language are handled, the more abstract, harder and less relevant they will seem to pupils, the longer the time required to teach them is likely to be, and the less likely it is that pupils will apply them effectively in practice. And boys in particular, are all too likely to switch off altogether.

(Frater, 2000: 110)

By contrast, in the schools with effective literacy policies, Frater found that 'teachers were professionally self-confident in approaching the National Literacy Strategy'. These teachers were able to draw upon the National Literacy Strategy Framework much more flexibly, constantly making 'connections between text-level work, and word and sentence-level study. And with them, *using language always carried the highest priority*' (*ibid.*, original emphasis). These findings are consistent with other evaluations of the National Literacy Strategy carried out by the government (Ofsted, 1999, 2000) and independently (Fisher, Lewis and Davis, 2000), which have found variability in the teaching of writing. Nor are those who drafted the National Literacy Strategy 'likely to have intended that any primary teachers might feel de-skilled or de-motivated' (Frater, 2000). Thus we see the model of literacy in the National Literacy Strategy being translated, by unconfident teachers, into an even more 'limited literacy' (Flower, 1994) than intended, particularly with respect to the teaching of writing. Frater argues for the need for teachers' opinions to be valued more highly by the community generally and by policy makers in particular. I would say that it is equally important that teachers have access to professional development that fosters understanding and confidence with educational principles that are supported by research. Without this there is little chance of standards being raised.

The implementation of the National Literacy Strategy, admittedly still at a relatively early stage, illustrates how a simplified pedagogy can emerge in the translation of policy into practice. This is, arguably, more likely to occur when the policy lacks explicit links to research evidence that would allow teachers to reconstruct the theoretical background necessary for an informed interpretation of the National Literacy Strategy: an interpretation that goes beyond the literal. The practice of simplified pedagogy is more likely to occur when teachers lack confidence due to low motivation and/or inadequate understanding of literacy development. It is also understandable that the content of training in a new policy initiative becomes simplified, due to the rush to implement policy and to the constraints of the training provision. However, there are clearly, here, a set of forces that might lead to a reductionist and over-simplified approach to the teaching of writing. Research evidence on the importance of teachers needing to connect up theory and practice in order to be effective comes from the Teacher Training Agency funded 'Effective Teachers of Literacy' project (Medwell *et al.*, 1998). The effective teachers identified in this project were well theorised, were able to verbalise strong connections between their theory and practice, and integrated skills teaching smoothly in meaningful contexts. By contrast, the less effective validation group teachers placed great emphasis on the teaching of skills, but were less well-theorised, and tended to teach the skills in a decontextualised manner (*ibid.*: 43)

Competing discourses in writing research

This chapter does not present a full review of research on effective teaching methods for developing children's writing (for which, see Smith and Elley, 1999; Beard 2000b, and this volume). It is not going to say that particular teaching methods lead directly to measurable improvements in children's writing. What it attempts instead is to review key developments in writing research and composition studies, in order to find a way through the 'competing discourses' (Fairclough, 1989) in this area, and to establish some key principles that are supported by theory. Some of this research has not been widely disseminated at the level of primary and secondary education. I would also argue that it is useful to look to the broader field of composition research to complement empirical studies that focus on effective writing behaviour, by providing a more complex picture of composition. As Coe (1994: 167) stresses, 'the process is best understood by describing not a writer's behaviour, but the system within which that behaviour makes sense'. In attempting to make sense of a range of research perspectives on writing it is hoped that some key principles will emerge that will help more teachers to have a grasp of the nature of the 'system' of composition.

Empirical studies of pedagogical effectiveness are important, and we need to have more of them. However, such studies need to be seen through the lens of an understanding of the fundamental processes of composition. Otherwise they will inevitably emphasise discrete skills, the 'basics' where accuracy can be easily measured, in the search for definitive answers: the much-demanded evidence for foolproof strategies for raising standards. There can be a tendency to privilege a quantitative, empirical approach that devalues other sources of evidence, such as messier, qualitative approaches, or the consensus that emerges from a range of perspectives.

At this point it is appropriate to raise the issue the generalisability of composition research to school contexts. Hilton (2001) criticises Beard (2000a) for applying Hillock's (1986) conclusions to primary pupils when they are intended for secondary age pupils. Clearly a distinction needs to be made between research on pedagogy, which must take account of pupils' prior experience of and relative familiarity with, for example, particular grammatical structures or genres, and research on fairly fundamental cognitive, social and cultural processes involved in composition. It is this latter area that is the focus of composition studies.

There have been several attempts, at various times, and in different ways, to map the field of writing research (for example, Hillocks, 1986, 1995; Bereiter and Scardamalia, 1987; Nystrand, Greene and Wiemelt, 1993; Smith and Elley, 1999; Applebee, 2000; Beard, 2000b). The rest of this section focuses on what we can learn about writing from different research discourses within the field of composition studies, presenting an overview, necessarily very selective and concise, of three major theoretical perspectives: cognitive, genre theory and sociocognitive. For each of these perspectives key concepts will be identified, as well as implications for the development of writing. Discussion of sociocognitive perspectives leads into a consideration of the work of Flower (1994) who, in the context of the broader standards debate, proposes a compelling theoretical framework for understanding composition. (For a fuller discussion of the 'intellectual history' of the field of composition studies up to the early 1990s, see Nystrand, Greene and Wiemelt, 1993. It is also worth pointing out that, although there are connections, composition studies is a distinct field from that of academic literacy or English for specific purposes.)

Cognitive models of composition

Writing fifteen years ago Wilkinson (1986: 35) stated that 'writing as a cognitive act has not had the attention it deserves' from United Kingdom researchers and educators, but that 'what we neglected was being developed in the United States', by which he means North America, as he makes significant reference to the early work of Bereiter and Scardamalia in Toronto. It seems that we in the United Kingdom have only begun to recognise the importance of this work in the last five years or so – and the work of Bereiter and Scardamalia (see 1987) is now getting the attention it deserves.

The cognitive perspective was dominant in the field of composition studies in the 1970s and 1980s, and typically focused on the behaviour and cognitive processes of individual writers. From a cognitive perspective, writing is seen as a problem-solving process. In fact, one of the main attractions for cognitive researchers was that it was an example of complex human problem-solving, and a major early focus, as in other areas of problem-solving research, was that of expert–novice differences. A dominant methodology is the use of concurrent 'think aloud' protocols, which, despite their limitations, proved a valuable means of gaining insight into the decision-making processes and metacognition of experts and novices while writing. There was acknowledgement of the intended audience and the context in which these individuals were writing, insofar as they were part of the writer's cognitive representation of the task. However, there was generally little or no attention to the wider social or cultural context of writing.

Cognitive perspectives on writing have been very valuable in clari-

fying the organisation of writing processes (planning, organising, translating and reviewing), and how these vary between individuals. These
differences have been explored most notably in the seminal work of
Hayes and Flower, a cognitive psychologist and a rhetorician, respectively (Hayes and Flower, 1981, 1984; Flower and Hayes, 1980). Most
of the cognitive research on writing at this time was done with undergraduate students, although some was done with high school students,
and Bereiter and Scardamalia (1987) developed a cognitive model of
writing alongside research on pedagogy in schools. Another important
contribution of the work of Hayes and Flower and Bereiter and
Scardamalia was that they provided a model for knowledge about the
content of writing – meaning – and about writing itself – rhetorical
knowledge – and, crucially, about the interaction between the two in the
composition process. A significant concept was that of 'knowledge-
transforming' writing (Bereiter and Scardamalia, 1987) through which
writers change their understanding of the content area as a result of
solving rhetorical problems.

It is important to note the distinction between cognitive process models
of writing at a theoretical level, and the 'process approach' to teaching
writing in the classroom (Graves, 1983) at a pedagogical level. The two
approaches have developed somewhat independent parallel paths.
Teachers in the United Kingdom have been more likely to be aware of the
'process approach' of Graves, but cognitive models of writing have had an
impact on our understanding of teaching and learning in writing, and thus
on pedagogy. This impact lies in two areas: a useable model of the writing
process and support for particular kinds of interventions. A focus on task
representation and constraints, planning, reviewing, and learning through
writing, through the interaction between content knowledge and genre
knowledge, supports an informed use of drafting, rather than what can at
worst be meaningless redrafting at whole text level – which can occur in
writers who do not have such understanding. To support writing development, this cognitive perspective implies the use of worked examples and
supported constraint reduction (essentially removing some of the demands
by providing scaffolds or deferring checking for grammatical correctness,
for example). Bereiter and Scardamalia (1987) developed effective classroom interventions based on their model, designing activities to encourage
reflective writing – again a means of scaffolding children's learning. (See
Levy and Ransdell (1996) for more recent research within a cognitive
perspective.)

Genre theory

In Australia, genre theory (see Cope and Kalantzis, 1993) grew out of
systemic linguistics (Halliday, 1985), and has had a significant impact on
the pedagogy of writing in Australia and, largely through the work of

Wray and Lewis (1997) and the National Literacy Strategy, in the United Kingdom as well. By contrast, the version of genre theory that originated largely in North America (Swales, 1990; Freedman and Medway 1994), which is different in some important ways, has not had as much impact in United Kingdom schools – not least because it emphasises the fluidity of genres and consequently limited possibilities of analysis, thus making it appear difficult to apply in classrooms. As well as having a strong theoretical and research base in applied linguistics, the Australian genre researchers worked with local teachers to develop a robust pedagogy for teaching children text genres important to school literacy, particularly in relation to six key examples: report, explanation, procedure, discussion, recount and narrative. The motivation of this work was the empowerment of disadvantaged groups by providing access to the genres of the dominant culture. Whilst teaching focused on the linguistic features of texts within the six genres, it was intended that this was always within a view of genres as social processes. Because of this attention to teaching genres through example texts, the Australian genre school has been characterised as static and prescriptive by North American genre researchers (Freedman and Medway, 1994), but this is an exaggerated dichotomisation of two perspectives that have a considerable amount of overlap, despite their differences in emphasis and level of linguistic analysis. However, the Australian genre school does have a structured model for explicit instruction, where the teacher takes on the role as expert in leading pupils through the stages of modelling (investigating the features of the genre model), joint negotiation (similar to shared writing in National Literacy Strategy terms) and independent writing. Thus the pupil is led through a scaffolded cycle from reading to independent writing within a critical, analytical framework.

The development of genre theory represented a shift in emphasis to seeing writing as social communication within particular cultural contexts: 'Whereas meaning in the 1970s was mainly a cognitive issue, by the 1980s, it had become "socialized" ... [partly in] direct reaction to the hegemony of cognitive research in the early 1980s' (Nystrand, Greene and Wiemelt, 1993). In the last decade, there has been a resurgence of interest in the cognitive aspects of writing. Sociocognitive, or social cognitive, perspectives on writing (for example, Berkenkotter and Huckin, 1993; Flower, 1994) have emerged in recognition that early cognitive models effectively partitioned off the 'social', as a set of external contextual factors. They have also built on recent developments in neo-Vygotskian theory, in situated cognition (Brown, Collins and Duguid, 1989) and in genre research. However, cognitive models that take into account social factors are not necessarily truly sociocognitive. Hayes (1996) has developed the original Hayes and Flower model of writing to produce 'a new framework for understanding cognition and affect in writing', which might be seen as belonging to this perspective, although he rejects the term 'social-cognitive', describing his model as 'individual-environmental'. It is thus more accurate to see this as a relatively unreconstructed cognitive model.

Sociocognitive models

Sociocognitive models of composition are concerned with 'how individual intention and agency insert themselves within culturally and socially organised practices' (Nystrand, Greene and Wiemelt, 1993). They emphasise the dynamic relationship between meaning, form, social context and culture, but see the act of composing as essentially cognitive, as Flower (1994) explains:

> The strong case for cognition lies, I believe, in the fact that the agent in even a socially extended process of making meaning is not society, community or a discourse; that is, meanings are not made by an abstract, theoretical construct but by individual writers, readers, speakers, and listeners who are interpreting inferred meanings around them, constructing their own, and attempting to share those meanings with or impose them on other members of their social or cultural collective. Individual meaning is not *sui generis*, but it is nonetheless a cognitive construction, created out of prior knowledge in response to the multiple layers of a writer's social, rhetorical, and cultural context.
>
> (Flower, 1994: 89)

Within a sociocognitive perspective, becoming literate depends on both knowledge of social conventions and individual problem-solving. We need to teach pupils strategic skills, rather than what Flower terms 'a pedagogy of correctness'. She suggests that in order to be literate pupils need the skills:

- to read a situation;
- to plan, organise, and revise;
- to build and negotiate meaning;
- to use and adapt conventions;
- to figure out what new discourses expect and how to enter them.

(adapted from Flower, 1994: 7)

An effective means of developing composition is thus through the use of collaborative writing to model these strategic skills when writing in an authentic context. We also need to investigate 'how children's understandings of the genres and functions within and across particular kinds of reading or writing activities affect the approaches used, the meanings conveyed and the learnings that ensue' (Langer, 1986: 143).

Although the sociocognitive perspective on writing can be seen as a synthesis of the cognitive and genre approaches, these do remain three distinct research discourses. These research perspectives cannot be fully reconciled at a theoretical level, but there is a considerable degree of overlap in their pedagogical implications. If we go beyond the character-istic discourses of the different perspectives, we can see that two key themes for developing writing receive particular support from across the range of research:

• scaffolding understanding of written communication – through activi-ties that model strategic writing skills and analysing genres in context
• scaffolding the writing process – through reducing constraints, providing structural support and collaborative writing.

The professional development of teachers

The importance of teachers' professional knowledge in developing pupils' writing, as in other areas of education, is widely accepted (Coe, 1994; Wray and Lewis, 1997; Smith and Elley, 1999; Beard, 2000b). Generally one would expect that teachers who are well-theorised – who have an informed and sophisticated understanding of the complexity of the writing process – will be able to teach 'the basics' of literacy in more meaningful contexts and thus more effectively than those who do not.

There has been a tendency to overlook composition studies and theoret-ical models of writing, especially when some of the supporting research has been carried out in non-school contexts, such as in the field of compo-sition studies. The fact that it can be easier to find 'hard' evidence for teaching technical skills, which lend themselves to more empirical approaches, than more complex compositional skills, means that discrete technical skills are sometimes over-emphasised, leading to a reductionist, componential approach. However, the previous section has attempted to show how the integrated models and theoretical perspectives of composi-tion can improve our broader understanding of the writing process. As a result of this, it should be possible both to readjust our ideas about the fundamental skills of writing and to have the professional confidence to teach technical skills in a more integrated way.

Interestingly, there is an analogy here between the teaching of writing in schools and the training of teachers of writing. The teaching of writing is a similarly complex process, in social and cognitive terms, to writing itself. It is inadequate for pupils to be taught a model of writing which simply reproduces the behaviour of good writers, or indeed the behaviour of 'novice' writers, as is sometimes the case, whether this is through an over-simplified drafting approach or an oversimplified genre approach. Similarly, teachers don't just need training to reproduce the behaviour – the moves or stages – of effective literacy teachers. They also need to understand the teaching of literacy at a strategic level – just as we need to teach writing strategically (Bereiter and Scardamalia, 1987; Flower, 1994).

Teachers need principles, rather than routines, in order to be (or to become) confident teachers of writing.

Conclusions: some principles for developing writing – and teachers of writing

It is not surprising that the research–policy–practice link is fragile. There is a tension between forces for simplification at the levels of policy and practice, and forces for complication at the level of research, where specialised and competing academic discourses can make it difficult to draw out implications for practice. Researchers and policy makers may be too tempted to try to find, or indeed fund, research to support elements of writing pedagogy in a piecemeal and retrospective way, and risk misapplying this through not having a sufficiently complex picture of writing. Teachers need to avoid the mechanical implementation of structured teaching, particularly at the word and sentence level. In order to discourage these trends we need to do two other things. First, we need to identify some fundamental principles about composition, which we can then use in teacher education and as criteria by which to both evaluate and orientate current initiatives in the teaching of writing. Second, we need to develop pedagogy by supporting more extensive research into the teaching of writing in meaningful classroom contexts.

I would like to suggest that we already have such a set of principles. Flower presents a set of 'strong claims' for 'a social cognitive alternative to the public story of literacy' (1994: 19–30; summarised below), which can serve as a powerful set of fundamental principles for understanding writing, and which reinstate thinking and learning in the writing process, as well as confirming the primary role of meaning-making in writing, at every stage.

1   *Literacy is an action.* Literacy is not a generalised ability a person possesses (or does not possess). Literacy is a set of actions and transactions in which people use reading and writing for personal and social purposes.
2   *Literacy is a move within a discourse practice.* When people engage in literate action, they are doing more than decoding or producing text. Like any social practice, it has a history with a set of expectations and conventions. A discourse practice cannot be reduced to a genre or a kind of text; it is a social and rhetorical situation in which texts play a specialised role.
3   *Becoming literate depends on knowledge of social conventions and on individual problem solving.*
4   *The new 'basics' should start with expressive and rhetorical practices.* From this perspective, what is basic is the how-to knowledge [that] goes by various names – heuristics, process plans, rhetorical or

problem-solving strategies, critical thinking skills – but in essence, they are action plans for carrying out a literate act. In this rhetorical tradition, the basic, foundational skills in learning to be literate are the skills one needs to read a situation; to plan, organize, and revise; to build and negotiate meaning; to use and adapt conventions; and to figure out what new discourses expect and how to enter them (Flower 1994: 27).

5   *Literate action opens the door to metacognitive and social awareness.* In other words, literacy as a social cognitive act creates some opportunities for strategic thinking and reflection that are absent in the pedagogy of textual conventions and correctness.

I will conclude by stressing that the most important way of developing pupils' writing is by developing teachers' understanding of writing. In the United Kingdom we have a mixed history of dissemination of theory and practice in the area of literacy. We can see that much of the National Literacy Strategy, particularly shared and guided writing at its best, is supported by the research on writing reviewed in this chapter, even if this is not always explicit in the framework itself. However, there is a danger that without a principled understanding of writing such as that offered by Flower (1994) we will, perhaps implicitly, disseminate a 'simple view' of writing, in the same way as Purcell-Gates (this volume) criticises the 'simple view of reading' in the United States. Teachers need the 'whole picture': a more integrated and fully developed model of writing rather than a set of activities, however well devised. I would like to argue that the importance of embracing complexity is what research tells us about how we should be developing writing:

> Under the pressures of outside evaluation and the exigencies of instruction, many administrators and teachers may opt for limited literacies, designating some feature (whether it be correctness, self-expression, or a disciplinary practice like literary analysis) as basic and turning it into the signifier and test of literacy. Complexity and dialectic are hard to sell.
>
> (Flower, 1994: 32)

References

Applebee, A. (2000) 'Alternative models of writing development', in R. Indriasano and J.R. Squire (eds) *Perspectives on Writing: Research, Theory and Practice*, Newark, DE: International Reading Association.

Beard, R. (2000a) 'Clarion call for another century', *Times Educational Supplement*, 6 October, Curriculum Special (p. 7).

—— (2000b) *Developing Writing 3–13*, London: Hodder & Stoughton.

Bereiter, C. and Scardamalia, M. (1987) *The Psychology of Written Communication*, Hillsdale, NJ: Lawrence Erlbaum.

36   Mary Bailey

Berkenkotter, C. and Huckin, T.N. (1993) 'Rethinking genre from a sociocognitive perspective', *Written Communication* 10(4): 475–509.
Brown, J.S., Collins, A. and Duguid, P. (1989) 'Situated cognition and the culture of learning', *Educational Researcher* 18: 32–42.
Bruner, J. (1985) 'Vygotsky: a historical and conceptual perspective', in A. Sinclair, R. Jarvella and W.J.M. Levelt (eds) (1987) *Making Sense: The Child's Construction of the World*, London: Methuen.
Coe, R.M. (1994) 'Teaching genre as process' in A. Freedman and P. Medway (eds) *Learning and Teaching Genre*, Portsmouth, NH: Boynton/Cook.
Cope, B. and Kalantzis, M. (1993) 'Introduction: how a genre approach to literacy can transform the way writing is taught', in B. Cope and M. Kalantzis (eds) *The Powers of Literacy: A Genre Approach to Teaching Writing*, London: Falmer.
Department for Education (DfE) (1995) *English in the National Curriculum*, London: DfE.
Department for Education and Employment (DfEE) (1998) *The National Literacy Strategy: Framework for Teaching*, London: DfEE.
—— (1999) *English in the National Curriculum*, London: DfEE.
—— (2000) *The National Literacy Strategy: Grammar for Writing*, London: DfEE.
—— (2001a) *KS3 Strategy Framework for Teaching English*, London: DfEE.
—— (2001b) *The National Literacy Strategy: Developing Early Writing*, London: DfEE.
Fairclough, N. (1989) *Language and Power*, Harlow: Longman.
Fisher, R., Lewis, M. and Davis, B. (2000) 'Progress and performance in National Literacy Strategy classrooms in England', *Journal of Research in Reading* 23(3): 256–66.
Flower, L. (1994) *The Construction of Negotiated Meaning: A Social Cognitive Theory of Writing*, Carbondale: Southern Illinois University Press.
Flower, L. and Hayes, J.R. (1981) 'A cognitive process theory of writing', *College Composition and Communication* 32: 365–86.
—— (1984) 'Images, plans and prose: the representation of meaning in writing', *Written Communication* 1(1): 120–60.
Frater, G. (2000) 'Observed in practice. English in the National Literacy Strategy: some reflections', *Reading* 34(3): 107–12.
Freedman, A. and Medway, P. (eds) (1994) *Learning and Teaching Genre*, Portsmouth, NH: Boyton/Cook.
Graves, D. (1983) *Writing: Teachers and Children at Work*, Portsmouth, NH: Heinemann.
Halliday, M.A.K. (1985) *An Introduction to Functional Grammar*, London: Edward Arnold.
Hayes, J.R. (1996) 'A new framework for understanding cognition and affect in writing', in C.M. Levy and S. Ransdell (eds) *The Science of Writing: Theories, Methods, Individual Differences and Applications*, Mahwah, NJ: Lawrence Erlbaum.
Hayes, J.R. and Flower, L. (1980) 'Identifying the organization of writing processes', in L. Gregg and E. Steinberg (eds) *Cognitive Processes in Writing*, Hillsdale, NJ: Lawrence Erlbaum.
Hillocks, G. (1986) *Research on Written Composition*, Urbana, IL: National Conference on Research in English/ERIC Clearinghouse on Reading and Communication Skills.
—— (1995) *Teaching Writing as Reflective Practice*, New York: Teachers College Press.
Hilton, M. (2001) 'Writing process and progress: where do we go from here?', *English in Education* 35(1): 4–11.

Langer, J.A. (1986) *Children Reading and Writing*, Norwood, NJ: Ablex.
Levy, C.M. and Ransdell, S. (1996) *The Science of Writing: Theories, Methods, Individual Differences and Applications*, Mahwah, NJ: Lawrence Erlbaum.
Lewis, M. and Wray, D. (2000) *Literacy in the Secondary School*, London: David Fulton.
Maybin, J., Mercer, N. and Stierer, B. (1992) 'Scaffolding learning in the classroom', in K. Norman (ed.) *Thinking Voices: The Work of the National Oracy Project*, London: Hodder & Stoughton for the National Curriculum Council.
Medwell, J., Wray, D., Poulson, L. and Fox, R. (1998) *Effective Teachers of Literacy*, Exeter: University of Exeter, for Teacher Training Agency.
Myhill, D. (1999) 'Writing matters: linguistic characteristics of writing in GCSE examinations', *English in Education* 33(3): 70–81.
Nystrand, M., Greene, S. and Wiemelt, J. (1993) 'Where does composition studies come from? An intellectual history', *Written Communication* 10(3): 267–333.
Office for Standards in Education (Ofsted) (1999) *The National Literacy Strategy: An Evaluation of the First Year of the National Literacy Strategy*, London: OFSTED.
—— (2000)*The National Literacy Strategy: The Second Year*, London: OFSTED.
Qualifications and Curriculum Agency (QCA) (1999a) *Improving Writing at Key Stages 3 and 4*, London: QCA.
—— (1999b) *Not Whether But How*, London: QCA.
—— (1999c) *Technical Accuracy in Writing in GCSE English Examinations: Research Findings*, London: QCA.
Smith, J. and Elley, W. (1999) *How Children Learn to Write*, London: Paul Chapman.
Swales, J.M. (1990) *Genre Analysis*, Cambridge: Cambridge University Press.
Wilkinson, A. (1986) *The Quality of Writing*, Milton Keynes: Open University Press.
Wray, D. and Lewis, M. (1997) *Extending Literacy: Children Reading and Writing Non Fiction*, London: Routledge.

3   As the research predicted?

Examining the success of the National Literacy Strategy

Roger Beard

A national target already achieved

The National Literacy Strategy (NLS) for England was launched at a London conference in 1997. During the conference, the opposition spokesperson for Education, David Blunkett, announced a target that, if his party came to power the following May, 80 per cent of 11-year-olds in England would reach Level 4 in reading by 2002 (the target was later adjusted to Level 4 in English). The ambitious nature of this target is underlined by the fact that in 1996 the percentage of pupils achieving Level 4 in reading was only 58 per cent. Level 4 is the standard in reading and writing expected to be gained by the average 11-year-old in their end-of-year national test. Speaking at the same conference, Professor Bob Slavin commented that the announcement reminded him of President Kennedy's 1962 target of getting a man on the moon by the end of the decade. Only, added Professor Slavin, the NLS target was more difficult.

Yet, three years later, the target for reading was achieved two years early. Progress towards the English target for 2002 had already been much greater than seemed feasible in 1997. Only the writing attainment of boys seemed likely to threaten the achievement of the target as a whole. At this high-profile national level, the National Literacy Strategy has already been a major success for English primary schools. It has brought about unprecedented requests for the sharing of its practices from other UK countries, from independent schools and from the secondary sector. The Strategy has been held up by international authorities on educational change as the most ambitious large-scale strategy of educational reform witnessed since the 1960s (Fullan, 2000). This chapter attempts to provide the careful analysis that the success of the NLS calls for. Its achievements fall into even sharper relief when set against earlier attempts to raise literacy standards at both local and national levels.

Some earlier attempts to raise standards

Previous more localised attempts to raise standards of literacy have not enjoyed anything like the degree of success of the NLS; many have been inconclusive. For instance, the Bradford Book Flood Project involved a substantial increase in book stocks but its evaluation noted that raising literacy standards involved a complex interplay of factors of which the provision of texts were but one part (Ingham, 1982).

Margaret Meek's *Achieving Literacy* was based on a similarly inconclusive study (Meek *et al.*, 1983). This involved the use of 'real books' to raise the standards of pupils whose reading development had been delayed. Indeed, the study's lack of success apparently led to the publication of the study being thrown into question, although this did not discourage Meek from going on to build her theories of 'how texts teach what readers learn' on related anecdotal evidence (Meek, 1988).

The Leeds Primary Needs Programme, whose evaluation report received prominent coverage in the national press in the early 1990s, involved a substantial investment of resources and in-service training over five years, totalling £15 millions, but it appeared to have little effect on standards. A key constraint appeared to be the promotion of a complex 'integrated day' pedagogy which 'presumed that the particular classroom layouts and patterns of organisation commended would promote children's learning more effectively than others ... . [The commended approaches included] multiple curriculum focus in teaching sessions, with different groups working in different curriculum areas and the kinds of teacher–pupil interaction associated with a commitment to discovery learning' (Alexander, 1992: 143). Unfortunately, during the time of the Primary Needs Programme, a slight decline in reading standards was found across the LEA (*ibid.*: 52). Robin Alexander's report culminates in his raising the 'problem of good primary practice', in which 'the good tends to be asserted but seldom demonstrated' (*ibid.*: 180). As will be shown later in the present chapter, this challenging of widely held assumptions has consistently run through primary and literacy education in recent years.

The Haringey Project, on the other hand, was much more successful in raising reading attainment. Pupils taking home books recommended by the teacher to read to their parents led to highly significant gains that were still evident five years later (Tizard *et al.*, 1982; Hewison, 1988). However, replications of the Haringey research in other contexts have been inconclusive (Hannon and Jackson, 1987; Tizard *et al.*, 1988). The issues raised by the discrepancy in findings have been discussed by Toomey (1993).

A previous central government policy for raising standards was focused on the introduction of a National Curriculum in 1989 and a concomitant programme of national testing. Ironically, the national testing programme has not been a reliable way of monitoring national standards over a sustained period of time. The change in the national testing criteria from statements of attainment to level descriptions in 1995 invalidated comparisons of the years before and after this point. The statements of attainment model had, in any case, been subjected to substantial technical criticism (Pumfrey and Elliot, 1991). The application of norm-referenced measures of reading in longitudinal studies have also failed to come up with evidence that the introduction of a National Curriculum has itself raised standards of reading (Davies and Brember, 1997; 1998).

Research and the National Literacy Strategy

Such a background makes the immediate success of the NLS, on such a large scale, all the more noteworthy. Above all, it reflects sustained hard work by thousands of teachers and pupils. It represents the pay-off from a substantial investment in education by central government, in training materials, in-service programmes and the appointment of several hundred literacy consultants in LEAs.

However, a more profound explanation of the success of the NLS may lie in the much maligned area of educational research. It is paradoxical that, soon after educational research was being subjected to substantial criticism (e.g. Hargreaves, 1996; Tooley and Darby, 1998; Woodhead, 1998), the likely success of the NLS was being predicted on the basis of a wide-ranging research review (Beard, 1999; see also Beard, 2000b), although what actually counts as 'educational' research is not always easy to determine. The review was, in turn, built on the reports from a literacy task force that contained two academics whose work had focused specifically on the research–policy interface.

School effectiveness research

The basis of the prediction lay in both generic and subject-specific domains. As was mentioned earlier, English primary schools have for many years been influenced by notions of 'good practice' that have become increasingly at odds with generic research findings on school effectiveness. These findings have added significance because they have been confirmed after advances in multilevel statistical modelling (Davies, 2000) and multiple studies which have been brought together in meta-analyses. Meta-analyses on school effectiveness and classroom effectiveness were central considerations in the research reviewed during the setting up of the National Literacy Strategy. Two meta-analyses in particular were singled out by the Literacy Task Force (LTF, 1997b): those by Jaap Scheerens (1992) and Bert Creemers (1994).

School effectiveness is a relatively new area of educational research, as is the use of meta-analyses in social research generally (Glass *et al.*, 1981). The effectiveness field is still characterised by debates, particularly on factor isolation (Goldstein and Woodhouse, 2000). Nevertheless, the following extract from Scheerens' analyses identifies a number of factors that, according to research and inspection evidence, were relatively uncommon in primary schools before the advent of the NLS.

Scheerens (1992) identifies two characteristics of school effectiveness that have 'multiple empirical research confirmation':

structured teaching, i.e.

- making clear what has to be learnt
- dividing material into manageable units
- teaching in a well-considered sequence
- using material in which pupils make use of hunches and prompts
- regular testing for progress
- giving immediate feedback

effective learning time.

This factor is partly related to the first, in that whole class teaching can often be superior to individualised teaching because in the latter the teacher has to divide attention in such a way that the net result per pupil is lower. Other aspects of effective teaching time are 'curricular emphasis', related to the time spent on certain subjects, and the need to inspire, challenge and praise so as to stimulate the motivation to learn and thus indirectly to increase net learning time.

The London study

As was indicated in the earlier references to the Leeds study, the emphasis in English primary schools has been more on the teacher facilitating learning by extensive use of individual and group work. Whole class teaching has often been denigrated as failing to cater for children's individual needs. Above all, English primary education has been unusual in the international context in promoting teaching approaches in which several subject areas are tackled a the same time. The relative ineffectiveness of this approach was highlighted in one of the first major school effectiveness studies which studied fifty primary schools over a three year period (Mortimore *et al.*, 1988), using measures of reading, writing, basic and practical mathematics, oral skills and classroom behaviour. The study identified the importance of 'limited focus' in lessons:

> pupils made greater progress when teachers tended to organise lessons around one particular curriculum area ... [Where] the tendency was for the teacher regularly to organise classroom work such that three or more curriculum areas were running concurrently, then pupils' progress was marred .... pupil industry was lower ... noise and pupil movement were greater, and teachers spent less time discussing work and more time on routine issues and behaviour control ... higher-order communications occurred more frequently when the teacher talked to the whole class.
>
> (Mortimore *et al.*, 1988: 253–6)

Mortimore *et al.* report that 'limited curriculum focus' is one of twelve factors which are characteristic of effective schools, including purposeful leadership by the head teacher, a work-centred environment and a positive climate. They also note features that were to become hallmarks of the National Literacy Strategy's Literacy Hour: explaining the purpose of the work to pupils and a balance of whole class and independent work (for which pupils were taught the related skills and guided in the allocated tasks). The researchers go on to identify the value of an audit of what has been achieved and learned, part of what in time was to become the plenary session in the Literacy Hour.

The authors are clearly aware of the tensions between their findings and the views of 'good practice' that were prevalent at the time. Like Alexander, they encourage a questioning of established assumptions:

> It appears that many experienced and extremely skilful teachers, whose normal practice has been to limit the curriculum focus of their lessons, have been led to feel guilty about their failure to manage more diverse activities ... Many teachers have felt that they ought to be able to handle a variety of topics a the same time. The implication of our data is that they should think again.
>
> (Mortimore *et al.*, 1988: 270, 287)

The Literacy Task Force

Some critics of the NLS have noted the apparent anomaly of the NLS *Review of Research and Other Related Evidence* being published after the decision was taken to implement the Strategy. Such criticisms fail to take account of the fact that school effectiveness research is clearly being drawn upon in both reports from the Literacy Task Force (LTF, 1997a and b). The Task Force contained two major authorities in the field, Michael Barber and David Reynolds. Reynolds, in particular, had consistently drawn attention to the tensions between British teaching practices and research findings on effectiveness, including issues raised by unnecessarily complex teaching arrangements (Barber, 1997; Reynolds, 1992; Reynolds *et al.*, 1994; Reynolds, 1998). This concern also continued to be expressed in reports of inspection evidence (e.g. Ofsted, 1997).

What may be seen as a greater anomaly than that referred to above is the fact that school effectiveness research seems to have been overlooked in many literacy education publications, despite the prompts that were sometimes given (e.g. Beard, 1990, 1991, 1992).

Reading process research

If generic research on school effectiveness partly predicted the success of the NLS, so did reading research, especially that concerned with the reading process and the role of phonic knowledge. Again, there is evidence of a substantial discrepancy between the model of reading assumed by influential teacher education publications and the conclusions from research, in this case particularly experimental research. These conclusions have been recently marked by an unusual consensus in what has often been a contentious area of investigation. At an international conference at the University of Glasgow in 1995, the morning session ended with one eminent British researcher commenting in a rather surprised tone of voice, 'We all agree!'. The focus of the agreement was the relative importance of word recognition compared with the use of contextual support in reading. Recent psychological research indicates that what characterises reading fluency is *context-independent* word recognition and *context-dependent* comprehension. This is well discussed by one of the speakers at the Glasgow conference, Charles Perfetti (1995). It may not be too much of an exaggeration to say that UK literacy education has, for many years, been disproportionately influenced by a model that is in many ways diametrically opposite.

For some years fluent reading was held to be a 'psycholinguistic guessing game' by some influential writers. This view assumed that fluent reading was characterised by increasing use of contextual cues and minimal use of visual cues (Goodman, 1967; Smith 1971). In the last twenty years a great deal of evidence has been put forward in support of the opposite view (see also Beard, 1995; Stanovich, 2000). The change in thinking has recently been starkly underlined by Jane Hurry in her literature review for the QCA on intervention strategies in early literacy:

> It is now very clear that Goodman and Smith were wrong in thinking that skilled readers pay so little attention to the details of print ... skilled readers attend closely to letters and words and in fact ... it is the less skilled readers who rely more heavily on contextual cues to support their reading.
>
> (Hurry, 2000: 9)

Recent research-based models of fluent reading suggest that reading involves the use of sources of contextual, comprehension, visual and phonological information which are simultaneously interactive, issuing and accommodating to and from each other (Rumelhart and McClelland, 1986; Seidenberg and McClelland, 1989; Adams, 1990; Reid, 1993; Stanovich and Stanovich, 1995; Perfetti, 1995). These experimental findings are brought together in the National Literacy Strategy in the 'searchlights' model. As the NLS Framework notes, most teachers are aware of these strategies for reading, but have often been over-cautious about the teaching of the phonic aspect of reading (DfEE, 1998a: 4). Again, there is a substantial research base to this issue and, again, influential views have had to be challenged and eventually superseded.

The role of phonic knowledge

Researchers have associated phonological awareness, children's ability to hear speech sounds, with early success in learning to read for some years. Children's phonological development follows a clear pattern, from being aware of syllables, to being aware of onsets and rimes within syllables, to being aware of phonemes (Treiman and Zukowski, 1996). There is also a significant connection between children's phonological development and their later reading success, linking oracy and literacy in highly specific ways. The central importance of phonemic processing in reading development has been increasingly highlighted by research on both sides of the Atlantic (e.g. Rieben and Perfetti, 1991; Gough *et al.*, 1992, Shimron, 1996; Macmillan, 1997; Byrne, 1998, McGuinness, 1998).

In contrast, the prevailing view in teacher education has been based on other perspectives. It has been widely assumed that learning to read has much in common with learning to speak. These assumptions have been combined with arguments against the use of systematic teaching of sound–letter correspondences (phonics). By 1992, publications which espoused such theories figured largely in initial teacher education book lists (Brooks *et al.*, 1992). The most recommended booklet on these lists was one espousing an 'apprenticeship approach' to teaching early reading, which referred to phonics as 'only one very small part of reading' (Waterland, 1985: 24; see also Beard and Oakhill, 1994).

It is difficult to estimate the effects that Waterland's ideas, and the ideas of those who espoused her views, had on the teaching of early reading. Inspection evidence suggests, however, that, through the 1990s, the teaching of phonic knowledge was sometimes unconvincing and at times haphazard (HMI, 1991; Ofsted, 1996a; Ofsted, 1998). In contrast, the National Literacy Strategy clearly draws on both the experimental research and the inspection evidence in its commitment to a strong and systematic teaching of phonics and other word level skills (DfEE, 1998a: 4), but within a balanced framework that ensures continuing attention to text and sentence level teaching as well. The importance of such a balance is shown in overseas literacy research that is discussed below.

Lessons from overseas literacy research

Inspection evidence and curriculum development research have also highlighted several other aspects where British primary education may have been out of step with thinking in other countries. Early reading in English primary schools has been largely taught by individualised methods in which the structure of commercial materials was often very influential. There was little use of regular direct class or group teaching of reading, even when the design of commercial materials suggested it (Ofsted, 1996c). As an earlier HMI report had pointed out, for most pupils in Key

Stage 1, reading to the teacher was often the most frequent experience of one-to-one teaching ... often less than five minutes per pupil. Schools generally provided too few opportunities for the pupils to see and hear the text of a story simultaneously (HMI, 1992: 16).

This state of affairs contrasted with the shared reading approaches which have been developed in New Zealand. In these, teacher and pupils simultaneously read aloud a large format text. The approach has been especially promoted in the writing of Don Holdaway (1979, 1982). He was particularly interested in developing methods which resembled the visual intimacy with print which characterises the pre-school book experience of parents reading with their children. Holdaway suggests that the use of 'big books' and shared reading enables the teacher to display the skill of reading in purposeful use, while keeping before pupils' attention the fact that the process is print-stimulated. Research suggests that, before the National Literacy Strategy, large format texts were not widely used for teaching reading in English primary schools (e.g. Cato, *et al.*, 1992; Ireson *et al.*, 1995; Wragg *et al.*, 1998; see also Beard, 2000c)

There was a similar story in relation to the teaching of skills for dealing with information texts. According to inspection evidence, these were taught rather patchily and sometimes left to chance (Ofsted, 1996a). Links between reading and writing were often not directly made (Ofsted, 1996b). This indicated that much might be gained from the approaches developed from Australian genre theory. The distinctive features of various genres are used first to raise awareness about their structures, then to model them in shared reading and writing and eventually to tackle them in collaborative or independent writing (Martin, 1989; Callaghan and Rothery, 1988; Cope and Kalantzis, 1993).

The EXEL project at Exeter University has also influenced the NLS. The project has drawn together a range of skills and strategies to form the EXIT model ('Extending Interactions With Text'). The model maps ten process stages and related questions from activation of previous knowledge, through establishing purposes and locating information, to interacting with a text and communicating the information to others (Wray and Lewis, 1997).

To assist children in the writing of non-fiction, the project has used a number of 'frames', skeleton outlines of starters, connectives and sentence modifiers, to help to 'scaffold' early attempts to write in particular genres (Lewis and Wray, 1995). The EXEL project focused on recounts, reports, procedures, explanations, persuasion and discussion, building on the work of Beverly Derewianka (1990). The potential of this curriculum development research was recognised by the Literacy Task Force (LTF, 1997b: 38) and subsequently many of its ideas were built into the NLS *Framework for Teaching* (DfEE, 1998a).

International comparisons

The potential of a national infusion of direct, interactive teaching which drew upon the above sources was further underlined by international comparisons of reading performance. Britain is located within a 'middle' group of countries which includes Belgium and Spain. In the middle and upper parts of the range of scores, children in England and Wales performed as well as those in countries much higher in the rank order (Brooks, Pugh and Schagen, 1996: 13). However, a distinctive feature of British performance is the existence of a long 'tail' of under-achievement which is relatively greater than that of other countries (*ibid*.: 10).

Dealing with the tail of under-achievement

There are several programmes in different parts of the world which are specifically targeted at disadvantaged students. These use combinations of teaching approaches which, until recently, were relatively rare in the UK, but which have subsequently been adapted by the NLS. For instance, Bob Slavin's *Success for All* programme is currently in use in nearly 500 schools in over 30 states in the USA. It is also used in an adapted form in Australia, Canada, Israel and Mexico (Slavin, 1996).

The main features of *Success for All* (more recently called 'Roots and Wings') are:

- a fast-paced, structured curriculum;
- direct, interactive teaching;
- systematic phonics in the context of interesting text;
- a combination of shared and paired reading and writing;
- early interventions for pupils who have not made expected progress after one year at school.

A similar strategy especially to address the needs of disadvantaged pupils is being implemented in Melbourne, Australia, in the Early Literacy Research Project (ELRP) (see Raban and Essex, this volume) led by Carmel Crévola and Peter Hill (1998), researchers whose work has also clearly influenced the NLS (LTF, 1997a: 19).

The National Literacy Project

Perhaps the most significant indicator of the likely success of the NLS came from the National Literacy Project. The National Literacy Project (NLP) was set up in England by the previous government in the spring of 1996 in fifteen Local Education Authorities. The rationale of the NLP drew upon the school management and teaching quality evidence from research and school inspections. Participating schools implemented two key structures, a *Framework for Teaching*, which translated the National

Curriculum into termly objectives, and the Literacy Hour, whose time allocation was based on the review of the National Curriculum (Dearing, 1994). The Framework and the Literacy Hour were earlier versions of what were subsequently to be included in the NLS.

Major gains in attainment

The NLP was evaluated by the National Foundation for Educational Research (Sainsbury *et al.*, 1998). Data were collected from 250 schools. The test results revealed a significant and substantial improvement over the eighteen-month period. Final test scores had improved by approximately six standardised score points for Y3/4 and Y5/6 pupils. This is equivalent to 8 to 12 months' progress *over and above* what is expected in these ages. For Y1/2 pupils the increase was nearly twice as large again, at 11.5 standardised score points.

It is unfortunate that a project that reported such startling successes and which had such positive messages for national policy was overlooked by critics who argue that the justifications for the NLS were post hoc. Early in 1997, the Literacy Task Force were clearly convinced that the Project was the harbinger of a major change in literacy education.

> The NLP's framework for teaching is firmly based on the Ofsted data, research evidence and international experience ... the work of the National Literacy Project seems likely to make a major contribution [to raising standards]. There is nothing to be gained from a new government coming in and overturning good work which is already in progress. On the contrary, the National Literacy Project provides a helpful beginning from which we can develop our strategy.
>
> (LTF, 1997a: 19–20)

The evaluation of the NLP provided clear indications of the substantial increase in reading standards that the NLS would be likely to bring about. The evaluation provided less detailed evidence on writing, beyond measures of spelling and punctuation. Later national test results raised different issues about the influence of the NLS influence on writing.

The question of writing

As was pointed out earlier, the main obstacle to the achievement of the 2002 target was shown to lie in children's writing attainment, especially that of boys. Again, a clear direction for literacy education is found in research findings, encapsulated in a meta-analysis. Provision for writing in schools has become better informed by research in recent years, particularly in relation to process and range (Beard, 2000a). However, a number of pedagogical aspects remain underdeveloped.

In line with its commitment to increasing the direct interactive teaching of literacy, the NLS has promoted greater use of shared and guided writing. The research basis of these methods appears not to be widely appreciated and it is worth spelling them out in detail. As with the school effectiveness research discussed earlier, a meta-analysis provides a clear sense of direction for literacy education.

Shared writing

The value of shared writing has been underlined by the research of Bereiter and Scardamalia (1987). On the basis of a sustained programme of over a hundred experimental studies, they make a number of recommendations:

- pupils (and teachers) need to be made aware of the full extent of the composing process;
- the thinking that goes on in composition needs to be modelled by the teacher;
- pupils will benefit from reviewing their own writing strategies and knowledge;
- pupils need a supportive and congenial writing environment, but will also benefit from experiencing the struggles that are an integral part of developing writing skill;
- pupils may also benefit from using various 'facilitating' techniques to help them through the initial stages of acquiring more complex processes (e.g. listing words, points that may be made, the wording of final sentences, etc.), in advance of tackling the full text.

Such procedures can relieve the pressure on children to produce a text, even a rough first draft, until they have assembled the support that they need.

Guided writing

The value of guided writing has been indicated in a meta-analysis by Hillocks (1986, 1995). Hillocks reviewed nearly 500 studies that assessed the effectiveness of one or more teaching approaches. He then used a set of criteria to select sixty well-designed studies for inclusion in a meta-analysis (research synthesis). He identified four broad teaching approaches. Their particular features are set out in Table 3.1.

Hillocks reports that the guided writing approach was two or three times more effective than the natural process/individualised approaches and over four times more effective than the presentational approach. According to Hillocks, the presentational approach is only minimally effective because it involves telling pupils what is strong or weak in writing performance, but it does not provide opportunities for pupils to learn

Table 3.1 Approaches to the teaching of writing

Approach	Teacher's role	Writing topics	Particular teaching strategies
'Presentational'	Imparting knowledge prior to writing	Assigned by teacher	Setting tasks and marking outcomes
'Natural Process' and Individualised	Engaging pupils in writing and fostering positive dispositions	Chosen by pupils	Providing general procedures e.g. multiple drafts and peer comments
'Guided Writing' (what Hillocks calls an 'environmental' approach)	Inducing and supporting active learning of complex strategies that pupils are not capable of using on their own	Negotiated	Developing materials and activities to engage pupils in task-specific processes

procedures for putting this knowledge to work. The process and individualised approaches are only moderately effective because they prompt ideas and plans for incorporation in particular pieces of writing, but do not ensure that pupils develop their own ideas and plans autonomously. This is especially so in the organisation of different kinds of writing. The guided writing approach is more effective because it presents new forms, models and criteria, and facilitates their use in different writing tasks. Problems are tackled in a spirit of enquiry and problem-solving.

Evidence from recent inspection evidence

School inspection evidence has suggested, however, that writing attainment is still relatively weak in many English primary schools. In a recent discussion paper, Her Majesty's Inspectorate (HMI) has drawn attention to inspection findings that suggest that the writing aspects of the NLS have not been as effectively implemented as its generic and reading aspects:

- there is insufficient teaching of writing;
- extended writing often comprises practising writing rather than being taught how to improve it;
- in literacy hours, there is often not an appropriate balance between reading and writing;
- skills learned in literacy lessons are insufficiently transferred into work in other subjects;
- there is an over-reliance on duplicated worksheets;
- there is an over-reliance on the use of a good stimulus to inspire pupils to write and insufficient back-up by the necessary teaching, for example in teacher-modelling.

The features of the best teaching of writing reported by HMI include the following, several of which are currently being taken up in the NLS *Grammar for Writing* initiative (DfEE, 2000), which was developed to bolster the teaching of writing in the 7–11 age range from 2000/1.

- a good technical knowledge of literacy (by the teacher);
- the selection of good quality texts to illustrate the particular writing skills being taught;
- the incorporation of word and sentence-level work into the teaching of writing;
- intervention at the point of composition to teach writing skills;
- the reinforcement and development of writing skills throughout the curriculum (HMI, 2000).

Conclusion

There has only been space in this chapter to discuss some of the main reasons why the success of the NLS represents the fulfilment of what could be predicted from a close reading of educational research. The chapter has also shown how the implementation of the NLS confronted some widely held views and introduced different emphases in primary teaching. Such changes inevitably cause unease. Sometimes they cause knee-jerk responses that a reflective reading of research findings might obviate.

The success of the NLS may also confirm that its contribution to the curriculum is not as a monolithic 'one size fits all' model, as has been suggested. Instead, it provides a highly flexible framework, offering endless permutations of shared, guided and independent work at text, sentence and word levels. It uses a rich range of text types outlined in the national curriculum and which schools have been able to adapt according to circumstances.

Neither is the NLS an excessively top-down model that threatens the flexibility of early years of schooling. Instead, it provides for such flexibility by yearly rather than termly objectives for the Reception age-range that can be used in ways that are felt to be developmentally appropriate.

Most importantly, the NLS has not yet been challenged by other research-based curriculum models for literacy education that could be adopted with similar or greater likelihood of success on a national scale. The NLS has already achieved the equivalent of getting a man on the moon. In so doing, it has raised standards and improved the life chances of many children.

References

Adams, M.J. (1990) *Beginning to Read: Thinking and Learning about Print*, Cambridge, Mass.: MIT Press.

Alexander, R.J. (1992) *Policy and Practice in Primary Education*, London: Routledge.

Barber, M. (1997) *The Learning Game: Arguments for An Education Revolution*, London: Indigo.

Beard, R. (1990) *Developing Reading 3–13*, London: Hodder & Stoughton.

—— (1991) 'Learning to Read like a Writer', *Educational Review* 43(1): 17–24

—— (1992) 'Review of Cairney T.H.', *Teaching Reading Comprehension*', *Journal of Research in Reading* 15(2): 142.

—— (1995) 'Learning to read: psychology and education' in E. Funnell and M. Stuart (eds) *Learning to Read: Psychology in the Classroom*, Oxford: Blackwell.

—— (1999) *The National Literacy Strategy: Review of Research and Other Related Evidence*, London: DfEE.

—— (2000a) *Developing Writing 3–13*, London: Hodder & Stoughton.

—— (2000b) 'Research and the National Literacy Strategy', *Oxford Review of Education* 26(3&4): 421–36.

—— (2000c) 'Long overdue? Another look at the National Literacy Strategy', *Journal of Research in Reading* 23(3): 245–55.

Beard, R. and Oakhill, J. (1994) *Reading by Apprenticeship? A Critique of the Apprenticeship Approach to the Teaching of Reading*, Slough: National Foundation for Educational Research.

Bereiter, C. and Scardamalia, M. (1987) *The Psychology of Written Composition*, Hillsdale, NJ: Lawrence Erlbaum.

Brooks, G., Pugh, A.K. and Schagen, I. (1996) *Reading Performance at Nine*, Slough: National Foundation for Educational Research.

Brooks, G., Gorman, T., Kendall, L. and Tate, A. (1992) *What teachers in training are taught about reading*, Slough: National Foundation for Educational Research.

Byrne, B. (1998) *The Foundations of Literacy: The Child's Acquisition of the Alphabetic Principle*, Hove: Psychology Press.

Callaghan, M. and Rothery, J. (1988) *Teaching Factual Writing: A Genre-Based Approach*, Sydney: Metropolitan East Disadvantaged Schools Programme.

Cato, V., Fernandes, C., Gorman, T., Kispal, A. with White, J. (1992) *The Teaching of Initial Literacy: How Do Teachers Do It?* Slough: NFER.

Cope, B. and Kalantzis, M. (eds) (1993) *The Powers of Literacy: A Genre Approach to Teaching Writing*, London: Falmer.

Creemers, B.P.M. (1994) *The Effective Classroom*, London: Cassell.

Crévola, C.A. and Hill, P.W. (1998) 'Evaluation of a whole-school approach to prevention and intervention in early literacy', *Journal of Education for Students Placed at Risk* 3(2): 133–57.

Davies, J. and Brember, I. (1997) 'Monitoring reading standards in Year 6: a 7 year cross-sectional study', *British Educational Research Journal* 23(5): 615–22.

—— (1998) 'Standards of reading at Key Stage 1: a cause for celebration? A seven year cross-sectional study', *Educational Research* 40(2): 153–60.

Davies, P. (2000) 'The relevance of systematic reviews to educational policy and practice', *Oxford Review of Education* 26(3&4): 365–78.

Dearing, R. (1994) *The National Curriculum and its Assessment: Final Report*, London: School Curriculum and Assessment Authority.

Department for Education and Employment (DfEE) (1998a) *The National Literacy Strategy: Framework for Teaching*, London: DfEE.

—— (1998b) *The National Literacy Strategy: Literacy Training Pack*, London: DfEE.

—— (2000) *Grammar for Writing*, London: DfEE.

Derewianka, B. (1990) *Exploring How Texts Work*, Sydney: Primary English Teaching Association.

Fullan, M. (2000) 'The return of large-scale reform', *Journal of Educational Change* 1: 5–28.

Glass, G.V., McGaw, B. and Smith, M.L. (1981) *Meta-Analysis in Social Research*, London: Sage.

Goldstein, H. and Woodhouse, G. (2000) 'School effectiveness research and education policy', *Oxford Review of Education* 26(3&4): 353–63.

Goodman, K.S. (1967) 'Reading: a psycholinguistic guessing game', *Journal of the Reading Specialist* 4: 126–35.

Gough, P.B., Ehri, L.C. and Treiman, R. (eds) (1992) *Reading Acquisition*, Hillsdale, N.J.: Lawrence Erlbaum.

Hannon, P. and Jackson, A. (1987) *The Belfield Reading Project Final Report*, London: National Children's Bureau.

Hargreaves, D.H. (1996) *Teaching as a Research-based Profession: Possibilities and Prospects*, London: Teacher Training Agency.

Her Majesty's Inspectorate (HMI) (1991) *The Teaching and Learning of Reading in Primary Schools 1990: A Report by HMI*, Stanmore: DES.

—— (1992) *The Teaching and Learning of Reading in Primary Schools 1991: A Report by HMI*, Stanmore: DES.

—— (2000) *The Teaching of Writing in Primary Schools: Could do better. A Discussion Paper by HMI*, London: OFSTED.

Hewison, J. (1988) 'The long term effectiveness of parental involvement in reading: a follow-up to the Haringey Reading Project', *British Journal of Educational Psychology* 58: 184–90.

Hillocks, G. (1986) *Research on Written Composition*, Urbana, Il.: National Conference on Research in English/ERIC Clearinghouse on Reading and Communication Skills.

—— (1995) *Teaching Writing as Reflective Practice*, New York: Teachers College Press.

Holdaway, D. (1979) *The Foundations of Literacy*, Sydney: Ashton Scholastic.

—— (1982) 'Shared book experience: teaching reading using favourite books', *Theory into Practice* 21(4): 293–300.

Hurry, J. (2000) *Intervention Strategies to Support Pupils with Difficulties in Literacy during Key Stage 1: Review of Research*, London: QCA.

Ingham, J. (1982) *Books and Reading Development*, 2nd edn, London: Heinemann.

Ireson, J., Blatchford, P. and Joscelyne, T. (1995) 'What do teachers do? Classroom activities in the initial teaching of reading', *Educational Psychology* 15(3): 245–56.

Lewis, M. and Wray, D. (1995) *Developing Children's Non-Fiction Writing: Working With Writing Frames*, Leamington Spa: Scholastic.

Literacy Task Force (LTF) (1997a) *A Reading Revolution: How We Can Teach Every Child to Read Well*, London: LTF (c/o University of London, Institute of Education).

—— (1997b) *The Implementation of the National Literacy Strategy*, London: DfEE.

Macmillan, B. (1997) *Why Schoolchildren Can't Read*, London: Institute of Economic Affairs.

McGuinness, D. (1998) *Why Children Can't Read*, London: Penguin Books.

Martin, J.R. (1989) *Factual Writing: Exploring and Challenging Social Reality*, 2nd edn, Oxford: Oxford University Press.

Meek, M. (1988) *How Texts Teach What Readers Learn*, Stroud: Thimble Press.

Meek, M., Armstrong, S., Austerfield, V., Graham, J. and Plackett, E. (1983) *Achieving Literacy*, London: Routledge & Kegan Paul.

Mortimore, P., Sammons, P., Stoll, L., Lewis, D. and Ecob, R. (1988) *School Matters: The Junior Years*, Wells: Open Books.

Office for Standards in Education (Ofsted) (1996a) *The Annual Report of Her Majesty's Chief Inspector of Schools: Standards and Quality in Education 1994/95*, London: HMSO.

—— (1996b) *Subjects and Standards: Issues for School Development Arising From OFSTED Inspection Findings 1994–5: Key Stages 1 and 2*, London: HMSO.

—— (1996c) *The Teaching of Reading in 45 Inner London Primary Schools: A Report by Her Majesty's Inspectors in Collaboration with the LEAs of Islington, Southwark and Tower Hamlets*, London: OFSTED.

—— (1997) *The Annual Report of Her Majesty's Chief Inspector of Schools: Standards and Quality in Education 1995/6*, London: The Stationery Office.

—— (1998) *The Annual Report of Her Majesty's Chief Inspector of Schools: Standards and Quality in Education 1996/97*, London: The Stationery Office.

Perfetti, C. (1995) 'Cognitive research can inform reading education', *Journal of Research in Reading* 18(2): 106–15. Reprinted in J. Oakhill and R. Beard (eds) (1999) *Reading Development and the Teaching of Reading: A Psychological Perspective*, Oxford: Blackwell.

Pumfrey, P.D. and Elliott, J. (1991) 'National Reading Standards and standard assessment tasks: an educational house of cards?' *Educational Psychology in Practice* 7(2): 74–80.

Reid, J. (1993) 'Reading and spoken language: the nature of the links', in R. Beard (ed.) *Teaching Literacy: Balancing Perspectives*, London: Hodder & Stoughton.

Reynolds, D. (1992) 'School effectiveness and school improvement: an updated review of the British literature' in D. Reynolds and P. Cuttance (eds) *School Effectiveness: Research, Policy and Practice*, London: Cassell.

—— (1998) 'Schooling for literacy: a review of research on teacher effectiveness and school effectiveness and its implications for contemporary educational policies', *Educational Review* 50(2): 147–62.

Reynolds, D., Creemers, B.P.M., Nesselrodt, P.S., Schaffer, E.C., Stringfield, S. and Teddlie, C. (eds) (1994) *Advances in School Effectiveness Research and Practice*, London: Pergamon.

Rieben, L. and Perfetti, C.A. (eds) (1991) *Learning to Read: Basic Research and Its Implications*, Hillsdale, N.J.: Lawrence Erlbaum.

Rumelhart, D.E. and McClelland, J.L. (eds) (1986) *Parallel Distributed Processing. Vol. 1: Foundations*, Cambridge: Mass.: MIT Press.

Sainsbury, M., Schagen, I., Whetton, C. with Hagues, N. and Minnis, M. (1998) *Evaluation of the National Literacy Strategy: Cohort 1, 1996–1998*, Slough: NFER.

Scheerens, J. (1992) *Effective Schooling: Research, Theory and Practice*, London: Cassell.

Seidenberg, M.S. and McClelland, J.L. (1989) 'A distributed, developmental model of word recognition and naming', *Psychological Review* 96: 523–68.

Shimron, J. (ed.) (1996) *Literacy and Education: Essays in Memory of Dinah Feitelson*, Cresskill, N.J.: Hampton Press.

Slavin, R.E. (1996) *Education for All*, Lisse: Swets & Zeitlinger.

Smith, F. (1971) *Understanding Reading*, New York: Holt, Rinehart & Winston.

Stanovich, K.E. (2000) *Progress in Understanding Reading*, New York: Guilford.

Stanovich, K.E. and P.J. (1995) 'How research might inform the debate about early reading acquisition', *Journal of Research in Reading* 18(2): 87–105.

Oakhill, J. and Beard, R. (eds) (1999) *Reading Development and the Teaching of Reading: A Psychological Perspective*, Oxford: Blackwell.

Tizard, B., Blatchford, P., Burke, J., Farquhar, C. and Plewis, I. (1988) *Young Children at School in the Inner City*, London: Lawrence Erlbaum.

Tizard, J., Schofield, W.N. and Hewison, J. (1982) 'Collaboration between teachers and parents in assisting children's reading', *British Journal of Educational Psychology* 52: 1–15.

Tooley, J. and Darby, D. (1998) *Educational Research: A Critique*, London: Ofsted

Toomey, D. (1993) 'Parents hearing their children read: a review. Re-thinking the lessons of the Haringey Project', *Educational Research* 35(3): 223–36.

Treiman, R. and Zukowski, A. (1996) 'Children's sensitivity to syllables, onsets, rimes and phonemes', *Journal of Experimental Child Psychology* 61: 193–215.

Waterland, L. (1985) *Read With Me*, Stroud: Thimble Press.

Woodhead, C. (1998) 'Academia gone to seed', *New Statesman*, 20 March.

Wragg, E.C., Wragg, C.M., Haynes, G.S. and Chamberlain, R.P. (1998) *Improving Literacy in the Primary School*, London: Routledge.

Wray, D. and Lewis, M. (1997) *Extending Literacy: Children Reading and Writing Non-fiction*, London: Routledge.

4   What do effective teachers of literacy know, believe and do?

David Wray and Jane Medwell

Introduction

This article reports the results of research, commissioned by the Teacher Training Agency in the United Kingdom, into the characteristics of teachers who could be shown to be effective in teaching literacy to primary school pupils. The findings are based on a close study of a sample of teachers whose pupils made effective learning gains in literacy and of a sample of teachers who were less effective in literacy teaching. The aims of this research were to:

- identify the key factors in what effective teachers knew, understood and did which enabled them to teach literacy effectively;
- identify strategies which would enable those factors to be more widely applied;
- specify aspects of continuing professional development which appeared to contribute to the development of effective teachers of literacy.

Effective teaching and effective teachers

The literature on effective teaching has a number of dominant themes, including school effect issues as well as issues related to the characteristics of effective teachers. The project reported here focused on the contribution made by the teacher to what children learnt in literacy. Research on school effectiveness suggests that variations in children's literacy performance may be related to three types of effect: whole school, teacher, and methods/materials. Of these three, the consensus is that the effect of the teacher is the most significant (Barr, 1984; Adams, 1990). Of the range of models put forward to explain the various components of school–teacher–pupil interactions, one we found particularly useful was the concept of 'curricular expertise', as advanced by Alexander, Rose and Woodhead (1992). By this they meant 'the subject knowledge, the understanding of how children learn and the skills needed to teach subjects successfully'. Effective teaching, they argued, depends on the successful combination of this knowledge, understanding and skill.

Most of the research into effective teaching is generic rather than specific to literacy teaching. In the 1970s a number of large-scale studies in the USA attempted to look at the effects of the teacher by searching for links between teacher classroom behaviour and pupil achievement (see Brophy and Good (1986) for a review). More recent studies have taken a more complex view of the classroom and used multi-faceted methods of research. Studies such as that of Bennett *et al.* (1984) looked at the classes of teachers deemed to be effective and Mortimore *et al.* (1988) studied teaching in junior schools.

Whilst the research offers little literacy-specific information it does give a range of findings concerning

- teacher classroom behaviour, such as classroom management, task setting, task content and pedagogic skills;
- teacher subject knowledge and beliefs, including content knowledge in a subject, an understanding of how children learn in that subject and the belief systems which interact with and enable such knowledge to be put into operation in the classroom.

Effective teaching and effective teachers of literacy

There have been numerous attempts to establish the nature of effective teaching in literacy. Most of these have begun by analysing the processes involved in being literate and from this put forward a model to guide instruction in literacy (for example, Chall, 1967; Flesch, 1955; Goodman and Goodman, 1979). The argument has been that effective teaching in literacy is that which produces effective literate behaviour in learners. This sounds like an eminently sensible position, but its main problem has been the difficulty researchers and teachers have found in agreeing on what exactly should count as effective literate behaviour, especially in reading. The major disagreement has centred around the relative importance given in views of literacy to technical skills such as word recognition, decoding and spelling or to higher order skills such as making meaning. Such lack of agreement has led to proponents of radically different approaches to teaching literacy claiming superiority for their suggested programmes, but using very different criteria against which to judge the success of these programmes.

An example of this can be found in recent debates about literacy teaching. The whole language approach, for example, emphasises language processes and the creation of learning environments in which children experience authentic reading and writing (Weaver, 1990). Whole language theorists and teachers stress that skills instruction should occur within the context of natural reading and writing rather than through decontextualised exercises. The development of literacy tends to be seen as a natural by-product of immersion in high quality literacy environments.

In contrast, other researchers and teachers argue that learning the code is a critical part of early reading and that children are most likely to become skilled in this when they are provided with systematic teaching in decoding (e.g. Chall, 1967). There is growing evidence that such teaching increases reading ability (Adams, 1990), especially for children who experience difficulties in learning to read (Mather, 1992; Pressley and Rankin, 1994).

There have been several studies comparing the effectiveness of teaching programmes using a whole language approach and programmes emphasising traditional decoding. The evidence suggests that teaching based on whole language principles (i.e. the use of whole texts, good literature and fully contextualised instruction) does stimulate children to engage in a greater range of literate activities, develop more positive attitudes toward reading and writing, and increase their understanding about the nature and purposes of reading and writing (e.g. Morrow, 1990, 1991, 1992; Neuman and Roskos, 1990, 1992). Evidence also indicates, however, that whole language teaching programmes have less of an effect upon early reading achievement as measured by standardised tests of decoding, vocabulary, comprehension, and writing (Graham and Harris, 1994; Stahl, McKenna, and Pagnucco, 1994; Stahl and Miller, 1989). Teaching which explicitly focuses on phonemic awareness and letter–sound correspondences does result in improved performance on such standardised tests (Adams, 1990). The picture emerging from research is, therefore, not a simple one and it appears that the nature of effective teaching of literacy changes according to the outcome measures used to evaluate it.

An issue which has potential bearing on our understanding of the nature of effective literacy teaching and which may offer a focal point around which conflicting research findings can be synthesised is the near impossibility of finding, and thus testing, 'pure' teaching approaches in literacy. Close examination of many recent studies which appear to support the explicit teaching of decoding and comprehension strategies suggests that, embedded in these programmes, there are often many elements of what could be described as whole language teaching, including, for example, the reading of high quality children's literature and daily original writing by children (Pressley *et al.*, 1991, 1992). Similarly, when the programmes described by whole language advocates are examined closely, it is quite apparent that they do contain a good deal of systematic teaching of letter–sound correspondences (for example, Holdaway, 1979). These teaching approaches, in fact, are tending to become more and more alike and commentators such as Adams (1991) have suggested that there is no need for a division between teaching approaches styled as 'whole language' or 'explicit code teaching' in orientation. What has emerged in recent years is a realisation that explicit decoding and comprehension instruction are most effectively carried out in the context of other components.

Such rapprochement between previously contrasting positions suggests that effective literacy teaching is multifaceted (e.g. Adams, 1990; Cazden,

1992; Duffy, 1991; Stahl *et al.*, 1994). That is to say that it integrates letter- and word-level teaching with explicit instruction in comprehension processes and sets all of these within a context meaningful to children in which they read and write high quality whole texts. Such an approach might be labelled eclectic in that it involves the use of a range of methods. Importantly, though, this implies an informed selection by the teacher from a range of teaching techniques and approaches on the basis of a detailed understanding of the multifaceted nature of literacy and of the needs of a particular group of children. It does not, as Rose (1996) points out, mean the naive use of a range of teaching methods in the hope that, like shotgun pellets, at least some of them will hit the target.

The likely characteristics and manifestations of effective teaching of literacy can therefore be described to some extent. The focus of our research was to consider what it was that effective teachers knew and believed about this teaching, and how this contributed to their effectiveness.

Designing the study

Our first step was to identify two main sample groups, one a group of primary teachers identified as effective in the teaching of literacy, and the second a control group of primary teachers randomly selected (the validation group).

A number of steps were taken to identify the effective literacy teachers. We first asked for recommendations from education personnel in a number of areas of the country. Having achieved a list of over 600 teachers recommended as effective in the teaching of literacy, we then checked such external data sources as we could locate about these teachers and their schools. National test data from each school and external inspection reports were combed for any indications that the literacy teaching of these teachers might not be as effective as we had been led to believe. A number of teachers were deleted from the list as a result. The head teachers of the remainder were contacted and asked (a) did they agree that the teacher in question was effective in teaching literacy, and (b) did they have objective evidence to indicate this was the case. The key criterion here was whether head teachers could supply us with evidence, in the form of standardised reading test scores, of above-average learning gains in reading for the children in the classes of these teachers. Satisfactory responses to both these questions led to the inclusion of that teacher in the final sample of effective teachers of literacy, which initially numbered 301 teachers.

Teachers in the validation group were selected to represent a range of effectiveness in teaching literacy. Primary schools in similar areas of the country and similar catchment areas to those of the effective teachers were chosen and the mathematics co-ordinators of 140 of these schools initially selected to be part of the validation sample. We thus had no reason to believe that these validation teachers were either effective or ineffective at teaching literacy. They were included as a control group.

Teachers in both groups were asked to complete a questionnaire designed to enquire into their beliefs about literacy and literacy teaching approaches, their feelings about children's needs in literacy development, their reported use of a range of teaching techniques and their professional development experience in literacy. Completed questionnaires were returned from 228 of the effective teachers (a response rate of 75.7 per cent) and 71 of the validation teachers (50.7 per cent).

We then identified sub-samples of the two main groups, that is a sub-sample of 26 teachers from the group of teachers identified as effective in the teaching of literacy and a sub-sample of 10 of the teachers from the validation group. These teachers were principally chosen on a volunteer basis but also to represent a range of school types and geographical areas. The teachers in both sub-samples were twice observed teaching and then interviewed about each of these teaching episodes. The first observation–interview focused on teaching strategies and classroom organisation, and the genesis of these in terms of the teachers' experiences of professional development. The focus in the second observation–interview was on lesson content and teachers' subject knowledge. During the second interview, teachers completed a 'quiz' designed to test their knowledge about aspects of literacy.

Main findings of the research

In the space available here all we can do is summarise the major findings of the research. Much greater detail about these findings can be found in Wray and Medwell (2001).

Teachers' subject knowledge in literacy

Both the effective teachers and the validation teachers knew the requirements of the United Kingdom National Curriculum for English well and could describe what they were doing in terms of these. The effective teachers, however, placed a greater emphasis on children's knowledge of the purposes and functions of reading and writing and of the structures used to enable these processes. They taught language structures and were concerned to contextualise this teaching and to present such structures functionally and meaningfully to children.

Even the effective teachers, however, had limited success at recognising some types of words (e.g. adverbs, prepositions) in a sentence and some sub-word units (e.g. phonemes) out of context. Units such as phonemes, onsets and rimes and morphemes were problematic for them and even using more everyday terminology for these units still did not guarantee success for the teachers in recognising them out of the lesson context.

Despite this apparent lack of explicit abstract knowledge of linguistic concepts, the effective teachers used such knowledge implicitly in their teaching, particularly that connected with phonics. It seems that these teachers knew the material they were teaching in a particular way. They appeared to know and understand it in the form in which they taught it to the children, rather than abstracted from the teaching context. This is an important finding, which we feel has implications for the content of teachers' continuing professional development.

Teachers were also asked to examine and judge samples of children's reading and writing. All the teachers were able to analyse the children's mistakes in these samples, but the way in which the two groups carried out this task was different. The effective teachers were more diagnostic in the ways they approached the task and were more able to generate explanations as to why children read or wrote as they did. In examining pieces of writing, the two groups eventually mentioned similar features, but the effective teachers were quicker to focus on possible underlying causes of a child's writing behaviour. Although both groups reached broadly similar conclusions about children's reading and writing, the effective teachers were able to offer many more reasons for their conclusions and to make these detailed judgements more quickly. This suggests a firmer command of subject knowledge relating to literacy processes.

Teachers' beliefs about literacy

The effective teachers of literacy tended to place a high value upon communication and composition in their views about the teaching of reading and writing. They were more coherent in their belief systems about the teaching of literacy and tended to favour teaching activities which explicitly emphasised the understanding of what was read and written.

The effective teachers translated their beliefs about purpose and meaning into practice by paying systematic attention to both the goals they had identified for reading and writing (the understanding and production of meaningful text) and to technical processes such as phonic knowledge, spelling, grammatical knowledge and punctuation. They tended to approach these technical skills in distinctive ways by using an embedded approach; that is, they gave explicit attention to word- and sentence-level aspects of reading and writing within whole text activities which were both meaningful and explained clearly to pupils. Teachers in the validation sample with less coherent approaches were less likely to show how technical features of reading and writing fitted within a broader range of skills. They did not necessarily ensure that pupils understood the connections between the aims and the processes of reading and writing.

Coherence and consistency emerged as being an important and distinctive characteristic of the effective teachers in several senses:

- their beliefs were internally consistent;
- their practice lived up to their aspirations;
- their beliefs included a belief in making connections between the goals of literacy teaching and learning activities and the activities themselves.

Teaching practices: connections and contexts

The effective teachers were generally much more likely to embed their teaching of literacy into a wider context and to understand and show how specific aspects of reading and writing contributed to communication. They tended to make such connections implicit and explicit. For example, when teaching skills such as vocabulary, word recognition and the use of text features, they made heavy use of whole texts or big books as the context in which to teach literacy. They were also very clear about their purposes for using such texts. They also used modelling extensively. They regularly demonstrated reading and writing to their classes in a variety of ways, often accompanying these demonstrations by verbal explanations of what they were doing.

Because of this concern to contextualise their teaching of language features by working together on texts, these teachers made explicit connections for their pupils between the text, sentence and word levels of language study.

The lessons of the effective teachers were all conducted at a brisk pace. They regularly refocused children's attention on the task at hand and used clear time-frames to keep children on task. They also tended to conclude their lessons by reviewing, with the whole class, what the children had done during the lesson.

Links with recent developments in literacy teaching

Developments in literacy teaching in the United Kingdom have recently been dominated by the design and implementation of a National Literacy Strategy aimed at ensuring higher literacy standards in children leaving our primary schools. This Strategy includes strong recommendations regarding the content and organisation of literacy teaching. In terms of the organisation of literacy teaching, its major innovation is the 'literacy hour' – a daily hour devoted to the teaching of literacy and sub-divided into whole-class teaching sessions followed by independent and group work sessions.

Although our research was begun before the National Literacy Strategy was devised, it was clear that there were several specific points of connection between the model of literacy teaching implicit in the Strategy and our research findings. We found that the effective teachers of literacy tended to teach literacy in lessons which were clearly focused on this subject (literacy hours). Within these lessons they used a mixture of whole-class interactive teaching and small-group guided work, with occasional individual teaching usually undertaken by a classroom assistant or volunteer helper. A good deal of their teaching involved the use of shared texts such as big books, duplicated passages and multiple copies of books, through which the attention of a whole class or group was drawn to text-, sentence- and word-level features.

Implications of the research

There are several implications emerging from the research in terms of future policy and practice in continuing professional development.

Access to in-service courses

There has been a long-standing tendency in the United Kingdom for literacy curriculum specialists to be targeted for in-service opportunities in literacy. Such specialists usually have positions of responsibility in their schools for co-ordinating literacy teaching and the expectation was that enhancements in their knowledge and expertise in teaching literacy would cascade down to their colleagues through in-school professional development work. There is evidence in our findings that this policy has had a positive effect on teachers who were literacy specialists. Most of the teachers in our sample of effective teachers of literacy currently held, or had held in the past, positions of responsibility for co-ordinating the literacy teaching in their schools. However, those teachers who had not been designated as school literacy co-ordinators had been somewhat restricted in the in-service opportunities available to them in literacy. We feel strongly that all teachers need professional development in this crucial area and recommend that literacy in-service work be targeted more specifically at non-experts.

The nature of professional development experience

Our findings suggest that a particularly valuable form of professional development was teachers' involvement in longer-term projects where they had to work out practical philosophies and policies regarding literacy and its teaching – for example, through doing and using research. This contrasts with the predominantly 'short-burst' nature of much current professional development experience. There are many professional development bonuses to be gained from a more active involvement of teachers in research and enquiry. Simple top-down training of teachers is less likely to result in significant development of teaching expertise.

The content of in-service courses

The most effective in-service content seemed from our findings not to be that which focused on knowledge at the teachers' own level, but rather that which dealt with subject knowledge in terms of how this was taught to children. This implies a more practical approach, and the teachers in this study confirmed that one of the most successful forms of in-service was that which gave them guided opportunities to try out new ideas in the classroom.

While we found little evidence that the effective teachers of literacy had an extensive command of a range of linguistic terminology, it seems likely that having a greater command might help them further improve their teaching of literacy. Such terminology could be introduced (or reintroduced) to teachers not as a set of definitions for them to learn but as the embodiments of linguistic functions with a strong emphasis upon the ways these functions might be taught.

The evidence from this project also suggests that the experience of being a literacy co-ordinator itself makes a significant contribution to teachers' development as literacy teachers. Schools need to consider how appropriate elements of this experience can be replicated for other teachers.

Conclusion

The research project described in this article is unique in the United Kingdom in focusing not on features of the teaching of literacy but on the characteristics of the teachers who perform this teaching well. There have also been very few comparable studies elsewhere in the world, the nearest equivalent being the research of Pressley, Rankin and Yokoi (1996) in the US. In the US study, however, effective teachers were chosen by nomination alone. Our research is distinctive in that we also used objective measures of teachers' effectiveness by looking at the learning outcomes they produced in their pupils.

We feel that we have made a significant contribution to understandings in this area and, we hope, have initiated a debate about teacher preparation, knowledge and development which has the potential to lead to major improvements in the quality of literacy teaching.

References

Adams, M.J. (1990) *Beginning to Read: Thinking and Learning About Print*, Cambridge, MA: MIT Press.

—— (1991) 'Why not phonics and whole language', in W. Ellis (ed.) *All Language and the Creation of Literacy*, Baltimore, MD: Orton Dyslexia Society.

Alexander, R.J., Rose, J. and Woodhead, C. (1992) *Curriculum Organisation and Classroom Practice in Primary Schools*, London: HMSO.

Allington, R. (1984) 'Content coverage and contextual reading in reading groups', *Journal of Reading Behaviour* 16: 85–96.

Barr, R. (1984) 'Beginning reading instruction: from debate to reformation', in David Pearson (ed.) *Handbook of Reading Research*, New York: Longman.

Bennett, S.N., Desforges, C., Cockburn, A. and Wilkinson, B. (1984) *The Quality of Pupil Learning Experiences*, London: Lawrence Erlbaum

Brophy, J. and Good, T. (1986) 'Teacher behaviour and student achievement', M.C. Wittrock (ed.) *Handbook of Research in Teaching*, London: Collier Macmillan.

Cazden, C. (1992) *Whole Language Plus: Essays on Literacy in the United States and New Zealand*, New York: Teachers' College Press.

Chall, J. (1967) *Learning to Read: the Great Debate*, London: McGraw-Hill.

Duffy, G. (1991) 'What counts in teacher education? Dilemmas in educating empowered teachers', in J. Zutell and S. McCormack (eds) *Learner Factors/ Teacher Factors: Issues in Literacy Research and Instruction: Fortieth Yearbook of National Reading Conference*, Chicago: NRC.

Flesch, R. (1955) *Why Johnny Can't Read*, New York: Harper Row.

Goodman, K.S. and Goodman, Y. (1979) 'Learning to read is natural', in L.B. Resnik and P.A. Weaver (eds) *Theory and Practice of Early Reading*, Hillsdale, NJ: Erlbaum.

Graham, S. and Harris, K.R. (1994) 'The effects of whole language on children's writing: a review of the literature' *Educational Psychologist* 29: 187–92.

Holdaway, D. (1979) *The Foundations of Literacy*, Auckland: Ashton Scholastic.

Mather, N. (1992) 'Whole language reading instruction for students with learning abilities; caught in the crossfire', *Learning Disabilities Research and Practice* 7: 87–95.

Morrow, L.M. (1990) 'Preparing the classroom environment to promote literacy during play', *Early Childhood Research Quarterly* 5: 537–54.

—— (1991) 'Relationships among physical design of play centres, teachers' emphasis on literacy play, and children's behaviours during play', in J. Zutell and S. McCormack (eds) *Learner Factors/Teacher Factors: Issues in Literacy Research and Instruction: Fortieth Yearbook of National Reading Conference*, Chicago: NRC.

—— (1992) 'The impact of literature based programmes on literacy achievement, use of literature and attitudes of children from ethnic minority backgrounds', *Reading Research Quarterly* 27: 251–75.

Mortimore, P., Sammons, P., Stoll, L., Lewis, D. and Ecob, R. (1988) *School Matters*, Wells, Somerset: Open Books.

Neuman, S.B. and Roskos, K. (1990) 'The influence of literacy enriched play settings on pre-schoolers engagement with written language', in J. Zutell and S. McCormack (eds) *Literacy Theory and Research: Analyses from Multiple Paradigms*, Chicago: NRC.

—— (1992) 'Literacy objects as cultural tools: effects on children's literacy behaviours at play', *Reading Research Quarterly* 27: 203–25.

Pressley, M. and Rankin, J. (1994) 'More about whole language methods of reading instruction for students at risk for early reading failure', *Learning Disabilities Research and Practice* 9: 156–67.

Pressley, M., El-Dinary, P.B., Gaskins, I., Schuder, T., Bergman, J., Almasai, L. and Brown, R. (1992) 'Beyond direct explanation: transactional instruction of reading comprehension strategies', *Elementary School Journal* 92: 511–54.

Pressley, M., Gaskins, I., Cunicelli, E.A., Burdick, N.J., Schaub-Matt, M., Lee, D.S. and Powell, N. (1991) 'Strategy instruction at Benchmark School: a faculty interview study', *Learning Disability Quarterly* 14: 19–48.

Pressley, M., Rankin, J. and Yokoi, L. (1996) 'A survey of instructional practices of primary teachers nominated as effective in promoting literacy', *Elementary School Journal* 96(4): 363–84.

Rose, J. (1996) 'What our schools must teach', *The Times*, 8 May 1996.

Stahl, S.A. and Miller, P.D. (1989) 'Whole language and language experience approaches for beginning reading: a quantitative research synthesis', *Review of Educational Research* 59: 87–116.

Stahl, S.A., McKenna, M.C. and Pagnucco, J.R. (1994) 'The effects of whole language instruction: an update and reappraisal', *Educational Psychologist* 29: 175–86.

Weaver, C. (1990) *Understanding Whole Language: From Principles to Practice*, Portsmouth NH: Heinemann.

Wray, D. and Medwell, J. (2001) *Teaching Literacy Effectively*, London: RoutledgeFalmer.

5 Developing literacy

Towards a new understanding of family involvement

*Clare Kelly, Eve Gregory
and Ann Williams*

After school, Jorna goes to Arabic classes from 5–7pm, four days a week. The book she takes from school, her elder sister helps her read. Her sister shows her the Bengali alphabet and they like to do drawing and writing together, turning it into a book. She likes to watch cartoons and Hindi films – her older brother brings them. She plays with the playhouse and listens to stories, but she can't move around too much because other people complain.

(Kelly, 1996)

Introduction

Over the past three decades, a particular paradigm of successful involvement by families in children's literacy has prevailed. Official education reports have stressed the importance of regular story-reading by parents from early infancy and the absence of this practice has been used by teachers and governments alike to explain early reading difficulties. As early as 1975, government reports informed parents that

> The best way to prepare the very young child for reading is to hold him on your lap and read aloud to him stories he likes, over and over again ... We believe that a priority need is ... to help parents recognise the value of sharing the experience of books with their children.
>
> (HMSO, 1975)

The maxim 'babies need books' has changed little during later decades. It has been promoted through a programme for providing disadvantaged families and their babies with books (Wade and Moore, 2000) and reiterated in a range of government reports (SCAA, 1996; DfEE, 1998) which envisage one route into literacy for all:

> Children who are read to regularly, hear stories, learn nursery rhymes, look at books, visit libraries and so on are much more likely to learn to read easily.
>
> (DfEE, 1997: p32)

Significantly, it is not enjoyment with any kind of print that counts. Both the official curriculum and the academic world in which teachers are trained sanction and reinforce certain types of reading. Home experiences such as those of Jorna above are excluded from the school model of success and even considered to be detrimental to school learning.

The crucial question for educators, however, is whether book and story-reading experiences at home are, in themselves, essential for successful cognitive and early reading development to take place? Or are they important simply because they reproduce what counts in early literacy tuition in British schools? In other words, does the problem of low achievement lie in inadequate parental involvement or in inadequate recognition by schools of the different strengths that children might bring with them from their homes and communities? The answer is important, since we know that a number of parents have always been and will always be unable to adopt school-based practices (Gregory, 1996; Greenhough and Hughes 1999). In this chapter we argue beyond the paradigm of *parental* involvement through *story reading* practice to consider a wider framework for family and community involvement.

Background

Although numerous studies from the English speaking world point to the advantages for young children of family involvement in their literacy development, their emphasis has always been firmly and almost exclusively upon *parents* working with children *in specific ways* and often using particular school-sanctioned materials. Current models of parental involvement in reading in the UK are generally based on the following assumptions:

Assumption One Parents need to perform school-devised activities using school materials and teaching methods. Successful parental involvement means that school reading and learning practices should be transmitted from school to home.

A number of studies in the UK point to the successful transmission of reading practices from school to home (see Hannon (1995) for a summary of these). Studies on the lack of parental involvement by lower social class parents during the 1970s (Newson and Newson, 1977) coupled with evidence of unsatisfactory reading standards by their children (HMSO, 1975) were also used to support a transmissionist argument; that improved performance might be achieved through involvement in school practices. A number of research studies and practical classroom projects detail the improved achievements of children from lower social class backgrounds when their parents learn and take over school practices (Hewison and Tizard, 1980; Tizard *et al.* 1982).

Assumption Two   The storybook-reading practice between parent and young child, as it takes place in Western schools, is the most valuable preparation for children's early literacy development. Although children may participate in other practices at home and in the community, these do not initiate children into crucial patterns for school success.

The official view of what counts as literacy has filtered down through the media to become the view of society at large. Large-scale research projects (Wells, 1985) have also provided evidence of a correlation between success in reading at school and story-reading experience from infancy at home. Some studies provide precise details of the nature of the cognitive and linguistic skills provided by story-reading interactions; linguistically, 'book-oriented' children are shown to be able to switch into complex structures involving longer 'idea units' or unit length (Scollon and Scollon, 1981) as well as 'appropriate' collocations and word-groupings, for example, 'the little red hen ... reaped the corn' (Dombey, 1983); cognitively, children are shown to learn to 'detach' themselves from the immediate audience to operate within the boundaries of the text from 'situation-dependent' to 'text-dependent' thought (Simons and Murphy, 1986). Some studies detail the way in which this process begins at a very early stage through 'lexical-labelling' (Snow and Ninio, 1986) whereby an adult and very young infant point to and label objects from a simple book.

Assumption Three   Home reading programmes are for parental involvement not wider family or community participation.

Current home-reading programmes assume *parental* involvement rather than involvement by the wider family or community in young children's reading. However, the role of siblings in children's learning has been the subject of various research studies; some reveal how young children learn social and emotional skills (Dunn, 1989) and cognitive skills (Cicirelli, 1976) from older siblings. Recent studies are beginning to highlight the special role which may be played by older siblings in linguistic minority families where parents do not speak the new language (Tharp and Gallimore, 1988; Zukow, 1989; Perez *et al.*, 1994; McQuillan and Tse, 1995) and to suggest that the ways in which children learn from older siblings in the home environment may have implications for school learning.

A wider theoretical framework for family involvement

The aim of this chapter is to question the above assumptions and to explode the myth that children's reading success depends upon experience with 'authorised' reading experiences at home. The theoretical framework informing this argument synthesises perspectives from the 'New Literacy Studies', cultural psychology and cultural anthropology. The New

Literacy Studies support an ideological model of literacy which signals explicitly that literacy practices are aspects not only of culture but also of power structures (Street, 1995; Baynham, 1995). Viewed in this way, school-sanctioned literacy – or 'Literacy', as referred to by Street (1995: 14) – is just one of a multiplicity of literacies which take place in people's lives, in different domains, for a variety of purposes and in different languages.

Cultural psychology offers a 'cultural mediational model of reading' (Cole 1996: 273) which recognises as vital the actual roles that significant 'experts' play in giving 'guided participation' (Rogoff, 1990) or 'scaffolding' (Bruner, 1986) to the learning of the novice.

However, an important argument of this paper is that young people are not trapped within existing home and community practices. The children whose voices we hear below reveal a complex heterogeneity of traditions whereby reading practices from different domains are blended, resulting in a form of reinterpretation that is both new and dynamic. Duranti and Ochs (1996) refer to this type of blending as *syncretic literacy*, which merges not simply linguistic codes or texts, but different activities. In this paper, we argue that *contrasting* home and school strategies and practices may provide children with an enlarged treasure trove, upon which they can draw in the official English school.

The study

The findings below are drawn mainly from a large bank of data, collected over seven years, on home, school and community reading practices among past and present generations of teachers and pupils in schools in Spitalfields, East London. This study attempted to piece together a complex jigsaw of the role of reading in the lives of families who, in many cases, do not fit those required by 'official' school demands. It examined the literacy histories and current practices in seven Bangladeshi British and six monolingual families whose five-year-old children attended two neighbouring schools and considered the nature of reading practices taking place in the children's lives, and how far the children transferred reading strategies from home to school and vice versa (Gregory, 1998; Gregory and Williams, 1998). Examples from monolingual children from other areas of London, whose family literacy practices are recognised as 'valid' within the current 'parental involvement' framework have also been collected and analysed.

Recognising differences: contrasting materials, mediators and purposes

Current views of what counts as partnership between home and school are illustrated in the following two examples of families where school reading practices are adopted and reinforced. For children from such families, experiences with books can often begin from an early age. The following vignette of Ben (33 months), sharing a book with his mother, while his sister Alice (15 months) looks on, illustrates how this practice offers an opportunity for close interaction between child and adult, but also enables a particular set of behaviours and expectations around books to be modelled and reinforced.

Mother	*Ben*
That's an easy one. Get a more difficult one.	

Ben looks through his books. His mother suggests 'Party'? Ben chooses another first and his mother reads its title: 'The Zoo'. Ben finally settles for 'Party', reading its title out loud.

Mother	*Ben*
	Hallo Alice.
No, Alice you can't have this book. Mummy and Ben are looking at this book *Susie and John are going to a party.* What's she doing, Ben?	
	That party ... that party ... That ... is it that one? (*pointing to the present*)
Yes! What colour is it?	
	Green.
Nooo!	
	Blue.
Bl-ue! What's she got on her feet?	
	White socks.
Are they on her feet?	
	No.
Now what's she doing?	
	Putting her shoes on.
Now, what's the boy doing?	
	Putting trousers on.
Are they short trousers or long trousers?	
	Long trousers.
Have a look. You can see his knees. Are they short trousers or long trousers?	
	Short.
Yes they are, aren't they.	

Belinda does not read the story through but pauses to consider the detail of the illustrations, using the book as a focus for developing Ben's language. She poses questions and checks Ben's responses if they are inappropriate. The emphasis here is on accuracy and serves the same function as the early lexical labelling behaviour previously referred to. This pattern of question – response – evaluation is a behaviour that Ben will recognise when he starts school and it is one that he is already beginning to internalise

Mother	Ben
	What's Ann doing?
What is Ann doing?	
	Opening her presents.

Such questioning techniques are just one characteristic of a school-oriented approach to literacy learning that may be adopted within the home. The following example illustrates how Isabel (aged 10) spontaneously adopts 'teacherly' behaviour when playing a game with her brother Alex (aged 4). The children are at home; the focus of the interaction is once more a book, although this time it is one that provides games, stories and quizzes for pre-school children. They have spent approximately fifteen minutes playing one game from the book. They have now chosen a page on rhymes:

Isabel	Alex
OK. Log and ... ?	
	dog!
Good boy! Wiz ... Lizard and ... ?	
	wizard!
I gave it away a bit there, didn't I? Carrot and ... ?	
	parrot
Well done! Coat and ... ?	
	dote!
Mmm ... Late and plate	
	Mmm ... Fence and paint No, no, no ... Fence and pence, pencil ...
Yes, pence, a pence, like one p. In other words, a pence.	
	Book and pook!
No, book and look!	
	Oh yeah. Door and poor. Yeah. Video and pedeo
	(*both children*) ... N-a-w ...

The activity continues until the children's father joins in and suggests they make joke rhymes.

Isabel	Alex
House and louse	
	Now I'm gonna tell one.
	Cupboard and hubbard.
	Mother Hubbard!
Yes!	

This playful scene between siblings, which lasts for over forty minutes, reveals the wealth of cultural and linguistic knowledge the two children share. They have a shared experience of nursery rhymes, a common understanding of rhyming words, and a deep knowledge of English. The encounter reflects the same pattern of interaction that was evident between Belinda and Ben and reveals the subtlety of Isabel's teaching style. She provides ample praise and encouragement for her brother, offering examples when he loses confidence, allowing him to experiment freely, yet correcting him when he makes a mistake. She pauses to allow him sufficient time to respond and suggests generalising beyond the page to their wider knowledge of rhyming words. In the following example, and on several other occasions, she explains words she thinks Alex may not understand:

Isabel	Alex
	Rabbit and habit!
That's a good one. Do you know what a habit is?	
Well, it's sort of ... How do you describe a habit?	
It's something, sort of, you do a lot of ...	

It is clear that the two children are already familiar with a school-oriented approach to literacy as they participate in this playful encounter, which provides a strong scaffold for Alex's learning. It is likely that when Alex and Ben start school shortly, they will recognise familiar patterns of interaction around books and stories and will be well placed to make a smooth transition into the world of the classroom. But what about children who do not have this shared understanding, whose experiences around literacy do not reflect those of the school and whose understanding of the nuances of English may still be developing?

Community classes: a different kind of learning

For most of the Bangladeshi British children in our Spitalfields study, education continues long after mainstream school has finished, as the following conversation between Ann Williams and six-year-old Ruhul demonstrates:

R	There are eighty-three children.
AW	Eighty-three children in your Arabic class! And when do you go to that?
R	Seven o'clock to nine o'clock.
AW	On?
R	A night.
AW	Every night?
R	Monday to Friday.
AW	Monday to Friday! You go for two hours every night! Aren't you tired?
R	I don't feel tired.
AW	And are you the youngest then?
R	Yes and I'm on the Qur'an.
AW	You're on the Qur'an now?
R	I'm on the last one.

Ruhul explains that he is reading the last primer before starting the Qur'an. He goes on to explain more about the structure of his classes.

AW	How many teachers are there for eighty-three children?
R	There's two.
AW	Only two? Who are they?
R	One is the Qur'an ... you know, all the Qur'an ... he can say it without looking.
AW	He can? What's his name?
R	I don't know. And one is ... he can ... he knows all the meanings.
AW	Does he? Does he tell you the meanings?
R	Yes he does.
AW	So do you just read the Qur'an for two hours? Is that what you do?
R	Yes but I don't sometimes, I talk sometimes.
AW	You don't!
R	I do.

Source: Williams and Gregory, 1999: 59

This conversation gives some idea of the demands made upon children who participate in very different home literacy practices. For these children, learning to read and write is a complex business involving several languages. The home dialect of the London Bangladeshis is Sylheti, an unwritten variety of Bengali and so parents feel that it is important that their children learn to read and write standard Bengali if they are to maintain their own culture. Finally, as practising Muslims, the children must read the Qur'an and therefore attend Qur'anic school and learn to read in Arabic. Already at age six, Ruhul realises that literacy is a serious business.

The class which Ruhul attended every day after school is typical of Qur'anic classes everywhere. The sessions are usually two hours long: few concessions are made to the young age of some of the children and even the smallest are expected to concentrate for long periods:

> In this particular class there are two male teachers, one of whom is working with the more advanced children who are tackling the complicated word structures of the Qur'an. The other group consists of younger children who are in a different part of the room with the second teacher, grappling with sounds and letters and oral verse. Everyone sits on the mat swaying to the sound of his/her own voice. Although on initial appraisal the noise level seems high, little of this is idle chatter. It is the expressed wish of the teachers that children read aloud, partly to assist their learning, but more importantly so that Allah can hear. Children are encouraged to develop a harmonious recitation in unison with the gentle rocking to and fro which accompanies the reading. They are told that Allah listens to his servants and is pleased if they take time to make their reading meaningful ... 'Now, repeat after me', the teacher requests, 'Kalimah Tayyabh, la ilaha ilallaho, mohammadan rasolallahe'. He tells them to look at him as they repeat ... I leave the room on the third recitation of the prayer and notice that the children have not wavered: all remain seated on the floor as they have done for the last hour and a half.
>
> (Rashid, 1996)

Teaching methods are traditional: the teacher reads a phrase and the children repeat after him until they are word perfect and the process continues with the next phrase.

In contrast with the monolingual group who engaged mostly in informal literacy practices outside school, the Bangladeshi British children spent on average thirteen hours per week receiving formal instruction in organised classes. Thus their home literacy differs from that of many monolingual children in many respects. First, it is conducted as group rather than individual or paired activities, and an individual's progress (towards the completion of the Qur'an, for example) is often marked by the whole group sharing sweets or other treats. Second, the purpose of reading is quite different from monolingual English children: learning to read and write in Bengali is seen as entering a cultural world and acquiring a language which was fought over during the violent struggle for independence from Pakistan in 1971: learning to read the Qur'an is necessary for taking on the Islamic faith and therefore an adult and serious occupation. Finally, even the task of reading at home in English is quite different for Bangladeshi British children. In this community, where some parents are literate in Bengali but not necessarily in English, home reading usually means children reading their school texts, not with mum or dad, but with those members of the family who are already fully proficient in English, i.e. the older sisters and brothers.

Reading between siblings: a syncretism of literacies

It was this 'booksharing' with older siblings that provided some of the most interesting insights into the young Bangladeshi British children's acquisition of literacy. The combination of cultures and learning styles the bilingual children were exposed to in their daily lives resulted in a unique method of tackling the school reading books at home. When the reading sessions were analysed, it became clear that the children were blending strategies learned in both their mainstream English school and in their Bengali and Arabic classes. This resulted in what we have termed 'syncretic literacy' (Gregory, 1998) with the repetitions and fast-flowing pace characteristic of the Qur'anic reading grafted onto strategies adopted from lessons in the English mainstream school, such as echoing, 'chunking' of expressions and predicting. The transcriptions also revealed that the older siblings employed a series of intricate and finely tuned strategies to support the young readers as they struggled with the text. In the early stages, when reading with a child who was just beginning to read, the supportive 'scaffolding' was almost total, with the older siblings providing almost every word for the beginning reader. As the younger child's proficiency increased, however, the scaffolding was gradually removed until the child was able to read alone. We were able to identify the following stages in the scaffolding of the young children's reading:

1 *Listen and repeat*: the child repeats word by word after the older sibling.
2 *Tandem reading*: the child echoes the sibling's reading, sometimes managing telegraphic speech.
3 *Chained reading*: the sibling begins to read and the child continues, reading the next few words until he or she needs help again.
4 *Almost alone*: the child initiates reading and reads until a word is unknown; the sibling corrects the error or supplies the word; the child repeats the word correctly and continues.
5 *The recital*: the child recites the complete piece.

The following two extracts illustrate stages (1) listen and repeat, and (3) chained reading:

(1) *Child*	*Sibling*
	The postman
The postman	
	It was Tum's birthday
was ....birthday	
	Ram made
Ram made	
	him a birthday card
him a birthday card	

(3) *Child*	*Sibling*
	Okhta (this one)
	It's
It's a whobber. Meg …	
	Mog
Mog catched a fish	
	caught
caught a fish	
They cook	
	cooked
cooked a fish	
	and
and Owl had a rest.	
Meg was looking	
looked out	

(Gregory, 1998: 43–4)

These home reading sessions are characterised by a very high number of turns and a fast flowing pace, strategies that we have already seen in practice in the Qur'anic classes. It is notable that in spite of the child's young age, the focus is on print rather than on any illustrations. Furthermore, the older sibling's insistence on accuracy from the outset indicates that this is not play but serious work in which the roles of learner and teacher are clearly defined and not negotiable. As we shall see below, the children of first generation immigrants take their role as mediator of new cultures, languages and literacies very seriously, even in play.

Combining experiences from home and school

Good morning class	
	Good morning Miss Wahida, good morning everyone.
I want to do the register.	
So, Sayeeda.	
	Good morning Miss Wahida.
Good morning Sayeeda	
OK. We've done your reading today.	
Now we are going to do Maths. OK.	

The scene is a flat in Spitalfields, Wahida, a Bangladeshi British child aged eleven, is playing schools with her eight-year-old sister Sayeeda. The pattern of the school day is reflected in the children's play. Maths is followed by a spelling test and a 'lesson' on homophones before assembly, followed by science, geography and art. Wahida demonstrates on the blackboard while

Sayeeda writes in an exercise book. The following extracts show how Wahida has adopted the strategies from her teachers and how skilfully she scaffolds the learning of her sister by syncretising the knowledge she has gained from attending two schools. One during the day and the other each evening.

Wahida	*Sayeeda*
Well done, Sayeeda. I'm going to give you a sticker later on. A head teacher's sticker. (*After clearing throat*) Now, we're going to do a spelling test. Are you ready, Sayeeda?	
	Yes Miss.
I'm going to give you at least 20 seconds for each of them, OK? The first one is tricycle, tricycle. Tricycle has three wheels, tricycle. The next one is commandment, Commandment, I COMMAND you to do as quickly as you can. Commandment Next one is technology. Technology is a subject ...	

The spelling test continues until Wahida demonstrates the correct spellings on the board as Sayeeda marks her own work. Then the focus moves to homophones:

Wahida	*Sayeeda*
Well done! Only two wrong. Now we're going to do homophones. Who knows what's a homophone is? No one? OK. I'll tell you one and then you're going to do some by yourselves. Like watch – one watch is your time, watch. And another watch is I'm watching you. OK? So Sayeeda, you wrote some in your book, haven't you? Can you tell me some please. Sayeeda, can you only give me three please.	
	Oh I have to give five.
No Sayeeda, we haven't got time. We've only another five minutes to assembly.	

It is hard to imagine that when Wahida began school at five, she spoke very little English. Six years on, she is using the appropriate language of the classroom and the lexis of particular subjects. It is clear she has internalised the social, cognitive and linguistic rules of the classroom and has made them her own. She has taken on a register that accurately reflects that of her teacher as she confidently conducts the class through both the rituals of the day (the register, lunchtime, assembly) and the conventions of the classroom (lining up, writing the date, marking work).

Wahida demonstrates her knowledge of teaching strategies as she gives direct instruction, encourages participation, provides demonstrations and structures the cognitive demands of different 'lessons', giving ample praise and encouragement to her pupil, who readily co-operates in this sophisticated game. In both the spelling lesson and the session on homophones, Wahida scaffolds Sayeeda's learning by contextualising words and providing examples of their meaning.

Wahida's emphasis on spelling and homophones accurately reflects the 'word level work' recommended for children of Sayeeda's age, as part of the Literacy Hour. It is possibly no coincidence that she chooses to concentrate on word-level work rather than sentence level which demands a sound knowledge of English grammar or text-level work which calls for greater interpretation of the meaning and underlying structure of texts. Some of the procedures she employs reflect the approaches that she would have experienced in her community school, where teaching methods focus more on listening, repeating and practising than on interpretation.

Wahida is syncretising what she knows from the different literacies of both school contexts in a way that is recognised by her sister. Wahida demonstrates how children, who come to school with experiences of literacy that do not conform to the official view, can learn to integrate the literacy of the classroom with their previous experience in a way that is creative and sophisticated and enables them to be effective literacy learners.

Conclusion

In the current educational climate there is a high priority rightly placed on children's attainment, but, as we have seen, most debates assume a particular route to literacy learning. Yet our studies show that children actively draw on, develop and integrate a range of 'funds of knowledge' (Moll *et al.*, 1992) from home, school and community to arrive at an understanding of how written language works.

The extensive nature of the literacy practices we have seen and the serious way in which children participate provide a strong argument for a shift in the way in which literacy is authorised and diversity is perceived within the culture of the school. If children's lived experiences are to be legitimised, it would seem important that teachers have time to listen to parents and families. The statement at the beginning of this chapter is a record of a discussion between the parent of a Year One child and a teacher who was able to acknowledge and extend the varied literacy experiences of her young pupil.

Our research suggests that parents should not exclusively be seen as the principal mediators of children's literacy. For many children, particularly those who have English as an additional language, older siblings play a very important role in providing models, supporting their brothers and sisters and giving them an understanding of what it means to be literate. They are especially well placed to understand and mediate the two worlds in which the younger children live.

Our studies reveal the strong link between work and play and the gap between children's experiences at home and what officially counts as learning. They have shown the wealth of learning that is going on in homes that do not subscribe to mainstream practices and the success that can arise if these children's experiences are recognised and built upon.

References

Baynham, M. (1995) *Literacy Practices: Investigating Literacy in Social Contexts*, London: Longman.

Bruner, J. (1986) *Actual Minds, Possible Worlds*, Cambridge, MA: Harvard University Press.

Cicirelli, V.G. (1976) 'Mother–child and sibling–sibling interactions on a problem solving task', *Child Development* 47: 588–96.

Cole, M. (1996) *Cultural Psychology: A Once and Future Discipline*, Harvard, MA: Harvard University Press.

Department for Education and Employment (DfEE) (1997) *The Implementation of the National Literacy Strategy*, London, DfEE.

—— (1998) *Homework: Guidelines for Primary and Secondary Schools*, London: DfEE.

Dombey, H. (1983) 'Learning the language of books', in M. Meek and C. Mills (eds) *Opening Moves*, Bedford Way Papers 17, Institute of Education, University of London.

Dunn, J. (1989) 'The family as an educational environment in the pre-school years', in C.W. Desforges (ed.) *Early Childhood Education, British Journal of Educational Psychology* Monograph Series No. 4, Edinburgh: Scottish Academic Press.

Duranti, A. and Ochs, E. (1996) *Syncretic Literacy: Multiculturalism in Samoan American Families*, University of California: National Center for Research on Cultural Diversity and Second Language Learning.

Greenhough, P. and Hughes, M. (1999) 'Encouraging conversing: trying to change what parents do when their children read with them', *Reading* 33(3): 98–105.

Gregory, E. (1996) *Making Sense of a New World: Learning to Read in a Second Language*, London: Sage.

—— (1998) 'Siblings as mediators of literacy in linguistic minority communities', *Language and Education* 12(1): 33–55.

Gregory, E. and Williams, A. (1998) 'Family literacy history and children's learning strategies at home and at school: perspectives from ethnography and ethnomethodology', in G. Walford and A. Massey (eds) *Children Learning: Ethnographic Explorations*, Stamford: JAI Press.

——— (2000) *City Literacies: Learning to Read Across Generations and Cultures*, London: Routledge.

Hannon, P. (1995) *Literacy, Home and School: Research and Practice in Teaching Literacy with Parents*, London: Falmer.

Her Majesty's Stationery Office (HMSO) (1975) *The Bullock Report: A Language for Life*, London: HMSO.

Hewison, J. and Tizard, J. (1980) 'Parental involvement and reading attainment', *British Journal of Educational Psychology* 50: 209–15.

Kelly, C. (1996) 'A closer look at parent–teacher discussions', *The Primary Language Record and the California Learning Record in Use: Proceedings from the PLR/CLR International Seminar*, Centre for Learning, El Cajon, California.

McQuillan, J. and Tse, L. (1995) 'Child language brokering in linguistic minority communities', *Language and Education* 9(3): 195–215.

Moll, L., Amanti, C., Neff, D. and Gonzalez N. (1992) 'Funds of knowledge for teaching: using a qualitative approach to connect homes and classrooms', *Theory into Practice* 31(2): 133–41.

Newson, J. and Newson, E. (1977) *Perspectives on School at Seven Years Old*, London: Allen & Unwin.

Padmore, S. (1994) 'Guiding lights', in M. Hamilton, D. Barton and R. Ivanic (eds) *Worlds of Literacy* pp. 143–56, Clevedon: Multilingual Matters.

Perez, D., Barajas, N., Dominguez, M., Goldberg, J., Juarez, R., Saab, M., Vergara, F. and Callanan, M. (1994) 'Siblings providing one another with opportunities to learn', *Focus on Diversity* 5 (1): 1–5 (Bilingual Research Group, University of Santa Cruz, California).

Rashid, N. (1996) in Gregory, E., Mace, J., Rashid, N. and Williams, A. (1996) *Family Literacy History and Children's Learning Strategies at Home and at School*. Final Report of the ESRC Project, R000221186.

Rogoff, B. (1990) *Apprenticeship in Thinking: Cognitive Development in Social Contexts*, Oxford: Oxford University Press.

School Curriculum and Assessment Authority (SCAA) (1996) *Desirable Outcomes for Children's Learning on Entering Compulsory Education*, London: HMSO.

Scollon, R. and Scollon, B.K. (1981) *Narrative, Literacy and Face in Interethnic Communication*, Norwood, NJ: Ablex.

Simons, H.D. and Murphy, S. (1986) 'Spoken language strategies and reading acquisition', in J. Cook-Gumperz (ed.) *The Social Construction of Literacy*, New York: Cambridge University Press.

Snow, C. and Ninio, A. (1986) 'The contracts of literacy: what children learn from learning to read books', in W.H. Teale and E. Sulzby (eds) *Emergent Literacy*, Norwood, NJ: Ablex.

Street, B. (1995) *Social Literacies: Critical Approaches to Literacy in Development, Ethnography and Education*, London: Longman.

Street, B.V. and Street, J. (1995) 'The schooling of literacy', in P. Murphy, M. Selinger, J. Bourne, and M. Briggs (eds) *Subject Learning in the Primary Curriculum*, London: Routledge.

Tharp, R. and Gallimore, R. (1988) *Rousing Minds to Life: Teaching, Learning and Schooling in Social Context*, Cambridge: Cambridge University Press.

Tizard, J., Schofield, W. and Hewison, J. (1982) 'Collaboration between teachers and parents in assisting children's reading', *British Journal of Educational Psychology* 52: 1–15.

Wells, C.G. (1985) 'Pre-school literacy related activities and success in school', in D.R. Olson, N. Torrance and A. Hildyard (eds) *Literacy, Language and Learning: The Nature and Consequences of Reading and Writing*, Cambridge: Cambridge University Press.

Wade, B. and Moore, M. (2000) 'A sure start with books', *Early Years* 20(2): 39–46.

Whiting, B.B. and Edwards, C.P. (1988) *Children of Different Worlds: The formation of Social Behaviour*, Cambridge, MA: Cambridge University Press.

Williams, A. (1997) 'Investigating literacy in London: three generations of readers in an East End family', in E. Gregory, (ed) *One Child, Many Worlds: Early Learning in Multicultural Communities*, London: Fulton.

Williams, A. and Gregory, E. (1999) 'Home and school reading practices in two East End communities', in C. Leung and A. Tosi (eds) *Rethinking Language Education*, London: CILT.

Zukow, P.G. (1989) 'Siblings as effective socialising agents: evidence from central Mexico', in P.G. Zukow (ed.) *Sibling Interactions Across Cultures: Theoretical and Methodological Issues*, New York: Springer Verlag.

6   The words in basal readers
A historical perspective from the United States

James V. Hoffman

Introduction

For the most part, generations of Americans have been successful in learning to read (Smith, 1965). Despite this track record of success, the methods and materials for beginning reading instruction have been under constant scrutiny. Debates over 'what's new' and 'what's best' have propelled changes. Sometimes the changes were tied to legitimate concerns over effectiveness, as with the dismal performance of children of poverty in response to traditional reading programmes. Sometimes, though, materials and methods that have held sway over practice faded away with no apparent reason only to be replaced by others. What appears to be rational and reasoned in some shifts is often followed by changes that defy explanation.

Historians have examined these changes, searching for explanations. Nila Banton Smith (1965) described patterns in change in materials and instruction associated with broad shifts in American society (e.g. independence from England). Others, researching at a more focused level, have traced patterns of change in specific features or components of instruction. Richard Venezky, for example, examined the changing role of letters and sounds in beginning reading instruction (Venezky, 1975). Regardless of the focal point one takes, the interplay between market, political, social and research forces can be seen in almost every major turn of events in the twentieth century. How these forces sometimes cancel each other out and at other times work in concert to jar practice toward major changes is both perplexing and revealing to those who study change.

For my part, I have puzzled over the 'words' used in beginning reading instruction and the changes that have taken place in word selection, word repetition, and the qualities of the texts that surround these words. You might think that after three hundred years of experience in teaching reading in America, and with over one hundred years of research, we would have some consensus on the issues surrounding words in readers. This is not the case. Words have become a point of heated debate in the United States in recent years as the 'whole language' and 'phonics' camps stake out their territory on what's good and what's bad in words. My analysis has focused specifically on the words appearing in basal reading textbooks (beginning reading scheme books, in the UK) because of the dominant role these texts continue to play in beginning reading instruction (Baumann *et al.*, 2000). In this chapter, I will focus on the issues and trends that dominated the last half of the twentieth century. This chapter is couched, therefore, in the context of a limited historical analysis of trends.

My goal is to present a conceptual map for 'words' in beginning reading texts that reflects my puzzling out of the past and current issues. I confess this to be a very parochial (i.e. United States) perspective on the words used in basal texts. However, I present my findings and my conception with the goal that other scholars in other social contexts might test out my conception within their own cultural experiences. Of course, it would be interesting to find some convergence. Though, even more enlightening would be the discovery of different paths, different trends and different issues.

A conceptual mapping of words in text for beginning readers

I begin at the end – with a map (see Figure 6.1).

The conceptual map is laid out in terms of two dimensions for considering the words used in beginning reading. The first dimension (forming the horizontal axis) reflects a continuum from words that are selected based on a principle of phonic regularity. On the far left of the continuum, words are considered optimal for beginning reading instruction based on the degree to which the sound–letter correspondences follow regular or consistent patterns as well as the degree of internal complexity (e.g. syllable structure, morphological structure). Towards the middle of the continuum, the frequency of the words in oral and written language is considered prominently in making a judgement about what is optimal. Moving to the right of centre on the continuum, we find a selection principle that values the use of the language of the child. At the farthest extreme on the right side of the continuum, the selection principle favours words drawn from literary texts. The continuum display is used to represent the fact that, while the texts in beginning reading materials may reflect a consideration and combination of all of these principles, some choices may require compromises on other principles. As an example, it would be impossible in English to select words that display high phonic regularity and that are also the highest frequency words in oral language. This horizontal axis on this continuum addresses primarily this question: what principle of word selection is most apparent and valued in these texts?

The second continuum (forming the vertical axis) reflects the qualities of the text that surrounds the words in beginning reading materials. The primary focus for this display is on the sentence level context for the words, but it can also include consideration of larger linguistic text structures (e.g. repeated patterns) as well as design features (e.g. illustrations). These are features that have been described in terms of predictable text structures (Rhodes, 1979). At the top of this axis, I represent the position

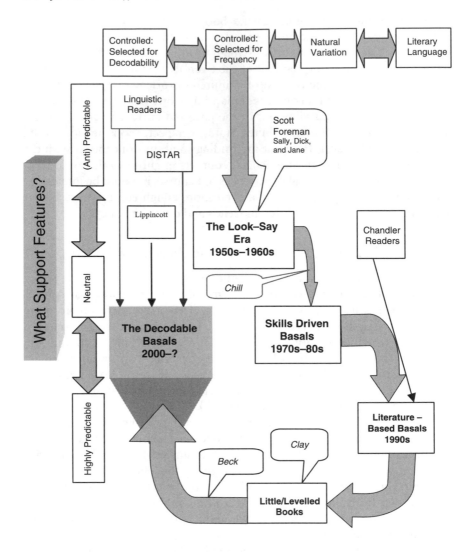

Figure 6.1   The words in first grade texts

that the least possible support offered outside the word is optimal. In this view, rich context and picture support are seen as diverting the developing reader's attention away from a focus on the critical within word features to support word identification. At the bottom of the axis, I represent the position that the texts for beginning readers should provide rich support in the form of linguistic (e.g. sentence level context), structural (e.g. repeated patterns and phrases; cumulative patterns; rhyme and rhythm patterns) and design features (e.g. picture support). The continuum is intended to reflect the relative strength of and the variety of different text structure supports that are offered. The middle ground on this continuum is less defined as a principled position. Rather, the middle ground represents the absence of attention (i.e. not designing away from but not designing text toward) external support. The vertical axis on this continuum addresses this question: how predictable is this text in supporting word identification?

Claiming territory: a historical perspective on issues

In this section, I will locate selected and representative materials that have been popular over the last half of the twentieth century on the conceptual map in Figure 6.1. The 'territorial' perspective is appropriate given the 'claims' for truth that have accompanied many of the positions taken on words in beginning reading materials. This section is divided roughly by fifteen-year intervals for the convenience of presentation, although the reality of change is much more fluid than suggested by this organisational structure. For the purposes of this report, I will be illustrative rather than exhaustive of the cases and patterns during this period. The first period will be described in greater detail than the other two periods since it provides the foundational perspective for the shifts that follow. The mapping of representative materials to Figure 6.1 relies on the programme descriptions in the text.

1955–1970 period: The Great Debate

Five distinct positions regarding the words used in materials for beginning reading instruction were present in this period. The first was clearly dominant and mainstream in terms of prevailing practice (see Austin and Morrison, 1963). The other four positions provide counterpoint perspectives that achieved varying levels of theoretical, research and practical support.

The look–say approach

Chall describes the late 1950s and early 1960s as a time of consensus in America regarding the texts for beginning reading instruction. The commonalities across the most popular basals of this time are striking. Vocabulary control and repetition was severe at the early levels. Consider the following description of the vocabulary plan for the primer level of Scott Foresman's *Fun with Our Friends* (Robinson *et al.*, 1965: 158):

> *Fun with our Friends* introduces 101 new words and reintroduces 75 words used in the Pre-Primers. The first five uses of all words, old and new, are bunched so that the young reader has rapidly repeated opportunities to meet the words in context and learn their distinctive forms. ... each word is used a minimum of ten times in the Primer.

The vocabulary selection for this programme, as with most of the other popular programmes of this time, is based on the highest frequency words in the English language (Chall, 1967). The assumption is that these words would be learned and taught as sight words. The severe restrictions on vocabulary, selected on the meaning–frequency principle, in the dominant basals of this period reflects the peak of trend toward greater and greater control that began in the early 1900s. Most of the texts for these basals, at the early levels, were written 'in-house' by the editors and/or programme authors. Because of limitations to vocabulary, the syntax is often distorted into a 'primer-ese' kind of discourse that does not correspond with the oral language structures young children bring to this text. Narratives are relied on almost exclusively in these texts. Poetry does not appear as a text structure in the early levels. The function of the illustrations is described in the teacher guide in terms of promoting 'imagery' and comprehension, not in terms of direct support for word recognition.

The sight word (look–say) method, the meaning–frequency principle for vocabulary selection, and the in-house narratives were the most popular beginning reading materials of the time (Mavrogenes, 1985). These programmes are located as a starting point on the conceptual map for the period (Figure 6.1) using the Scott Foresman *Sally, Dick, and Jane* series as the example. With reference to support for word recognition, this approach is more towards the top of the vertical scale. This placement reflects the mismatch of syntax from the oral language of the students to the written 'primer-ese'. On the horizontal scale, this approach is positioned in terms of severe vocabulary control following the meaning–frequency selection principle.

The linguistic approach

Leonard Bloomfield was a staunch critic of the reading instruction in public schools during this period of developing consensus (Bloomfield, 1942). For Bloomfield writing and reading are simply overlays to our oral language systems of speaking and listening. Learning to read was learning about the principles for the mapping. It has nothing to do with comprehension of thinking. For Bloomfield, the focus should be on teaching the code primarily through practice in controlled text. The most important feature of control for Bloomfield was regularity:

> Our first material must show each letter in only one phonetic value; thus, if we have words with 'g' in the value that it has in get, got, gun, our first material must not contain words like gem, where the same letter has different value.
>
> (Bloomfield and Barnhart, 1961: 39)

The method relies heavily on exposure to minimal pairs (e.g. bad and had; rat and sat) as well as on exposure to phonograms (e.g. Nan, can, fan, Dan). Meaning was downplayed as unimportant in learning to read and potentially distracting away from attention to the text itself. The same position was held toward syntactical patterns that reflected oral language, i.e. not important. Similarly, no picture support was allowed because of its distracting effects. Because of Bloomfield's prominent stature in the field of linguistics, the method became known as the linguistic method and was picked up on by numerous publishers in various programmes (e.g. the Palo Alto Linguistic Readers, the Miami Linguistic Readers). The linguistic readers find a secure place in the top left-hand corner of Figure 6.1. This positioning reflects the combined stance toward regularity in word selection and the negative stance toward contextual support.

The phonic–linguistic approach

In the *First Grade Studies*, Bond and Dykstra (1967) used the term phonic–linguistic to describe an approach to beginning reading that stressed systematic, sequential and synthetic phonics instruction accompanied by practice in texts that reflected the skills that have been taught. The Lippincott basal programme was used as an experimental condition in the *First Grade Studies* to reflect this orientation. In a typical lesson following this phonic–linguistic orientation, students might be taught the /sp/ blend through explicit instruction. This lesson would build directly on other phonic elements that had been taught previously. Control and repetition of vocabulary was less an issue in this approach than frequent encounters with target elements in text. As a general rule, the rate of introduction of new words was far greater in the phonic–linguistic programmes than in the look–say programmes .

It is also worth noting that many of these phonic–linguistic programmes stress the teaching of spelling as an important part of the teaching of the code. This was certainly true of the Lippincott and the DISTAR programmes. The phonic–linguistic approach is located in the same quadrant of Figure 6.1 as the linguistic method.

Language experience based approaches

The language experience approach is almost antithetical in spirit to published commercial texts. Advocates for language experience call for the use of the learner's personal language, culture and community as the primary sources of texts for beginning reading instruction. At practically every point during the twentieth century we can find language experience promoted over traditional approaches (Farnham, 1895; Lee and Allen,

1963; Stauffer, 1965). There were however, during this period, several significant attempts to bridge the language experience philosophy with commercially prepared materials. In practically every case, these efforts were directed toward the needs of culturally 'different' children. These are children who do not meet all of the assumptions imbedded in traditional materials for linguistic competence and social experiences.

Research had documented the failure of these children to learn with traditional programmes and materials. Language experience was a viable option, but the needs were widespread and the effective use of language experience called for skills that many teachers did not possess.

What these programmes had in common was the belief that texts that reflected the linguistic knowledge of the reader should be used as a bridge into traditional texts for students who were linguistically different. Though never reaching high levels of commercial success, these language-based materials do fill a gap in the range of alternatives. This view is located in Figure 6.1 to reflect the valuing of the oral language of the child. There is no evidence, though, that these texts went much beyond the use of familiar language structures and familiar topics to make them predictable.

Literature-based approaches

The fifth option available during this period shares the commitment of a language experience approach in valuing the language of children, but it places a greater emphasis on using the language of literature to create a supportive text. Bill Martin's *Sounds of Language* series embodied this philosophy. The *Sounds of Language* series was created in response to the Texas basal adoption in the mid-1960s.[1] Martin's *Instant Readers* were combined into a levelled programme with a teacher's guide (Patterson, 2000).

Martin's (1972) directions suggest that the teacher might proceed with this text through, first, a 'read to', then a 'read along', to a 'read alone' progression. Analysis at the sentence and the word level would follow. As with the other options available in the 1955–1970 period, the literature-based approach of Bill Martin had an historical precedent in the 'Story Method' (e.g. Cole and Christies' *Story Hour Readers*, 1913). I have placed the *Sounds of Language* series as the most extreme in terms of the use of predictable structures as well as the use of a literary vocabulary.

Jeanne Chall (1967) described the tail-end of this period in American history in terms of 'The Great Debate'. For her, the most important division in this period was dichotomous between those who advocated an emphasis on code versus those who advocated an emphasis on meaning. In my representation of the period in terms of positions on the words in texts, the debate is slightly more complicated but no less intense. Two facts are clear regarding this period. First, there was serious division within the field on which approach worked best with students. Second, these deep divisions were not resolved through public polemics (Flesch, 1955), or scholarly reviews (Chall, 1967), or research investigations (Bond and Dykstra, 1967). Chall wanted materials and methods to change based on the findings from research. But, in the end, market-place forces shaped the changes that were to follow.

1970–1985 period: the great deluge

It is difficult to characterise this next period in terms other than 'more' – of everything. With no clear winner emerging from 'The Great Debate', the mainstream programmes and materials moved to take the 'best' from all of the conflicting approaches in the previous period to assume an eclectic philosophical base. While words are the focus for this chapter, the 'more of everything' applies to more than just words in this period. Basals, as a matter of survival, accommodated and adapted to meet the challenges from other perspectives. Most of the mainstream basal programmes took a position of adding to the number of skills taught and adding to the number of words included in the programmes.

By the early 1980s the average number of unique words in basals reached 542 (Perry and Sagen, 1989). By the late 1980s, the average number of words in the first grade programmes of most dominant basals approached 900 unique words (Hoffman *et al.*, 1994). This more than doubled the number of unique words in the programmes from the 1955–1970 period. The meaning frequency selection principle still governed in these programmes. Only the number of words increased. There was no fundamental shift in the rationale. With the increase in vocabulary, the syntax in these readers moved slightly away from the distorted 'primer-ese' of *Sally, Dick and Jane* to approximate more 'natural' language patterns.

The number of skills taught grew as well (Popp, 1975). In the case of skills, basals were responding to the direct challenge from 'skills-based management systems'. These management systems (e.g. The Wisconsin Design (Otto and Askov, 1971); Fountain Valley (Brick, 1976)) were designed to be used independent of practice materials (i.e. readers) and advocated the teaching and testing of the component skills of reading in a sequential pattern. The skills mastery perspective was incorporated into expanding inventories of skills in the scopes and sequences of mainstream basals (Johnson and Pearson, 1975).

Interestingly, despite the increase in the number of skills being taught, the match between the skills taught and the words appearing in the texts remained low in the mainstream basals. Analyses of the alignment of skills to vocabulary revealed a severe discrepancy in the traditional basals that continued to select vocabulary on the meaning frequency principle. Beck (1981) examined the first grade programmes from eight different publishers: four code-emphasis and four meaning (i.e. the more traditional and more widely used) emphasis basals. She calculated the percentage of words that could be decoded based upon the previous instruction in all of a word's constituent elements. Basal texts that assumed a phonics first orientation were found to be more decodable than traditional basals. Decodable levels for the four code emphasis programmes ranged from 69–100 per cent. Decodable levels for the four meaning emphasis basals ranged from 0–13 per cent for the first third of the year and a range of 38–59 per cent with an average of 48 per cent for the remainder.

By the mid-1980s, the mainstream 'eclectic' basals had not only survived the assault from detractors but had consolidated and strengthened their hold on beginning reading instruction (Anderson *et al.*, 1985). These eclectic programmes are located on Figure 6.1 to reflect a slight shift toward the right in terms of a vocabulary selection principle and slightly more toward the bottom in terms of surrounding support as compared to the Look–Say basals of the previous period.

It is important to acknowledge an unusual event during this period, proving the point that too radical changes might lead to disaster. The experience of Scott-Foresman in this transitional period has become a classic lesson for basal publishers in responding to the challenges of staying current and staying competitive. Scott-Foresman went from the highly controlled 'look–say' Dick and Jane programme in the 1955–1970 period to a literature-based philosophy with Scott-Foresman Systems (Robinson, 1971). Severe vocabulary controlled and skills instruction disappeared in this series. A magazine format for the selections replaced the traditional reader. In the market place, Scott-Foresman paid the price for such a radical departure, dropping from its dominant position to the status of a minor player.

1985–2000 period: the great divide

The forces for change found converging support in the academic, policy and practice arenas during this period. Within the academic community, emergent literacy and developmental models displaced 'readiness' and mastery perspectives (Sulzby and Teale, 1991); schema theory and reader response theory displaced component skills notions of comprehension (Anderson and Pearson, 1984; Beach and Hynds, 1991); and complementary models of composing and reading displaced isolated views of language use and skill development (Tierney and Pearson, 1983). Within the practice community, the 'whole language' movement gained momentum and identity as a grass-roots base for reform of teaching (Goodman, 1989; Watson, 1989). Teachers asserted their voice in making significant decisions regarding the students in their classrooms. Finally, the policy community took an assertive position in support of change.

The remarkable changes in basals seen during this period can be understood in terms of two states' textbook adoption: California in early 1990 and Texas in 1993. State textbook adoption policies have been in use since the early twentieth century. Policy intents and practices vary from one state to another (see Farr *et al.*, 1987). For some states these policies are fairly simple and designed to insure that the prices charged by publishers are not above the prices charged in other states. In other states these policies involve a critical review of textbooks to be sold in the state to ensure that the programmes are aligned with the state's curriculum standards. Textbook adoption policies in these states are used to define the qualities and features of programmes that state tax dollars can be used to purchase. In states where the textbooks are purchased by the state using state tax dollars the review appears to be more substantive and critical (e.g. Texas and California) as compared to states where local tax dollars are used to purchase textbooks. In recent years politicians have been using the textbook adoption policy control mechanism as one of the tools to spark reform and insure greater standardisation of the curriculum. This leverage can be used to shape the basal development process itself (see Hiebert, 2002, this book).

The California basal adoption of the early 1990s was based on the principles and philosophy represented in the California literature framework. This innovative state curriculum framework called for an increased reliance on authentic children's literature in instruction and a diminishing reliance on skills teaching (California State Department of Education, 1987). Prominent basal publishers made critical decisions in this uncertain textbook market. In particular, Houghton–Mifflin did not submit their mainstream programme (i.e. the one marketed nationally) to the California adoption. Instead, they packaged sets of tradebooks ('real' books in the UK) into grade level packets and submitted these for adoption. Other major competitors made some accommodations away from the traditional format of the 1980s and toward the literature-based framework, but nothing as dramatic as the Houghton–Mifflin California programme (Wepner and Feeley, 1993). Adoptions by districts in California in the 1990 adoption favoured the Houghton–Mifflin literature sets by an overwhelming factor – estimated to be as high as 70 per cent of the total market.

On the heels of the California adoption came the Texas adoption of 1993. The textbook proclamation for the 1993 Texas adoption took the California push toward literature even further. All selections in these programmes were to be drawn from authentic children's literature. 'Authentic' was operationally interpreted to mean published previously in the tradebook form. The changes in vocabulary from the previous period were dramatic. The number of unique words across all programmes submitted for the 1993 adoption was 1,834 words as compared to an average of 962 for the 1987 programmes (Hoffman *et al.*, 1994). Vocabulary control had all but disappeared at the first grade level. In its place, there was an increased reliance on predictability as a source of support for the reader. Picture support, rhyme, repeated patterns and phrases, cumulative stories and other predictable features were embedded throughout these programmes. These programmes are represented in Figure 6.1 toward the right (literature) side in terms of vocabulary selection and on the bottom in terms of strong surrounding support for word identification.

The divide between the mainstream and the skills-focused programmes that had survived the previous period created an enormous gap in the market. That gap was soon to be filled. Back in California, the experience with the literature-based basals in classrooms produced concerns over the accessibility of these texts for the low-skilled, struggling readers. The demand for accessible text to augment the literature-based basal texts was met with an influx of 'levelled' little books (Peterson, 1991). These little books designed for use within a reading recovery philosophy were carefully levelled in terms of decoding demands as well as offering high levels of predictability to support the reader. The little books/levelled books are located in the bottom right quadrant to reflect their emphasis on predictable text support in highly accessible text (Mennon and Hiebert, in press).

2000 and beyond: the great detour

As we enter the new millennium, there are hints of what is to come. State textbook adoption processes are shaping beginning reading materials in a direction cycling back into the gap created in the previous period. In November of 1997, the state of Texas invited publishers to submit new programmes. One requirement was that first grade students be provided with opportunities to read from texts in which the majority of words are decodable. Decodable texts are defined as 'engaging and coherent texts in which most of the words are comprised of an accumulating sequence of letter–sound correspondences being taught' (Dickson, in press). Decodable texts contain a significant proportion of regularly spelled words to which students can apply the knowledge of the letter–sound relationships they are learning. Originally, the average of all decodable texts was to exceed 51 per cent of the words. This figure was later augmented by the Texas State Board of Education to an 80 per cent decodable words criterion level.

The construct of decodability applied in the Texas proclamation for basal texts is more closely aligned with the work of Beck (1981) and Stein, Johnson and Gutlohn (1999). This conception of decodability rests not so much on specific word (phonic) features as it does on the relationship between what is taught in the curriculum (i.e. the skills and the strategies presented) and the characteristics of the words read. Rather than ranging on a continuum from high to low decoding demands/complexity, the Texas definition yields a yes/no decision on decodability for each word. Following this model, the word 'cat' is decodable only if the initial c, the medial short a, and the final letter–sound associations have been taught explicitly within the programme skill sequence. A word like 'together' might be defined as decodable if all of the 'rules' needed to decode the word had been taught explicitly, prior to its encounter in the text. Foorman's *et al.* (1998) research findings were used to argue for the importance of decodable text even though there was no direct testing of the importance of this variable on student learning. Serious concerns over the validity of the research base for this conception of decodabilty have been voiced (Allington and Woodside-Jiron, 1998).

Five publishers submitted programmes that conformed to the requirement for decodability, as well as the other criteria set forward by the state of Texas. Our recent analysis of these programmes suggests that major changes have taken place in contrast with the 1993 literature-based basals (Hoffman *et al.*, 2000). The decodability levels of the 2000 texts are much less demanding than the 1993 texts. There has been a shift away from word selection on the meaning frequency principle to word selection based on the match between the words included and the phonics skills taught. The number of unique words and total number of words has not changed dramatically from the 1993 series, but the control over vocabulary at the early levels is much greater. The level of predictable text support has declined from 1993 to 2000. Further, the engaging qualities of the literature (e.g. content, language and design) have also declined.

The notion that these changes represent a 'great detour' reflects my sense that the shift is a significant reversal in the direction that had been part of the mainstream movement toward broader use of literary vocabulary with rich contextual (predictable) support systems. The term detour also reflects my view that this reversal may be temporary because it has been the result of political forces and not the market place forces that had shaped adoptions prior to this time.

Caveats

This review has focused specifically on words in the texts for beginning readers – in particular on the words in basals and other levelled texts. There is the potential, in such a limited enquiry, for important considerations to be interpreted as unimportant by virtue of the fact that they were not discussed here. I cannot conclude this review, therefore, without a note on limitations. First, I have not considered the ways in which these particular kinds of texts might be combined with work in other texts (e.g. tradebooks) to create a variety of texts and tasks for beginning readers. Basal texts have struggled under the demand that they be and include just about everything a reader and a teacher might need. This is an unrealistic expectation and one that has been a source of concern for those who wish to see a wide variety of texts available for developing readers.

Second, I have placed the issue of meaning and engaging texts in the background rather than the foreground of the discussion. There is general agreement and research support for the value of texts that are engaging for students as a source of motivation, as an opportunity for critical thinking, and a context for developing flexible reading strategies that match reader purposes (Guthrie and Alvermann, 1999). I believe that issues related to words and beginning reading texts and meaning are connected in reality but somewhat independent conceptually. It is possible to envision Figure 6.1 with a third dimension that would relate to the engaging qualities of the texts. It is likely that the slope of such a figure would move from low engaging in the top left quadrant to high engaging in the bottom left. This is an empirical issue. In fact, our research has demonstrated that the litera-ture-based basals of the 1993 Texas adoption texts tend to be higher in engaging qualities (Hoffman *et al.*, 2000). However, it is not a necessity. There are examples of texts from the linguistic–phonic perspective that are highly engaging. There are texts from the literature-based perspective that are not. It is simply more difficult to create texts that are higher on engaging qualities when the limits on word selection and support are greater.

Mapping the future

This analysis suggests where we have been and where we are with respect to the words used in beginning reading instruction. The data is descriptive of the trends not evaluative of the effects of these changes on teaching prac-tices or student achievement. This analysis suggests that the changes over the past fifty years have been more than just a pendulum swing of change. Even the 'Great Detour' is not a return to a previous position but a relative relocation that retreats on some principles but not entirely to old territory.

The changes have been substantial and influenced by a combination of theoretical, market and political forces. Clearly, the trend has been toward an increased influence on the words in texts by political forces. The leverage of the state textbook adoption policies has been particularly influ-ential over the past two decades.

Troubling in this movement is the short-circuiting of market forces. Consumers of texts, the teachers and students who use them, are now out of the loop in demanding changes that meet needs. Publishers are driven by policy mandates, not by the market place, in shaping programmes. Troubling in this movement is the shortsightedness of policy makers in forcing particular changes in textbooks without regard for the big picture. Mandates for literature-based texts to improve content and interest led to an abandoning of control over accessibility and levelling of text. Mandates for increased decodability have led to a decrease in predictable text features as well as a decrease in text quality. Perhaps, most troubling in this movement is the absence of data collected on the effect of these changes on teaching and learning.

We can only hope that careful tracking of the trends and conceptualisa-tions that reflect the qualities of these changes can become the basis for shaping the future direction of texts in ways that build on experience.

Note

1 In Texas, the state approves a list of programmes that school districts may chose from. Programmes that qualify for this list have been reviewed by the state education agency for compliance to state requirements. Funding for the purchase of textbooks is provided by the state and supported through state revenues. These 'state textbook adoption policies' vary from one state to another. Texas and California lead the states in having the most rigid requirements and, because of the large markets involved, have the greatest influence on publishers.

References

Allington, R.L. and Woodside-Jiron, H. (1998) 'Decodable text in beginning reading: are mandates and policy based on research?', *ERS Spectrum* 16(2): 3–11.

Anderson, R.C. and Pearson, P.D. (1984) 'A schema-theoretic view of basic processes in reading comprehension', in P.D. Pearson, R. Barr, M. Kamil, and P. Mosenthal (eds) *Handbook of Reading Research* (pp. 255–92), New York: Longman.

Anderson, R.C., Hiebert, E.H., Scott, J.A. and Wilkinson, I.A.G. (1985) *Becoming a Nation of Readers: The Report of the Commission on Reading*, Washington, DC: National Institute of Education.

Austin, M. and Morrison, C. (1963) *The First R: The Harvard Report on Reading in Elementary Schools*, New York: Macmillan.

Baumann, J.F., Hoffman, J.V., Hester, A.M. and Moon R. (2000) 'The first R, yesterday and today: US elementary reading instruction practices reported by teachers and administrators', *Reading Research Quarterly* 35(3): 338–77.

Beach, R. and Hynds, S. (1991) 'Research on response to literature', in R. Barr, M. Kamil, P. Mosenthal and P.D. Pearson (eds) *Handbook of Reading Research*, Vol. II (pp. 453–89), New York: Longman.

Beck, I. (1981) 'Reading problems and instructional practices', in G.E. MacKinnon and T.G. Waller (eds) *Reading Research: Advances in Theory and Practice*, Vol. 2 (pp. 53–95), New York: Academic Press.

Bloomfield, L. (1942) 'Linguistics and reading', *The Elementary English Review* XIX(4) (April): 125–30 and XIX(5) (May): 183–6.

Bloomfield, L. and Barnhart, C. (1961) *Let's Read*, Detroit, MI: Wayne State University Press.

Bond, G.L. and Dykstra, R.R. (1967) 'The cooperative research programme in first-grade reading instruction', *Reading Research Quarterly* 2: 10–141.

Brick, M. (1976) 'Fountain Valley reading support system for teachers', *Reading Improvement* 13(2): 66–70.

California State Department of Education (1987) *Handbook for Planning an Effective Literature Program: Kindergarten Through Grade Twelve*, Sacramento.

Chall, J. (1967) *Learning to Read: The Great Debate*, New York: McGraw-Hill.

Cole, I. and Christie, A.J. (1913) *Story Hour Readers Manual*, New York: American Book Company.

Dickson, S. (in press) *Texas Education Agency Basal Analysis Plan Related to Decodability*, adapted from TEA technical report in preparation, Austin, TX: Texas Education Agency.

Farnham, G.L. (1895) *The Sentence Method of Reading*, Syracuse: Bardeen.

Farr, R., Tulley, M.A. and Powell, D. (1987) 'The evaluation and selection of basal readers', *Elementary School Journal* 87(3): 267–82.

Flesch, R.F. (1955) *Why Johnny Can't Read: And What You Can Do About It*, New York: Harper.

Foorman, B.R., Fletcher, J.M., Francis, D.J., Schatschneider, C. and Meehta, P. (1998) 'The role of instruction in learning to read: preventing reading failure in at-risk children', *Journal of Educational Psychology* 90(1): 37–55.

Goodman, Y. (1989) 'Roots of the whole language movement', *Elementary School Journal* 90(2): 113–28.

Guthrie, J.T. and Alvermann, D.E. (1999) *Engaged Reading: Processes, Practices, and Policy Implications*, New York: Teachers College Press.

Hoffman, J.V., Sailors, M., Patterson, B. and Mast, M. (2000) 'The decodable basals', paper presented at annual meeting of National Reading Conference, Scottsdale, AZ.

Hoffman, J.V., McCarthey, S.J., Abbott, J., Christian, C., Corman, L., Dressman, M., Elliot, B., Matherne, D. and Stahle, D. (1994) 'So what's new in the new basals? A focus on first grade', *Journal of Reading Behavior* 26(1): 47–73.

Johnson, D.D. and Pearson, P.D. (1975) 'Skills management systems: a critique', *Reading Teacher* 28(8): 757–64.

Lee, D.M. and Allen, R.V. (1963) *Learning to read through experience*, New York: Appleton-Century-Crofts.

Martin, Bill, Jr. (1972) *Sounds I Remember* (pp. 3–4), New York: Holt, Rinehart & Winston.

Mavrogenes, N.A. (1985) 'William Scott Gray: Leader of teachers and shaper of American reading instruction', doctoral dissertation, University of Chicago.

Mennon, L.A. and Martin, M.A. (in press) *Little Books and Phonics Texts: An Analysis of the New Alternatives to Basals*, CIERA Technical Report, Ann Arbor: University of Michigan.

Menon, S. and Heibert, E.H. (2000) *Literature Anthologies: The task for First-Grade Readers*, CIERA Report 1.008, Ann Arbor, MI: CIERA.

Otto, W. and Askov, E (1971) *The Wisconsin Design for Reading Skill Development*, ERIC Document ED051966.

Patterson, B. (2000) 'On the wings of words: a life history of Bill Martin Jr', unpublished doctoral dissertation, University of Texas at Austin.

Perry, L.A. and Sagen, P.S. (1989) 'Are basal readers becoming too difficult for some children?', *Reading Improvement* 26(2): 181–5.

Peterson, B. (1991) 'Selecting books for beginning readers', in D.E. DeFord, C.A. Lyons and G.S. Pinnell (eds) *Bridges to Literacy: Learning from Reading Recovery* (pp. 119–47), Portsmouth, NH: Heinemann.

Popp, H. (1975) 'Current practices in the teaching of beginning reading', in J. Carroll and J. Chall (eds) *Toward a literate society* (pp. 101–46), NY: McGraw-Hill.

Rhodes, L.K. (1979) 'Comprehension and predictability: an analysis of beginning reading materials', in R.G. Carey and J.C. Harste (eds) *New Perspectives on Comprehension* (pp. 100–31), Bloomington, IN: Indiana University School of Education.

Robinson, H.M. (1971) *Coordinating Reading Instruction*, Scott Foresman Reading Systems, Glenview, IL: Scott Foresman.

Robinson, H.M., Monroe, M., Artley, A.S., Huck, C.S. and Jenkins, W.A. (1965) *Fun With Our Friends: The New Basic Readers*, Curriculum Foundation Series, Chicago, IL: Scott Foresman.

Smith, N.B. (1965) *American Reading Instruction*, Newark, DE: International Reading Association.

Stauffer, R.G. (1965) 'A Language Experience Approach', in *First Grade Reading Programs, Perspectives in Reading* No. 5 (pp: 86–118), Newark, DE: International Reading Association.

Stein, M., Johnson, B. and Gutlohn, L. (1999) 'Analysing beginning reading programs: the relationship between decoding instruction and text', *Journal of Remedial and Special Education* 20(5) (Sept/Oct.): 275–87.

Sulzby, E. and Teale, W. (1991) 'Emergent literacy', in R. Barr, M. Kamil, P. Mosenthal and P.D. Pearson (eds) *Handbook of Reading Research, Vol. II* (pp. 727–58), New York: Longman.

Tierney R. and Pearson, P.D. (1983) 'Toward a composing model of reading', *Language Arts* 60(5): 568–80.

Venezky, R.L. (1975) 'The curious role of letter names in reading instruction', *Visible Language* 9(1): 7–23.

Watson, D.J. (1989) 'Defining and describing whole language', *Elementary School Journal* 90(2): 129–42.

Wepner, S.B. and Feeley, J.T. (1993) *Moving Forward With Literature: Basals, Books, and Beyond*, New York: Maxwell Macmillan.

Discussion

Research into the teaching of literacy

Maureen Lewis

At a conference in London, Michael Fullan, from the University of Ontario and currently head of the team undertaking the external appraisal of the National Literacy and Numeracy Strategies for the DfES, told the following joke:

> A professor of education was visiting the most improved and successful school in a deprived area of the city. He spent the morning observing classes, spoke to teachers and pupils and examined the school's excellent test results. He saw well-motivated pupils reading with enthusiasm, writing with great skill and undertaking creative problem solving in maths. At the end of his visit he was asked what he thought of it all.
>
> 'Ah. It's all very fine', he said, 'But will it work in theory?'

The roar of laughter from the mainly practitioner audience spoke not only of their enjoyment of the story but also perhaps gave some insight into the image of theoreticians held by some of those who spend all their time working in classrooms. These tensions between theory and practice have been polarised in this country over the last few years by those who claim that much educational research is over-theorised, irrelevant and of little value to classroom teachers and policy makers (Woodhead, 1998; Hargreaves, 1996; Tooley and Darby, 1998). The chapters in this first part of the book illustrate how, on the contrary, research should and indeed does shape policy and classroom practice. The discussions put forward in each of these chapters demonstrate the role of research in both challenging and shaping orthodoxies, and give direct examples of the role of research in influencing policy makers and practitioners.

The governments of the three nations represented in this book (UK, USA and Australia) are each concerned to raise standards in literacy in their countries and each has used research to help shape its policies. In England the government has set challenging targets for the standards of literacy that are to be achieved by the nation's children. The strategy it has implemented has drawn on research and good practice and two of the chapters in this section (Beard and Bailey) offer different perspectives on this – Beard arguing that the National Literacy Strategy (NLS) was firmly grounded in research from its inception and Bailey arguing that some aspects of the NLS are more firmly grounded in research than others. In the USA, the Secretary of Education has compared the challenge set to teachers in raising reading standards as equivalent to the challenge to land the first man on the moon (Paige, 2001a). America, too, has drawn on research to inform an 'Education Blueprint' (Paige, 2001b) for achieving its reading standards goal. In 1997, a national panel on reading (NRP) was convened by the federal government, charged with assessing the status of research-based knowledge about reading, including the effectiveness of various approaches to teaching children to read. The NRP met over a period of two years. The full report is now available on the internet (NICHD, 2000) and its findings are helping to shape federal literacy policy. In Australia, the government published *Literacy for All: The Challenge for Australian Schools. Commonwealth Literacy Policies for Australian Schools* (Commonwealth Government, 1998) and again drew on research data to guide its decisions in shaping 'The Literacy Plan'. What is apparent in all three nations is a shared recognition that literacy education is a priority and that each government has also indicated the central importance it places on research in guiding its approach.

Such a commitment to research by national governments can only be applauded – even though there will always be debate about which research is selected and which is rejected – but whilst acknowledging the importance of research in influencing government policy we must also acknowledge the inherent tensions that might arise. Ernest (1998), quoting Levin, argues that research and policy are and should be in conflict because they represent different aims and cultures. On the one hand, he argues, policy is short term and decision orientated. On the other hand, research is long term and knowledge orientated. In addition, he argues that good research is very cagey about claiming to provide sure-fire solutions to problems and is very careful about over-generalising or assuming that applications are easily made. It is for these very reasons that research reviews which investigate research findings over time and synthesise the findings from several studies are particularly significant. It is just such research overviews that seem to be influencing policies at the moment. This is not to say, however, that research can never have an immediate and direct impact upon classroom practices.

Each of the chapters in this section is strongly grounded in literacy research, either by offering research overviews or by describing a specific piece of research. The authors illustrate for us the different ways research can be used. The research described in these chapters extends our knowledge of literacy practices by drawing upon international as well as national findings; gives us a wealth of evidence to guide or critique policy regarding literacy teaching; helps us identify effective practices in literacy teaching;

reminds us of the importance of recognising that children's literacy prac-tices go beyond the classroom and are influenced by the social-cultural practices within their homes and communities; and also reminds us of the complex relationship that exists between how literacy teaching is perceived and the texts we offer pupils. Importantly, all these chapters (implicitly or explicitly) ask the thoughtful reader to examine their own assumptions about literacy and literacy teaching and to weigh these against the evidence offered.

Several authors in this section argue that we can now draw on research from different perspectives to arrive at a consensus view about the teaching of literacy. Harrison argues that there is a consensus view emerging on the teaching of reading. Hoffman, too, indicates where consensus might lie in the teaching of reading and decries the use of research to justify huge swings in the approaches adopted by some states. Many educationalists view the growing consensus on how to teach reading as a welcome respite from the 'reading wars' of the 1980s and early 1990s. Wray and Medwell in their chapter on effective teachers of literacy indi-cate aspects of effective literacy teaching that few would dispute. Many of the characteristics of effective literacy teachers that they identify – such as having a good knowledge of literature – will readily be adopted into a consensus view of effective teaching.

Challenging assumptions and orthodoxies is another crucial aspect of research if our knowledge is to grow and we are not to ossify into doing things in certain ways because we have always done them in that way. Kelly's chapter explicitly challenges the assumptions we often make about school and community literacy practices. Hoffman's chapter illustrates how different orthodoxies in how to teach reading have been established and challenged, and the impact these differing orthodoxies have had on books and related practices for teaching children to read. Beard robustly challenges some of the established orthodoxies in both reading and writing from the 1970s and 1980s in his chapter.

However challenging people's (often deeply held) assumptions is diffi-cult. People who have given much time and thought to particular theories and approaches defend their views and often resist change. In the UK the focus for heated debate appears to be shifting from disputes about the teaching of reading to disputes about the teaching of writing. Bailey outlines some of the areas of dispute in her chapter on writing. There is some indication in Bailey's chapter that, just as the 'reading wars' polarised views into 'phonics' versus 'real books', the critics of the National Literacy Strategy approach to writing may be polarising the argu-ment into 'grammar' versus 'writing process'. 'Grammar' is a pejorative term in this context and the NLS is caricatured as promoting mechanistic and decontextualised teaching of grammar and other aspects of writing and ignoring writing process. Such polarisation is unhelpful and gives a distorted account of how the teaching of writing is exemplified in recent government advice. There *is* an important debate to be had about the teaching of writing and how we can best combine the teaching of compositional and transcriptional aspects of writing – and there is a need for all those who engage in this debate to examine their own assumptions. There is also an urgent need for new research and evidence to inform the debate. For example, it is interesting to reflect that following the promotion of the National Literacy Strategy's new guidance on the teaching of writing during this year (DfEE 2000, 2001) there has been a 3 per cent rise in writing scores in national test results for 11 year olds (DfES, 2001) after several years of writing scores remaining static. It is early yet to give too much weight to this evidence as longer-term evidence of rising writing standards are needed, but it is an indication that new approaches should be carefully considered.

The role of national tests in both measuring and shaping what counts in literacy is taken up in Part II and the question of how one measures rising standards is examined. In this next section, and in the section that concludes the book, the importance of research in providing us with the evidence to reflect upon the literacy experiences and achievements of our pupils continues as a recurring theme. Taken together, all the chapters in this collection amply disprove the claim that 'educational research is over-theorised, irrelevant and of little value to classroom teachers and policy makers'.

References

Commonwealth Government (1998) *Literacy for All: The Challenge for Australian Schools Commonwealth Literacy Policies for Australian Schools (1998)* (available at www.detya.gov.au/schools/publicat.htm).

Department for Education and Employment (DfEE) (2000) *Grammar for Writing*, London: DfEE.

—— (2001) *Developing Early Writing*, London: DfEE.

Department for Education and Skills (DfES) (2001) *National Curriculum Assessments for 7, 11 and 14 year olds in England, 2001* (available at www.dfes.gov.uk/statistics).

Ernest P. (1998) 'What is the purpose of educational research? Reply to Discussion Paper 3' (available at www.bera.ac.uk/debate/reply).

Hargreaves, D.H. (1996) *Teaching as a Research-based Profession: Possibilities and Prospects*, London: Teacher Training Agency.

National Institute of Child Health and Human Development (NICHD) (2000) *National Reading Panel Report* (available at www.nationalreadingpanel.org).

Paige, R. (2001a) Keynote speech by Roderick Paige, USA Secretary for Education, at the International Reading Association International Conference, New Orleans, May 2001.

—— (2001b) *Transforming the Federal Role in Education so that No Child is Left Behind* (available at www.whitehouse.gov/infocus/education).

Tooley, J. and Darby, D. (1998) *Educational Research: A Critique*, London: Ofsted.

Woodhead, C. (1998) 'Academia gone to seed', *New Statesman* 77(20 March): 51.

Part II

What counts as evidence?

7   The irrelevancy – and danger – of the 'simple view' of reading to meaningful standards

Victoria Purcell-Gates

Public and political pressure for high-stakes assessments linked to rigorous standards in the United States has unfortunately been accompanied in many arenas by a regressive move to conceptualise the construct to be assessed – reading – in a simplistic manner. This conceptualisation is referred to as the 'Simple View of Reading', and its re-emergence in educational and research circles in the United States is, in my view, disturbing, perplexing, and – ultimately – dangerous. The 'Simple View of Reading' posits that the process of reading involves only two components and that they are additive and linear: (1) decoding and (2) comprehension. This stance is disturbing because it is linked to political moves that appear to be power plays by special interest groups whose special interests do not include marginalised people, but rather those who have long held power and influence. It is perplexing because it represents several giant steps backwards, ignoring research and knowledge that has been accumulated over the past two decades of the ways sociocultural and cognitive factors interact and transact to influence academic success, including reading achievement. It is ultimately dangerous because it is not unlikely that the results of this simplistic view of learning to read, with its current link to high-stakes testing and new standards, will result in the reification – but this time under a 'scientific' mantle – of the academic marginalisation of underachievement of those groups of people who since time immemorial have represented the bottom quartile of achievement in our schools. It could very well lock non-mainstream students ever more solidly into categories of achievement that label them as 'not good enough', 'below average', 'not proficient', or whatever the norm-referenced or criterion-referenced term of choice is.

We need standards

Before I go further, though, let me briefly affirm the need for standards. This argument against a simplistic view of reading is not one against standards – by which I mean criteria or targets against which achievement is to be judged. If we do not have standards for achievement in education, we have no compass, no goal, nothing to guide or inform our teaching, nothing to promise our students, no real purpose for the institution of education.

Further, we need standards now because too many of our students appear to have invested valuable life time in the activity of schooling with very little payoff. It appears that, for many of our students, no promise was made or kept by the institutions of education. And with no promise or goal, it stands to reason that no organised effort will be invested in keeping the unmade promise. With rare exceptions, whole groups of students in the United States leave our schools with skills and abilities, and hopes and expectations for a 'good and prosperous' life, significantly lower than other whole groups of children.

We all know who these children are: they are, for the most part, the children of poor, marginalised, lower-class families. The achievement gap between the 'haves' and the 'have-nots' is an old, unwavering, solid fact of education. It has never been closed despite thousands of words of rhetoric paid to it, millions of dollars thrown at it and hundreds of legislative actions taken on its behalf. This virtually straight-line relationship holds across nations, in developed and developing countries, across forms of government, across forms of education and teaching methods and across time (Kaestle *et al.*, 1991).

This unconscionable achievement gap is why we need standards – standards that are taken seriously for all children; standards that can guide and shape instruction as required by local contexts; promises that can be made and kept. I offer as an example of such standards those created jointly by the National Council of Teachers of English and the International Reading Association for Reading and Language Arts. The following sample exemplifies their tone and scope: 'Students read a wide range of print and nonprint texts to build an understanding of texts, of themselves, and of the cultures of the United States and the world; to acquire new information; to respond to the needs and demands of society and the workplace; and for personal fulfilment. Among these texts are fiction and non-fiction, classic and contemporary works' (NCTE/IRA, 1996: 27).

However, the nature of many of the state standards that have been imposed in the US is troubling, as are the ways in which they have been put in place. Unlike the NCTE/IRA standards, state standards are being imposed by politically-appointed bodies on schools and, thus, on colleges of education from without in the form of high-stakes achievement tests – the MEAP (Michigan Educational Assessment Program), the TAAS (Texas Assessment of Academic Skills), and so on. The 'high stakes' include promotion to the next grade, graduation from high school, and, in some cases, permission to drive a car!

The new moral panic

While some may argue that high stakes are needed for schools and school attendees to take standards seriously, I am disturbed by factors that have contextualised this new standards/assessment move. One of the more disturbing is the dubious claim that literacy levels are declining. The American public has been convinced, through an effective orchestration of public pronouncement, news releases, talk shows, commentaries, and so on, that a serious literacy crisis exists among the American people – not just children but adults as well! According to this theme, close to one half of the products of state schools do not possess literacy skills sufficient to function in the 'new information society'. Within this, the general opinion has been formed that children are failing to learn to read in school and that strong action must be taken by government to counteract the forces of sloth and poor teaching.

However, this claim is not backed by data. Berliner and Biddle in their award-winning critique of the myths of educational decline (1995) point out that (a) SAT scores have risen steadily since 1976, especially for students from minority homes; (b) since 1977, the National Assessment of Educational Progress (NAEP) scores indicate stable achievement combined with modest growth for students from minority groups and 'less advantaged' backgrounds. They suggest that 'some critics confuse what education has accomplished with what one might want it to accomplish' (Berliner and Biddle, 1995: 28), and that claims that stable or modestly growing achievement scores are not good enough 'cannot be substantiated because they are based on unanchored perceptions of national need and on predictions that are not necessarily sound' (*ibid.*: 27–8).

Arguably the most famous case of falling scores in America, and the one that was widely used for the call for school reform, is that of the state of California, where in 1994 the NAEP scores placed California almost last among the fifty states in reading. This was immediately taken up by a vociferous group as an indictment of the reading instruction that had been very loosely in place in California for several years, termed Whole Language or Literature-Based Reading Instruction. What this group failed to acknowledge was the unprecedented influx of immigrants to this state, fleeing persecution and poverty, many of whom had received no education in their homelands and all of whom spoke a language different from English. They failed to document what reading instruction was like in those schools with the lowest scores. They failed to provide data as to how many classrooms in California actually *used* Whole Language and, for those that did, what form it took. They actually failed to document anything with actual data. Regardless, this fall in test-score status was somehow generalised to the entire country in the popular imagination and, before we knew it, we had a national literacy crisis on our hands, and Whole Language, Literature-Based, Meaning-Focused (whatever you want to call instruction that embeds phonics instruction within meaningful literacy activities) was dubbed the cause.

The above suggests to many an organised and orchestrated movement, opportunistically responding to public fears, to influence public belief. At the very least it reflected a confluence of actions on the part of the federal government, state governments, special interest groups and the media. It all came together in a seeming second to form public belief and then to act on that with legislative mandates. Any attempts to moderate the discourse and to move the impending train onto a more informed track were quickly waylaid.

Another piece of the dubious nature of the high-stakes assessment/standards movement was the way in which influential panels were mandated, funded, shaped and used to document the supposed problem as well as its scientific answer. About the same time that the special interest groups in California and Texas were beginning to take control of the literacy instruction in their states, and that the popular press and media were inflaming the public with their sky-is-falling rhetoric, a panel was being formed by the National Research Council and the National Institute of Child Health and Development. The National Research Council is a policy advisory body to the federal government formed by the National Academy of Sciences and the National Academy of Engineering. The National Academy of Sciences describes itself as 'a private, nonprofit, self-perpetuating society of distinguished scholars engaged in scientific and engineering research, dedicated to the furtherance of science and technology and to their use for the general welfare' (Snow, Burns and Griffin, 1998: iv). The National Academy of Engineering 'was established in 1984, under the charter of the National Academy of Sciences, as a parallel organisation of outstanding engineers [and] shares with the National Academy of Sciences the responsibility for advising the federal government' (*ibid.*). The appointed committee consisted of some literacy researchers with first-hand knowledge of children, schools and teaching, others from the neurological research field, and some policy people.

Despite a high level of mistrust from the literacy community, due in part to their sense of exclusion, the committee did a reasonable job in identifying and synthesising the research that would inform early reading and drew implications from this literature for instruction. They basically concluded what good teachers have always known: home language and literacy experiences dramatically affect the degree of success children will achieve in school literacy learning; children need to learn how to decode with accuracy early on in their formal instruction; children need to read a lot as soon as they can from highly engaging texts. Drawing as they did from the dyslexia research, there was a great deal of focus placed on the need for beginning readers to possess 'phonemic awareness' (the knowledge that words can be reduced to theoretically isolable units or phonemes, and the ability to do this) before they could benefit from phonics instruction which teaches them to map letters to phonemes or phonemic units.

However, the troubling part of this is the way in which this report was used. While its basic conclusion implicated a 'balanced' approach to beginning literacy instruction, only its conclusions regarding phonemic aware-ness and direct, systematic teaching of phonics were highlighted by the press and the policy mavens. Rather than acknowledge the complexity of the learning to read process, which was reflected, implicitly at least, in the report, the powerful special interest groups used this report to 'document' again the need to replace Meaning-Based early reading instruction with direct, systematic teaching of phonemic awareness and phonics. This is also being used to justify the use of high-stakes assessments of this knowl-edge at state and local levels and the threat of them at the national level. Ready-to-go, expensive, code-based instructional programmes hit both the educational and the trade markets. The rest of the report is now almost completely lost in the public's mind. These manipulations of the public will are some of the troubling aspects of the procedures surrounding the high-stakes assessment and standards movements. Let me move on to the problems with the new-old simple view of reading.

Giant steps backwards

Within this disquieting sense of manipulation is the real question: why this move *back* to a simplistic notion of what is involved in learning to read and write – to a time when *literacy* was known as simply *reading*? What is missing from this simplistic picture is any notion of culture – of the ways that language and literacy are acquired and develop within sociocultural contexts, of the acknowledgement that academic and literacy achievement is highly correlated with sociocultural group membership. This perplexes me the most. Why act as if we have not explored and come to appreciate the deep and abiding ways that the sociocultural affects the cognitive (Gee, 1992; Heath, 1983; Purcell-Gates, 1995; Vygotsky, 1962)? Let me argue for a bit for why this stance results in irrelevant impacts of research on educational outcomes.

First of all, I challenge anyone to describe a scenario in which any mental process occurs outside a sociocultural context. From birth, we perceive objects, learn about them, think about them, act upon them, forget about them – *while we are in the world*. And the world is organised socially and culturally. It is not possible to truly think of the sociocultural and the cognitive as separable. The relationship between the two is not additive or linear. Rather, their relationship is nested and transactional, with the cognitive occurring always and forever within a sociocultural context. The obvious conclusion from this is that research into a cognitive process like reading, to have any veridical relationship to reality, to life, must reflect this contextualisation of the cognitive by the sociocultural.

But does this really apply to cognitive processes like word recognition? Do the basic cognitive processes like perception and recognition change, or look different, if their sociocultural contexts change? I know that at least some reading researchers deny that they do. Their assertion, therefore, is that the process of word recognition operates the same whether one is reading from a list of unrelated words, reading from a list of related words, reading words in the context of a single sentence, reading words in the context of a paragraph, reading words in the context of a novel, doing any one of these reading tasks in a lab in front of a computer screen as a subject in an experiment, within an fMRI machine with your head in a locked position reading from a reflected image, reading in a classroom during round-robin reading, reading in a classroom during free reading, reading at home from a recipe book during a cooking event, or reading in bed before drifting off to sleep. According to many researchers of the sub-components of reading, this process is unaffected by context, linguistic or situational. But, I have to ask, from the perspective of an unrepentant empiricist: how do we know? So far, the only data used to support the conclusion that the word recognition process is the same regardless of context is based on experiments conducted under carefully controlled conditions within the context of experimental labs. And I know of at least one study of first graders that discovered differential strategy use for word reading within the same children depending on whether they were reading independently, reading with a group, or reading with a peer – three different sociocultural contexts (McIntyre, 1992).

I would like to see more research done on the word recognition process as it operates under differing contextual conditions. There are enough indications from existing research to suggest that this process, if not fundamentally different, at least operates within a range of differences, as the context of the word changes. While work by Stanovich, West, Schwantes, and others (Schvaneveldt, Ackerman and Semlear, 1977; Schwantes, Boesl and Ritz, 1980; Stanovich and West, 1978, 1981) demonstrates convincingly that younger, less able readers rely on linguistic context to a greater degree than do readers for whom the word recognition process has become automatic, models of perception and recognition of real-world objects, including words, include the effects of context not as trivial but almost in a deterministic sense.

For perception of real-world objects, Palmer (1975) and others have demonstrated that objects will be recognised both faster and more accurately if they are encountered in congruent contexts. For example, when shown a picture of a living room, or a kitchen, complete with furnishings, subjects recognise a toaster faster and more accurately (that is, with fewer 'misses' or errors) in the picture of the kitchen as compared to the picture of the living room. Note that our conceptions, or schemas, of which objects more typically belong in a kitchen, a living room, a bedroom, and so on, come from our experiences living in our own specific, socioculturally organised worlds. When shown a picture of a cooking fire in different contexts, for example, I suspect that most of us here would recognise it faster and with fewer errors in the context of a campground than in the context of a 'kitchen'. But the people I worked with in the rural areas of El

Salvador as I studied the workings of a women's literacy class, would, I suspect, recognise it faster in the context of a kitchen than a campground since they cooked three times a day over a cooking fire placed on a raised platform and located inside their kitchens which were one-room structures built of sticks (Purcell-Gates and Waterman, 2000). I doubt if any of the women in the literacy class had ever even seen an electric toaster!

Regarding the recognition of letters and words, I point to Rumelhart's (1975) and McClelland and Rumelhart's (1982) interactive model of word recognition, a model that is still valid and is implicit, I believe, in much of the work that is still being done on word recognition. According to this model, as confirmed by a series of carefully designed and executed experiments, context aids the perception of letters as they are processed in the perceptual system. Context at the semantic level, the syntactic level, the lexical level, the letter cluster level, the letter level and the feature level significantly enables perception and recognition of letters and words. Note, again, that that which determines what constitutes congruent context – that is, context at all, at the semantic, the syntactic, the lexical, the letter cluster, the letter, and the feature levels – is determined by our experiences living in the world, in our own specific, socioculturally organised worlds.

Luria (1983) linked the written language encoding system to young children's grasp of the specific function of print as an aid for recalling messages. Dyson (1991) points out that Luria illustrated in detail how a functional and interactive context – a socioculturally organised context – might lead to the grasp of the function of print as an aid for recalling messages and the beginning of the child's search for ways of precisely differentiating meanings through letter graphics. In other words, experiencing the act of using print within an authentic, interactive, sociocultural context enabled the cognitive task involved in learning letter–sound encodings which enabled that print function – writing down messages.

Even within Schema Theory – that quintessentially cognitive, psycho-centred theory – the effect of context is at the forefront. It accounted for context effects, especially the context of expectation and background knowledge on all levels of cognition, from basic processes like letter recognition to more cognitive ones like comprehension and interpretation of text. And several researchers at the time went on to confirm the obvious conclusion from schema theory, that comprehension of text was affected by cultural perspectives.

The foregoing arguments were directed at those who view the world primarily through a cognitive lens. Other arguments against the simple view of reading, though, flow from the work of sociocultural researchers who have described the clear cognitive consequences of differing sociocultural ways of thinking about reading, writing and words (Heath, 1983), and of differing dialects and languages that do not share political and social power with the language of academic literacy (Purcell-Gates, 1995).

The danger of the simple view of reading

By denying the complexity of learning to read and write, we are missing critical research questions, and thus we run the very real risk of rendering our research results irrelevant – irrelevant to the actual problem, not the created problem described earlier. By assuming a purely cognitive lens and rejecting the sociocultural one, we cannot make any headway towards understanding why sociocultural group membership is the strongest predictor of academic achievement. Assuming only the cognitive lens, we have to pretend that sociocultural factors do not exist because we can't 'see' them through our lens. We are left with the conclusion that only teaching method is the operative factor (haven't we 'been there and done that'?), and, if the teaching method found to be the most beneficial to middle-class children does not work as well with low-SES children, then there must be something wrong with those children – back to the old, ethnocentric deficit theories!

Let me first list some of the flawed research conclusions that have led us, I believe, along this slippery slope – one destined to end, I fear, with the further academic alienation of traditionally educationally under-served sociocultural groups. First, there is the strong belief that research has documented that parents from low-SES groups (and many in the US assume this means ethnic minorities) do not know how to talk to their children. This ranges from the belief that these parents do not talk to their children at all to the belief that, while they do say things, they don't say the 'right' things in the 'right' way – that is, as middle-class parents do.

Conclusions drawn from this type of research implicate poor children's vocabulary, syntax and phonemic awareness. And what data is this based on? This is primarily based on data that come from (a) small samples of middle-class children from disproportionately represented academic homes and (b) larger samples of poor children and their parents who are asked to engage in culturally obscure tasks for the sake of research.

These types of studies also assume that because reading is a language activity, one's oral language performance is the precursor and determiner of one's literacy ability. By assuming this 'language ability writ large' stance, this research strand totally ignores the sociolinguistic research that documents the deterministic role that such social factors as setting, purpose and speaker–listener relationships have on language production. Further, this research ignores the documented linguistic differences between speaking and writing – differences that reflect these sociolinguistic factors (Purcell-Gates, 2001). In other words, readers do not read their oral language, no matter what form that oral language may take, and certainly no one reads the oral language used in homes between parents and children. Blaming the oral language of poor families for the school failures of poor children misses the boat by more than a mile.

Another line of mistakenly applied research conclusions I wish to address is that which is currently driving reading policy in the US. Few are aware that the 'solid body of research' on early reading touted by NICHD is research on the causes of dyslexia. Similar concerns about dyslexia helped to focus activists behind the California rush to impose a systematic direct instruction model of phonics teaching and to discredit meaning-based literacy instruction. I must ask, what is the neurological condition of dyslexia doing driving the general education agenda?

According to the federal definition of this learning disability, dyslexia is a relatively rare neurologically-based condition that makes it unusually difficult to learn to read and write.[1] People who have this condition are born with it and it is not considered to be curable. Rather, dyslexics require a different type of reading instruction – one that involves very systematic and rule-governed instruction in letter–sound relationships.

Knowing that it is the research on the underlying causes of dyslexia that is driving the current early reading instruction reform movement helps to answer some of the questions regarding this movement, but not all. Because all learning disabilities, including dyslexia, are presumed to be neurologically-based and not the result of cultural differences (National Joint Committee on Learning Disabilities, 1989 in Myers and Hammill, 1990), sociocultural factors are not included in the research lens used by researchers studying it. But how did we segue from a specific type of diffi-culty in learning to read to the entire population of learners who experience difficulties in learning to read and who thus experience prob-lems, or slower development, with academic literacy throughout their schooling?

The impression I have gained from a reading of the public documents is that, while different 'causes' of reading disability exist (at least hypotheti-cally), including biological ones (i.e. dyslexia), (a) it is still a matter of contention that learning disabilities have a neurological aetiology,[2] and (b) it is too hard to sort this out now. Therefore, the Preventing Reading Difficulties in Young Children committee stated that their recommenda-tions extend to all children, regardless of their level of risk of experiencing difficulties in learning to read and regardless of the presumed cause of such difficulty (Snow, Burns and Griffin, 1998). From a group that touts the necessity of empirical data to back conclusions, this is problematic.

And this leads to some dangerous implications coming from this simple-view-of-reading, cognitive-only-lens movement that is driving school reform with its control over instruction, teacher education, and high-stakes assessment:

Danger 1:   We will put a type of instruction into place in all classrooms for all children that has been verified as effective only for a small percentage of children.

Danger 2:   We will fail to understand the sociocultural factors that contribute to the systematic failure of whole groups of children in our schools because the research lens being validated and funded does not include these factors.

Danger 3:   Because the possibility of an untested instructional programme and/or a simplistic educational programme applied to problems that are neither recognised nor understood will fail, high-stakes assessments will drive another nail in the coffin of academic underachievement for further generations of children from low-status social and cultural groups.

Danger 4:   This nail may prove to be the one made of steel due to the public's uninformed and non-critical understanding of 'science', and rules of implication.

An argument for complexity

I wish to end with an argument and call for embracing complexity. When we consider literacy development for different people in different contexts from different sociocultural worlds for different purposes, we are in a complex arena. To deny this is not only foolish, it is foolhardy and borders on the unethical. We cannot allow the politicians and their policy appointees to act as if a young learner from a low-literate family who speaks a mountain dialect will learn to read in the same classroom, with the same instruction, and in the same way to the same level as one from a highly-literate family who speaks like those in power. We cannot allow them to insist, as they are now beginning to do in the United States, that all teachers accept this supposition and teach all children to read in the same way and then pay the consequences when it does not 'work'.

Rather, I believe that we must first insist that our existing knowledge of the complexity that results from sociocultural contexts of learning be integrated into policy decisions and, secondly, that this knowledge base be expanded with more research that can ultimately hone and sharpen policy for reading instruction. We need empirical data to answer crucial questions like: (a) How do beginning readers take from their instruction to learn to effortlessly and effectively process print for meaning? (b) Why do beginning readers from homes of poverty accomplish this more slowly and less well? Does it make a difference whether these children are taught by community insiders or outsiders? Why? (c) What exactly do learners from mainstream affluent homes know that allows them to accomplish this process faster and better in mainstream schools? How did they learn this? (d) How do you explain the almost straight-line relationship between family income and reading achievement around the world? (e) If successful learners go through different processes, or follow different paths toward literacy depending on the focus of their instruction, then how is it that they arrive at the same place, if they do?

We need studies that will tell us: (f) not only what cognitive and linguistic skills learners need to begin to read successfully, but how they learned those skills, in what contexts, under what conditions, within what types of interactions with whom; (g) what is the relationship, if any, between what I call the *actualisation* of literacy learning (i.e. literacy in practice outside school settings) and the ways in which literacy was taught and experienced by learners in school. We need to design a study that would accommodate and explain the work Shaywitz and Shaywitz (1996) are doing with the neurology of dyslexics, as well as the work done by Rosalie Fink on successful adult dyslexics (1998), who explain their success as professionals – and overcoming the debilitating effects of dyslexia – with the fact that at some point in their lives as students they became actual readers in response to personal intense motivations to read extensively on their own on a topic of personal interest.

Unless we reject the politically motivated calls and manipulations for simplistic solutions to created and misrepresented problems and instead embrace the world of learning and development in all of its complexity, we will continue to contribute to the real literacy problem: the under-representation of poor and marginalised people among the academically successful.

Notes

1   Best estimates put the incidence at between 2–6 per cent of the general population (Myers and Hammill, 1990).
2   The history of research into learning disabilities is a long and chequered one, plagued from the beginning by real problems of differentiating types and subtypes of LD. Its legacy is this notion that LD as a construct is questionable. However, most teachers who have ever worked with learners with diagnosed learning disabilities and researchers who study them in neurology labs agree that for some learning difficulties no other explanation exists besides a neuro-logically-based difference in processing information.

References

Berliner, D.C. and Biddle, B.J. (1995) *The Manufactured Crisis: Myths, Fraud, and the Attack on America's Public Schools*, New York: Addison-Wesley.

Dyson, A.H. (1991) 'Viewpoints: the word and the world – reconceptualizing written language development or do rainbows mean a lot to little girls', *Research in the Teaching of English* 25: 97–123.

Fink, R.P. (1998) 'Literacy development in successful men and women with dyslexia', *Annals of Dyslexia* 48: 311–47.

Gee, J.P. (1992) *The Social Mind: Language, Ideology and Social Practice*, New York: Bergin & Garvey.

Heath, S.B. (1983) *Ways With Words: Language, Life and Work in Communities and Classrooms*, Cambridge: Cambridge University Press.

Kaestle, C.F., Damon-Moore, H., Stedman, L.C., Tinsley, K. and Trollinger, W.V., Jr. (1991) *Literacy in the United States*, New Haven, CN: Yale University Press.

Luria, A. (1983) 'The development of writing in the child', in M. Martlew (ed.) *The Psychology of Written Language* (pp. 237–77), New York: John Wiley.

McClelland, J. and Rumelhart, D. (1982) 'An interactive activation model of context effects in letter perception: Part 2. The contextual enhancement effect and some tests and extensions of the model', *Psychological Review* 89: 60–94.

McIntyre, E. (1992) 'Young children's reading behaviors in various classroom contexts', *JRB: A Journal of Literacy* 24: 339–71

Myers, P.I. and Hammill, D.D. (1990) *Learning Disabilities: Basic Concepts, Assessment Practices, and Instructional Strategies*, 4th edn, Austin, TX: Pro-Ed.

National Council of Teachers of English and International Reading Association (NCTE/IRA) (1996) *Standards for the English Language Arts*, Urbana, IL: National Council of Teachers of English.

Palmer, S. (1975) 'The effects of contextual scenes on the identification of objects', *Memory and Cognition* 3: 519–26.

Purcell-Gates, V. (1995) *Other People's Words: The Cycle of Low Literacy*, Cambridge, MA: Harvard University Press.

—— (2001) 'Emergent literacy is emerging knowledge of written, not oral, language', in J. Brooks-Gunn and P.R. Britto (eds) *The Role of Family Literacy Environments in Promoting Young Children's Emerging Literacy Skills* (pp. 7–22), San Francisco, CA: Jossey-Bass.

Purcell-Gates, V. and Waterman, R. (2000) *Now We Read; We See; We Speak: A Portrait of a Freirean-based Adult Literacy Class*, Mahwah, NJ: Lawrence Erlbaum.

Rumelhart, D.E. (1975) *Toward an interactive model of reading*, Technical Report No. 56, Center for Human Information Processing, La Jolla, CA: University of California, San Diego.

Schvaneveldt, R., Ackerman, B. and Semlear, T. (1977) 'The effect of semantic context on children's word recognition', *Child Development* 48: 612–16.

Schwantes, G., Boesl, F. and Ritz, R. (1980) 'Children's use of context in word recognition: a psycholinguistic guessing game', *Child Development* 51 (Summer): 730–6.

Shaywitz, S.E. and Shaywitz, B.A. (1996) 'Unlocking learning disabilities: the neurological basis', in S.C. Cramer and W. Ellis (eds) *Learning Disabilities, Life-long Issues* (pp. 255–60), Baltimore, MD: Paul H. Brookes.

Snow, C.E., Burns, M.S. and Griffin, P. (eds) (1998) *Preventing Reading Difficulties in Young Children*, Washington, DC: National Academy Press.

Stanovich, K.E. and West, R. (1978) 'Automatic contextual facilitation in readers of three ages', *Child Development* 49: 99–118.

—— (1981) 'The effect of sentence context on ongoing word recognition: tests of a two-process theory', *Journal of Experimental Psychology: Human Perception and Performance* 7: 658–72.

Vygotsky, L.S. (1962) *Thought and Language*, Cambridge, MA: Harvard University Press.

8 Understanding national standards in reading

Sue Horner

Understanding national literacy

Any large-scale national drive to raise standards needs to attract consensus in a number of areas. There needs to be agreement that standards are too low, that public spending can and should be put into raising them and that schools and teachers should prioritise the nominated areas, regardless of what else they do.

In England, in 1997, the areas of literacy and numeracy were designated as the priorities nationally for all primary schools. The National Literacy Strategy and, a year later, the National Numeracy Strategy were put in place, with a structure of national, regional and local staffing and specially designated funding.

The system for specifying what is to be taught and for assessing the standards of pupils' work at key points in their schooling were already in place (Horner, 1998). The National Strategies added more detail to the curriculum to be taught by producing frameworks of objectives for teaching. The success of the strategies is measured by pupils' performance in national tests at age 11. Targets are set for national achievement, which become translated into targets for each school.

Given the pressure on these tests, the credibility of such measurements rests on a range of factors such as their validity, reliability, comparability over time and consistency of approach. The tests need to be understood, particularly by teachers, so that the dimensions of literacy that are to be expected at the target levels are clear and pupils helped to achieve them.

This chapter explores how the tests are made explicable and usable for teachers. The Qualifications and Curriculum Authority, which is responsible for the tests, has developed a range of ways to show what the tests are testing, including at question level. There are other ways that teachers learn about the tests, including annual reports on pupils' performance in the tests (*Standards Reports*), which are sent to all schools.

This chapter focuses on reading, since there are directly comparable instruments in other countries, and international studies, such as PISA and PIRLS, are also available for context and comparison. The underlying construct of reading is described and the way this is reflected in questions explained. The nature of difficulty in questions is also related to reading skills. The transparency of the testing is reinforced in the publication of reports on how pupils answered the questions (e.g. QCA 2001) , and this is outlined in the last section of the chapter.

National tests of reading

In England all children undertake formal assessments of their reading and writing at the end of the second, sixth and ninth years of schooling, that is, at ages 7, 11 and 14 respectively. These assessments are keyed to statutory requirements for what should be taught and an eight-level scale describing progress across the age range.

During the 1990s the tests for the various ages were developed on different time scales and to different models, showing sensitivity to the experience and expected performance of pupils at each age. These assessments have become very high-stakes, as the government has used them to set demanding targets for pupil performance in them. From the starting point in 1996, when 57 per cent of pupils achieved the target levels, the government set the expectation that, in 2002, 80 per cent of pupils should reach that level. The progress towards that aim is shown in Figure 8.1.

In the period from 1996 to 2000 the percentage of the cohort achieving the target level at age 11 rose from 57 per cent to 75 per cent. In order to be sure that the demands of the assessments are maintained over time there are rigorous equating measures in place. These are necessary since the results of the tests are published and schools ranked and rewarded on the basis of their pupils' performance.

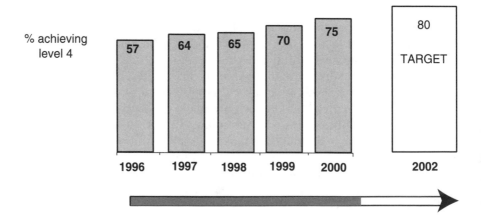

Figure 8.1   Progress towards government target for achievement in literacy

The development of the tests, their trialling and pretesting and subsequent analysis of how pupils performed are documented elsewhere (see Sainsbury, 2000 and this volume; Whetton *et al.*, 2000). The technical systems are extensive, with different statistical measures applied at various points. What I want to focus on here is not the technical properties of the tests, but the construct of reading that underpins them.

The national curriculum for English and its accompanying scale of pupil performance set out dimensions of reading. Within a wide range of texts, the skills outlined include strategies for reading for meaning, selecting and retrieving information and ideas, and skills of inferring and deducing. They also include responding to and commenting on the language and structure of texts and their purposes and contexts. The salience of these aspects of reading varies at the different ages, but their significance in defining the broad scope of what counts as reading should not be underestimated, especially when considering the curriculum backwash from such high-stakes tests.

During 2000 a review of the national assessment arrangements has been undertaken and we intend to develop a framework for the tests which shows clearly the continuities, as well as the different emphases, in the nature of the reading assessed at each age. We do not see the framework as limited to what can be assessed in short, formal tests, but see it as applicable in ongoing assessments and as particularly useful for diagnosing pupils' strengths and weaknesses.

Reading assessment focuses

We have now defined the aspects of reading to be assessed as pupils' ability to:

1   use a range of strategies, including accurate decoding of text, to read for meaning;
2   understand, describe, select or retrieve information, events or ideas from texts and use quotation and reference to text;
3   deduce, infer or interpret information, events or ideas from texts;
4   comment on the structure and organisation of texts, including grammatical and presentational features at text level;
5   identify and comment on the writers' uses of language, including grammatical and literary features at word and sentence level;
6   identify and comment on writers' purposes and viewpoints and the effect of the text on the reader;
7   relate texts to their social, cultural and historical contexts and literary traditions.

In principle, any reader at any age may give evidence in any one of these assessment focuses, since they are not specifically age- or ability-related:

- pupils aged 7, 11 or 14 can show they can select and retrieve information (focus 2) particularly in non-fiction texts;
- young children can suggest the reason for the use of a presentational feature such as a word printed in capital letters (STOP!), while an older pupil may comment on the use of subheadings or layout (focus 4);
- a young child can distinguish texts where the purpose is to describe or explain from those which aim to give instructions. A secondary school pupil may be showing skills also related to focus 6, by commenting on how the writer's views are shown through the portrayal of character or the choice of language when conveying action.

The first three focuses are more likely to be emphasised when assessing 7-year-olds and the others may well be more prominent when assessing older students. But this is not simply a question of a hierarchy of skills. All readers must be using strategies to decode and make meaning from texts, but for experienced readers much of such activity is automatic, and the strategies are only likely to become evident when the reader is confronted with a text which has unfamiliar words or more complex ideas. In the assessment for 7-year-olds, focuses 1 and 2 are likely to be more prominent because that is the curriculum emphasis for those children, ensuring they can use phonic, graphic and contextual clues and also use their word recognition skills when reading different texts.

When students are older what becomes more valued is the ability to evaluate and respond critically to a text, using reasons and evidence. This moves beyond inference and deduction into being able to distinguish layers of meaning and recognise such features as deliberate ambiguity or implicit bias. Being able to see how the social or literary context of a text influences its meaning is also usually thought of as an advanced skill, but some children in primary school are able, for example, to reflect on whether stories, such as those by Richmal Crompton, are old-fashioned and how stories set some time ago may or may not be relevant to children now.

These assessment focuses are relevant in reading at all ages, but their emphasis varies as the curriculum changes and pupils become more skilled. So how can they then be used to give a framework for assessing national standards?

Using the assessment focuses

In developing the tests the first priority is to identify texts which are interesting to the pupils, varied in form and suitable for constructing questions. As questions are being devised the assessment focuses begin to become useful. Of any particular question we can ask not only 'What is the answer?', but also 'Which focus is this related to?' and 'Does it really assess that focus?'. The focuses immediately offer a way to reflect critically on the questions and their potential answers, helping to establish whether it is a worthwhile question and to identify what sort of contribution it can make to the overall pattern of the test.

Once a range of questions has been devised and informally trialled, the selection of questions for the next stage has to be made. At this point the balance of the test can be considered through looking at the numbers of questions and marks assigned to the different focuses. This is not a mechanical process with pre-set notions of the precise balance of focuses in any test. To some extent the focus of the questions is related to the type of text. For example:

- A page of diagrams and labels showing the sequence of a spider spinning a web suggests questioning mostly related to strategies in reading for meaning (focus 1) and understanding and retrieving information (focus 2). There may also be scope for looking at presentational features (focus 4) in terms of layout, headings and structure of the information;
- A contrasting text, such as a version of a traditional tale, may offer more possibilities of questions on uses of language, including literary features (focus 5) and how the story relates to its literary tradition (focus 6).

While there may be no specific balance of assessment focuses required, it is, of course, important to look at the balance and the way the questions cluster and are distributed across the test as a whole. Over time, patterns change, which indicates the balance of the assessment focuses at the different ages. In general the tests for 7-year-olds include most questions on focuses 1, 2 and 3, with a few questions related to other areas. The tests for 11-year-olds have a proportion of marks on focuses 2 and 3, but also range more across the other areas. The tests for 14-year-olds are less explicitly linked to focuses 2 and 3, although pupils will use these skills in answering questions related more to focuses 4, 5 and 6. These differences in emphasis reflect the demands of the eight-level scale to which the tests are calibrated.

Question difficulty

The level of difficulty of any particular question derives from a complex relationship between the text, the assessment focus, the amount of structure in the question and where the question comes in the test. Offering a structure in the question may enable pupils to tackle aspects which are difficult if they are left to work them out for themselves. The level of scaffolding or independence in using reading skills is an important dimension across the years:

- A multiple-choice question for 7-year-olds may enable them to identify the purpose of a text;

- Eleven-year-olds can be asked what a particular sentence shows about a writer's purpose – for example, a sentence in the first person and a colloquial style can be identified as describing an experience for a younger person;
- Fourteen-year-olds may be invited to identify the writer's purpose and give evidence for their views, drawing on the complete text.

These questions all relate to the same assessment focus, but the differing levels of structure in the questions suggest the movement from a strongly guided reader to an independent one. This also illustrates how it is not possible to view the assessment focuses as a hierarchy – structuring the questions can enable younger pupils to show understanding of more complex concepts than might otherwise be possible.

Retrieval of information on, for example, scientific evidence for a theory from a complex text is likely to be difficult. Retrieval of a synonym for a single word to answer a question on the same page as the answer (as in a Year 2 test) is much less difficult. Implicit in these dimensions of questions is the level of independence with which pupils are expected to tackle texts and questions. Independence relates to the level of support in the question and the ability to orchestrate different reading skills in order to answer a question. Older and more skilled readers are also asked to range across a text or texts, without necessarily being given specific references, in order to accumulate points to be assembled into answers. This involves using criteria of relevance, and also a more evaluative view of what is read. In skilled readers, independence in understanding a text and how it works is likely to be accompanied by critical and evaluative comments on the effectiveness of it.

Understanding and reporting on national performance

At the same time as the tests are sent into schools, the marking guides are also sent. This means that the system is transparent and the marking is carried out to pre-agreed and published expectations. The tests of 11-year-olds are marked by teachers and others from different schools. The marking is checked and then the scripts are returned to schools so that teachers can see exactly how their pupils did. If teachers are not content with the marking of their pupils' work they can ask for a review. This happens most often when one or two marks will make the difference to a pupil achieving the target level.

To help teachers understand the tests and how their pupils performed in them, a *Standards Report* is published each year and sent to schools. The report has a number of elements:

- summary data, showing the changes in the English scores over time
- key messages, including significant trends such as the differential performance of boys and girls
- detailed analysis of pupil performance by assessment focus
- implications for teaching and learning, which indicate priority areas in teaching reading and writing
- technical data, such as question facilities.

The main body of the report describes how pupils answered the questions, with examples of acceptable and unacceptable answers, related to the marking guidelines. The questions on the various assessment focuses may be found at different points during the test, so the report brings these together to look at patterns. For example, children who are likely to achieve the national expectations should achieve highly on the questions focused on *understanding and retrieving information*. They should also be able to *deduce, infer or interpret information, events or ideas*. They will also show some skill in responding to questions on features at text, sentence and word levels, and in identifying writers' purposes.

Teachers are able to look at their own pupils' scripts and see if there are particular patterns in the answers which could be related to teaching. One school found that their pupils did not succeed in answering a question focusing on comparing texts, and the teachers realised they had not taught this. Similarly, some classes may be more familiar with working on fiction, and the results may show they need more help with non-fiction texts. These reports enable teachers to be more reflexive, and consider the impact of their teaching. Many use previous years' tests as a way of helping pupils understand what they will be asked to do, and since teachers have the marking guides, they are able to be clear about good answers.

Conclusion

The tests are high stakes for teachers, schools and the government. In order for them to be educationally defensible it is important that the tests are understood and the results are credible. The rationale and assessment focuses are published, the marking guides are public at the same time as the tests, pupils' scripts are returned to schools, and a report on performance by a nationally representative sample of pupils is sent into all schools. All these aim to maintain an open system, where the measure of performance is available for scrutiny and challenge, and is also accessible to teachers and pupils.

References

Horner, S. (1998) 'Assessing reading in the English National Curriculum', in Harrison, C and Salinger, T. (eds) *Assessing Reading 1: Theory and Practice* (pp. 84–95), London and New York: Routledge.

Qualifications and Curriculum Authority (QCA) (2001) *Standards at Key Stage 1 English and mathematics*; *Standards at Key Stage 2 English and mathematics*; *Standards at Key Stage 3 English*, London: QCA.

Sainsbury, M. (2000) 'The life cycle of a question', paper presented at Qualifications and Curriculum Authority assessment conference, Chester, November 2000.

Whetton, C., Twist, E. and Sainsbury, M. (2000) 'National tests and target setting: monitoring consistent standards', paper presented to American Educational Research Association Annual Meeting, New Orleans, April 2000.

9   Validity in literacy tests

Marian Sainsbury

Introduction

As a contribution to considering 'what counts as evidence', this chapter will address testing and other formal assessment procedures, looking in some detail at the kinds of evidence they can provide. In evaluating children's progress, some accepted measure of their attainment is essential, and many research studies make use of test scores as part of their findings. Similarly, the great majority of public debates about raising standards in literacy take for granted the nature of the instruments by which those standards are measured.

Yet these tests are not fixed, predetermined guarantors of objective evidence. The information that tests can provide varies according to many factors: the kind of questions that are asked, the circumstances in which the tests are administered and the rules for marking and scoring, for example. What can and what cannot be inferred from a particular set of test results is a question at the heart of validity theory, and answers are often multifaceted and ambiguous (Messick, 1989). In looking at what counts as evidence, it is essential to consider what kinds of tests are available, and what they can reveal about pupil attainment.

This chapter will survey and review some of the features of the test development process and its products, and the overlapping collection of theoretical frameworks into which the work fits. It will try to establish what is known and what further research needs to be done, in order to continue to ensure that tests of literacy are able to bear the very considerable weight that is currently placed upon them.

Constructs and performances

Underlying the entire test development process is the notion that it is possible to take a sample of behaviour and, from that sample, to gain information about a wide range of knowledge, skill and understanding. The questions in a test, or the requirements of an assessment task, are not of particular interest in themselves, but are intended to stand for a much broader and deeper area of interest, a construct which represents some valued educational outcome (Haertel, 1985). Educational constructs typically include ideas about the nature of the subject itself, as a discipline, as well as ideas about how children learn in that curriculum area.

These constructs are essentially wide-ranging, complex and abstract in nature. Yet tests to find out about pupils' learning must necessarily require something concrete and specific. This can be envisaged as a span (Figure 9.1), in which the difference between the 'test/task' end and the 'construct' end is seen in terms of increasing generality, complexity and abstraction (Sainsbury and Sizmur, 1998).

CONSTRUCT   TEST/TASK PERFORMANCES

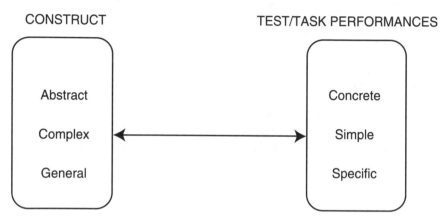

Abstract   Concrete

Complex   Simple

General   Specific

Figure 9.1   The span between construct and performance

The work of the test developer can therefore be conceptualised as a quest for a set of test items or performance tasks that will give the best possible information about important aspects of the construct – the search for validity.

Validity, reliability and manageability

At the same time, other imperatives must be observed. Teachers are understandably reluctant to spend large amounts of time administering tests or to undertake time-consuming and cumbersome performance tasks, so the manageability of the assessment instrument is always a concern. The other main demand upon the test developer is for reliability: the test results should be consistent, irrespective of the time and place of administration and of the identity of the administrator and the marker. This is particularly the case in a high-stakes system where confidentiality and security are essential requirements for reliability.

Of course, it is unrealistic to suggest that all these demands can be met in full by any assessment instrument of any kind. Validity and reliability require as full an assessment as possible, which clearly works against manageability. Validity may require tasks which replicate as closely as possible performance in the real world, which detracts from reliability as all real-world situations are different. Reliability may demand simple objective answers which cannot represent the construct fully, setting up a tension with validity. So the work of the test developer is always to draw the best possible balance between these conflicting demands in the light of the purpose of the assessment. This requirement – fitness for purpose – underlies all test development work.

The construct with which this book is concerned is the construct of literacy, arguably the most central and important 'valued educational outcome' of all. In the construct of literacy, ideas about the nature and purpose of reading and writing are intermingled with ideas about the ways in which children learn the subject. All of these reflect aspects of the contemporary social, political, philosophical and educational context within which they are situated.

Whilst bearing in mind the constraints of manageability and reliability, this chapter will principally concern itself with validity and with the way in which literacy is currently defined. In order to delineate what is included in this construct of literacy, the National Curriculum programmes of study and the National Literacy Strategy framework for teaching form useful points of reference. Between them, they articulate an accepted view of literacy as it is currently taught in this country. The main argument will be that contemporary definitions of literacy are considerably more complex than previous ones. Since tests must validly reflect the construct, the demands placed upon test development in recent years – since the introduction of the National Curriculum – have been considerable. A great deal of innovative work has taken place over a relatively short period of time in seeking to meet these demands.

Traditional constructs of literacy

Children's ability to link the spoken word with the written word has always been regarded as fundamental to literacy. Some traditional reading tests restricted themselves to addressing this limited definition of the construct. The Schonell test, for example (Schonell, 1945), which was widely used in Britain right up to the 1980s, simply required children to pronounce a series of single words. Its well-known first line is *tree little milk egg book*, and higher levels are represented by words such as *sepulchre* and *idiosyncrasy*. This minimalist approach to defining reading encountered fierce criticism (see, for example, Stierer, 1989), and, despite its enviable manageability, would have few defenders nowadays. It clearly makes no attempt at all to address whether children have any understanding of the words they read.

A fuller definition of the construct of reading is addressed by a range of tests which require sentence completion. One popular example of this in

Britain is the Suffolk Reading Scale (Hagley, 1987). Here, children are offered a sentence with one missing word and must choose the correct option from a series of five. The difficulty level varies, with sentences such as:

He hit the ball with the [*date / hat / boy / bit / bat*].

near the beginning, progressing to:

The [*automatic / audacious / autocratic / augmented / auspicious*] occasion was marred by the inclement weather.

towards the end. Answering successfully requires children to read the words, and also requires understanding of the meaning of the local context of the single sentence.

Modern theories: increasing complexity

This is very far, however, from the complexity that seems to be a feature of the contemporary construct. Here, the establishment of the link between the spoken word and the written word is also viewed as crucial, and the 'searchlights' model in the National Literacy Strategy in England sets out how phonic and grammatical knowledge, together with word recognition and contextual understanding, contribute to achieving this. At these early stages of literacy learning, however, understanding and response are already an important part of the construct. Even with young children, the area of interest is whether they have understood the meaning of a text, and not simply whether they can pronounce the words in it. This part of the contemporary construct is underpinned not just by psychological theories, but also by literary ones, and in particular those often referred to as reader-response theories.

According to these theories, meaning is made in the interaction of reader with text. The reader actively engages with the written words, not just following each sentence, but anticipating and retrospecting, adjusting and summarising meanings at various points in the text (Iser, 1974; Rowell *et al.*, 1990). Particularly important in this process is an element of 'filling gaps'. The text does not contain every piece of information necessary for understanding, and the reader must therefore supply what is missing from his or her own experience. Depending upon the text, there may be many opportunities for filling gaps at various levels of depth and sophistication. Most texts for children require them to use some chains of reasoning of their own, for example to supply the link between causes and effects, or characters and their motivation for action. In some books, even for the youngest children, there is scope for reflection upon profound human and philosophical questions, as the work of Anthony Browne or Jenny Wagner, for example, demonstrates (Stephens, 1992; Watson, 1993).

A further layer of complexity is introduced by the fact that reading and understanding must apply to a wide range of text types. Different types of text – information, instruction, narrative, poetry – call forth different types of engagement. The purpose for which the reader reads typically varies with these different types of text, and therefore the kind of background knowledge that the reader must bring to fill the gaps varies too (Duthie, 1996). To tackle a variety of text types, knowledge about the world and about people must be complemented by knowledge about texts themselves – what their purposes might be, and how they are typically organised and use language in order to meet those purposes. A further dimension of this, which is rapidly gaining in prominence, is the whole area of electronic texts and the different kinds of reading involved in gaining meaning from a computer screen.

Correspondingly, the requirements for writing do not simply set out that children must learn to write words using the conventional spellings. Over and above this, they should bring to their writing the knowledge of text types that they have gained from their reading. As writers, they work to produce texts for particular purposes, reviewing and revising their drafts with structure, audience and purpose in mind.

There is, moreover, an attitudinal strand adding a further dimension to the construct. The general requirements of the National Curriculum for English in England open with a statement that pupils should become 'enthusiastic, responsive and knowledgeable' readers. Young readers and writers are not only learning about different text types, but need to appreciate for themselves the purposes of reading and writing, their uses and value.

Thus an analysis of the National Curriculum demonstrates that literacy, as defined there, is a highly complex construct. These considerations, however, are not confined to the English National Curriculum, but are echoed in international literacy scholarship. In their preface to the third volume of the *Handbook of Reading Research* (Kamil *et al.*, 2000), the editors identify as their first main theme the broadening of the definition of reading. They identify 'the need to present reading from the perspective of multiple social-science disciplines, as well as from the perspectives of neurology and critical literary theory' (*ibid.*: xi).

The complexity of the contemporary construct, in which (at least) reader response, knowledge of text types, values and attitudes are added to the skill of word recognition, is what places particular demands upon those seeking to devise valid tests of literacy. Traditionally, in England, the demonstration of understandings of these kinds was not required until the end of the secondary years of education, where essays are the typical response mode.

Those devising literacy tests for primary-aged children in recent years have, therefore, been faced with unprecedented challenges. In Figure 9.1, the more complex the construct at the left-hand extreme, the more difficult it is to make valid links to the right-hand extreme of the diagram where concrete, specific test items and task performances must give valid information about that construct. In the rest of the chapter, some examples will be given of the kinds of research activity that are implied by these considerations, and of some features of the resulting assessments.

Developing mark schemes: recognising varied responses

The first example will illustrate the way in which mark schemes in reading tests are developed with a view to crediting a range of appropriate responses from young readers. Since meaning is made in the interaction of reader and text, and since the reader can only arrive at that meaning through using aspects of his or her own experience, a variety of different responses is likely to be acceptable. For almost all questions in almost all reading tests, there is no one right answer. This is already very different from most traditional models of reading test.

This example describes in detail some of the issues that emerged during the development of a single question from the level 3 test at Key Stage 1 that was used in England in 1998. This test was part of the statutory national assessment of seven-year-old pupils in that year, and was aimed at above-average children of that age. The example has been selected because in this case the processes of analysis were documented in full. Similar processes are necessary for all questions in all reading tests that require a 'gap' in the text to be filled from the pupil's own experience. The test was developed by the School Curriculum and Assessment Authority (SCAA, now part of the Qualifications and Curriculum Authority, QCA), and the analyses described below were carried out as part of the pre-testing commissioned by SCAA (Burley, 1997).

The story text in this booklet was Charles Keeping's *Miss Emily and the Bird of Make-believe* (1978). Miss Emily buys a lovely golden bird from an unscrupulous market trader, Jack Ratty. She finds that the bird is an ordinary city sparrow that Jack Ratty has painted gold, confronts him with the truth and makes sure that he stops this cruel practice. Near the beginning of the story, we read this paragraph:

> She hadn't gone very far when she saw a large crowd of children gathered round a street trader. It was Mister Jack Ratty. He was making the children laugh, playing his one man band and dancing round a barrow. The barrow was loaded with plants and cheap toys, and there was one beautiful coloured bird in a golden cage. 'How lovely,' thought Miss Emily, and she drew nearer to look.

A pre-tested version of this test had the question:

> How did Jack Ratty make people want to come to his stall?

Although this is a relatively simple question, it gave rise to some fairly extensive analyses which illuminate the way that text, question and mark scheme need to be carefully developed in the light of qualitative and quantitative evidence. To answer the question, children need to use their knowledge of what might make a market stall attractive, as they read the paragraph above.

The statistical discrimination analysis of this question first suggested that it was not functioning as well as expected. The mark scheme applied in the pre-test credited answers that referred to three actions of Jack Ratty's: making the children laugh; playing his one-man band; and dancing around his barrow. To investigate whether this was causing difficulties, children's answers on a sample of 500 test scripts were further analysed. Rather than marking the answers right or wrong, a code was assigned to each different answer, and the frequencies of the codes were analysed. This analysis revealed a much wider variety of inferences than the original mark scheme recognised.

The answers listed in the mark scheme were indeed the most common, with 54 per cent of children identifying at least one of the three listed actions. However, there proved to be a substantial proportion of children, 42 per cent, who, not unreasonably, attributed the attractiveness of the stall to the goods on sale. Of these, about half framed their answers in terms of an action of Jack Ratty's, giving answers such as:

He loaded up his stall with brightly coloured birds, plants and things;

He sold lots of cheap toys.

Some even gave answers that drew upon their knowledge of the story as a whole:

He painted ordinary sparrows to make them look attractive.

The other half simply answered by listing the contents of the stall, without referring to something Jack Ratty did:

There were lots of bright coloured birds.

This analysis identified the range of ways in which children might use their own experience to fill this gap in the text. The results allowed us to recommend that the wording of the question should be changed slightly to make it clear that an action of Jack Ratty's was required:

What did Jack Ratty do to make people want to come to his stall?

The mark scheme was broadened to credit answers which referred to placing attractive objects on the barrow, as well as making the children laugh, playing the one-man band and dancing. When it was pre-tested again, 78 per cent of children answered correctly according to the new mark scheme, and the discrimination statistic was much improved.

This lengthy work to refine what is really a very simple question highlights the challenge when working with more demanding texts. At Key Stage 2, the national tests for eleven-year-olds routinely ask children to make inferences across the entire text, and up to three marks can be awarded for differing qualities of understanding and response. The development of mark schemes that can give credit for a range of legitimate inferences, whilst ruling out all inappropriate answers, is a major undertaking.

An interactive reading task

A completely different approach to assessing reading and response is exemplified by the Key Stage 1 level 2 reading task for seven-year-olds of average attainment. Here, the challenge is to provide a valid assessment for young children who are not yet fluent readers and writers. The solution, unusually in the current National Curriculum assessment system, consists of an interactive assessment task, rather than a formal pencil and paper test. Teacher judgement of ephemeral responses is used, rather than a detailed mark scheme and written evidence.

This is an assessment which has survived since the early days of National Curriculum assessment, when the original notion of the 'standard assessment task' envisaged something close to normal classroom practice. The task is individual, and requires the child to choose a book from a carefully selected list, to talk about the choice, to read aloud and to discuss what has been read. The teacher makes a running record of the child's performance, noting miscues and strategies. The assessment is made on the basis of a judgement of the independence and accuracy of the reading aloud, and on the quality of the discussion of the book's content.

This task can claim a high degree of validity in that it is a very close representation of the way the child reads from day to day in the classroom. The reading material is an attractive, authentic book; the teacher has the opportunity to identify some of the reading strategies at work, as well as the degree of accuracy, and understanding is shown through interactive discussion. This allows the teacher to ensure that the child understands what is being asked and to follow up the child's comments with further questions to probe understanding. For most children of this age, conversation is a natural way to show what they have understood. Different responses to the text are credited according to the teacher's judgement, which can take account of the features of the text and of the personality of the individual child.

The manageability of this task, on the other hand, is comparatively poor. Teachers have to spend 15–20 minutes with each child in individual conversation in order to make the assessment. For this purpose, supply (substitute teacher) cover has to be provided at great cost to the nation, and this alone has brought the survival of the task into question regularly since its introduction. There is evidence that teachers are willing to take on these demands because they are, on the whole, pleased with the quality of the information the task provides.

The task's approach to reliability is also interesting. Since children read from any one of a list of twelve books, consistency does not mean ensuring that all read the same passage. The passages are very carefully compared against a number of criteria and subjected to large-scale trials to confirm their comparability. But essentially, the task approach is to claim that consistency lies in the fact that all children have the opportunity to read something of interest to them, and so to demonstrate their optimum performance. Similarly, the children do not respond to identical questioning, but rather are allowed to show what they know by means of interaction in which further questions are asked, inviting them to expand upon their answers.

Teacher assessment

This task is amongst the least formal of all the assessments that teachers have to administer under the National Curriculum. The statutory assessment system, however, also carries a requirement for teacher assessments. Much of this assessment is now likely to take place within the context of the literacy hour introduced into virtually all primary schools in England since 1998 as part of the National Literacy Strategy. Teacher assessment can be seen as a further movement in the direction of informality, with corresponding implications for validity and reliability.

Ongoing assessment allows the teacher to look not just at a single sample of the child's performance, but at a whole range of performances, all of them in authentic classroom conditions. This has enormous potential for enhancing validity. These assessments can include, for both reading and writing, a whole range of texts of different types and with different content. The text types defined for each term under the National Literacy Strategy provide a systematic check on this. Children's ability to respond to a text by bringing ideas and understanding from their own experience can be assessed in the context of the books they find most engaging. It can be demonstrated through talk and drama as well as in writing. Their motivation to read and write, and their understanding of the purposes and value of literacy, can also be noted as they occur in structured lessons and in day-to-day conversation.

Reliability is also enhanced, in the sense that the teacher has a range of observations on which to base judgements, rather than a single performance. On the other hand, assessment will not be made in the same circumstances, but will vary from child to child and from teacher to teacher. It is this perceived shortcoming that prevents teacher assessment from having greater status in the national assessment system. Nevertheless, its contribution to the validity of the system as a whole should not be underestimated (Stobart, 1999).

Conclusions

This brief survey of aspects of the national testing system has attempted to bring out some of the research and development implications of recent radical changes to the construct of literacy in education. Rather than restricting itself to children's ability to pronounce words or to demonstrate comprehension of a limited local context, this construct now includes layers of response, textual analysis, attitudes and values that were not there before. There is a national curriculum in which the construct is articulated, and tests are expected to yield information about the construct as it is currently defined, and not about something narrower. To return to the theme of this section, what counts as evidence depends directly upon what is tested. Any evidence about standards is only as strong as the measure that is used. The aim in recent years has been to develop measures that reflect the construct as fully as possible, so that the inferences that are made from the test scores truly reflect the nature of literacy in the contemporary world.

The specific examples from test development research have demonstrated some of the issues involved and some of the variables that test developers work with. It is clear, however, that there is a continuing need for fundamental research to underpin assessment. As more becomes known about the nature of literacy, the test development process must continue to evolve in order to reflect this increasing understanding. At the same time, there is a need for a greater awareness amongst educationalists, teachers and the public at large of the breadth and depth of the construct that is currently described as literacy.

References

Burley, J. (1997) *Key Stage 1 Level 3 Reading Test for 1998: Error Analysis*, Slough: National Foundation for Educational Research (unpublished report).

Duthie, C. (1996) *True Stories: Nonfiction Literacy in the Primary Classroom*, York Harbour, ME: Stenhouse Publications.

Haertel, E. (1985) 'Construct validity and criterion-referenced testing', *Review of Educational Research* 55(1): 23–46.

Hagley, F. (1987) *Suffolk Reading Scale*, Windsor: NFER-Nelson.

Iser, W. (1974) *Implied Reader: Patterns of Communication in Prose Fiction from Bunyon to Beckett*, Baltimore, MD: Johns Hopkins Press.

Kamil, M.L., Mosenthal, P.B., Pearson, P.D and Barr, R. (eds) (2000) *Handbook of Reading Research: Volume III*, Mahwah, NJ: Lawrence Erlbaum.

Keeping, C. (1978) *Miss Emily and the Bird of Make-believe*, London: Hutchinson.

Messick, S. (1989) 'Validity', in: R.L. Linn (ed.) *Educational Measurement*, 3rd edn, London: Collier-Macmillan.

Rowell, J.A., Moss, P.D. and Pope, S. (1990) 'The construction of meaning from text: possible effects of different reading strategies', *Educational Psychology* 10(1): 39–55.

Sainsbury, M. and Sizmur, S. (1998) 'Level descriptions in the National Curriculum: what kind of criterion referencing is this?', *Oxford Review of Education* 24(2): 181–93.

Schonell, F. (1945) *The Psychology and Teaching of Reading*, Edinburgh: Oliver & Boyd.

Stephens, J. (1992) *Language and Ideology in Children's Fiction*, London: Longman.

Stierer, B. (1989) 'Reading tests', in *Centre for language in Primary Education: Testing Reading*, London: CLPE.

Stobart, G. (1999) 'The validity of National Curriculum assessment', paper presented at British Educational Research Association Annual Conference, University of Sussex, Brighton, 2 September 1999.

Watson, V. (1993) 'Multi-layered texts and multi-layered readers', *Cambridge Journal of Education* 23(1): 15–24.

10 Trying to count the evidence

Greg Brooks

Clearing the ground

In the title of this book, *Raising Standards in Literacy*, the term 'standards' needs clarification, since it has (at least) two meanings which are in tension with each other. The older meaning, still the predominant one in North America, is 'criteria for judging success'. The newer meaning, perhaps the more frequent now in Britain, is 'levels of attainment'. The tension between the two meanings is best seen in the virtually annual contradictory reactions to rising pass rates in public examinations in Britain. Some welcome the rise as showing that standards have risen (and so they have, in the sense that levels of attainment have gone up), while others bewail it as showing that standards have fallen – by which they mean that the criteria for success must have been lowered. The truth might of course partake of both.

Here I am taking 'standards' in the newer sense, and will therefore focus on evidence that levels of attainment have been raised and how this was brought about. In searching for such evidence I shall be ignoring two other possible sets of evidence:

- I shall not be looking at information on current levels of attainment, whether high or low or middling. This is because such information provides no evidence on how to improve attainment. Information on current levels of attainment might provide evidence that those levels are too low, and therefore need to be raised – but this is as much of a truism in the information age as it always was, and can be taken as an assumption;
- I shall also not be looking at information on whether levels of attainment are rising or falling or remaining stable over time. This information is well documented for literacy in Britain (Brooks, 1998), and in any case still does not provide evidence on how to improve attainment.

However, I shall draw attention to two conclusions from my analysis (Brooks, 1998) of trends over time in literacy:

- judged by the results of national monitoring surveys since the first in 1948, levels of attainment in reading among school pupils appear to have remained in general very stable;
- there also seems to be evidence going back to the generation born around 1920 that the proportion of adults with poor literacy skills has been fairly stable, at about a fifth.

If these conclusions are reliable, then it would seem to follow that raising overall standards of attainment is a monumentally difficult task. Consider: it is widely believed (e.g. by Turner, 1990) that at some point in the 1960s 'traditional' methods of initial literacy teaching, especially phonics, were largely abandoned and replaced by 'progressive' approaches. To doom-sayers who believe that reading standards have been steadily declining, the abandonment of phonics was the cause and restoration of phonics will be the cure. But to advocates of 'progressive' methods, phonics was part of the problem and its reintroduction would be retrograde. If either group were right, levels of attainment should have altered in step with the change of emphasis in instruction, but in opposite ways: levels of attainment should have fallen if the 'traditionalists' were right, and should have risen if the 'progressives' were right. But, as I have shown, in general neither was the case.

(The wobble in the average reading attainment of 8-year-olds in England and Wales – down between 1987 and 1991, then back up again between 1991 and 1995 – is an exception, but probably had causes much closer in time than the supposed, and much earlier, abandonment of phonics – see Brooks, Schagen and Nastat, 1997).

Therefore, either the switch in teaching emphasis was less widespread than is generally believed – and Cato *et al.* (1992) found that most teachers said they used a mixture of methods – or the impact of different methods on levels of attainment is small or difficult to detect, or some combination of these. Whichever, raising levels of attainment at system level will be difficult to achieve and/or to detect (cf. Hiebert, this volume) – and proving causation even more so.

Other evidence that I shall not be examining is information on changes in attitudes to literacy and in literacy-related behaviour. With attitudes to literacy I include reading and writing preferences and habits. By literacy-related behaviour I mean, for example, frequency of using a library and number of books owned or in the home. I exclude these things because they are not direct indicators of attainment.

So my focus is very clearly only on evidence that particular interventions have raised levels of attainment. Having defined that focus, I now give examples for four aspects of literacy learning: pre-school, initial, helping struggling learners and adult literacy. I give more detail on the first of these topics than on the rest because it is less well documented else-where. I do not attempt to analyse the literature on the impact of the

iteracy Strategy in England, since that is massively documented
including some of the other papers in this volume.

...he link between pre-school experience and early literacy development

General intervention studies

There have been a couple of recent reviews of this topic (Brooks, 2000; Evangelou and Sylva, 2001). The first significant conclusion is that children who attend some form of quality pre-school provision make better early progress in literacy than children who attend little or no pre-school provision, *even when possible confounding factors* (such as socio-economic status, parents' level of education) *are allowed for*. This conclusion arises from two large-scale studies. The first is the EPPE (Effective Provision of Pre-School Education) study in England which included about 3,000 children (see House of Commons, 2000); the second is a survey of 6-year-olds in Malta (Mifsud *et al.*, 2000a, b) involving over 5,000 children.

These studies should not be taken to mean that earlier introduction of the formal teaching of literacy will solve all problems – the pre-school provision in question was predominantly informal. Also, both these studies were correlational, and therefore cannot prove causation. Fortunately, there are just enough intervention or training studies to prove the point. These are listed in Table 10.1. Two (Carolina Abecedarian, Parents as Teachers) started working with children as newborns, the rest from age 3 or 4.

Seven of these eight studies show that wide-ranging, high-quality pre-school interventions do benefit children's early literacy attainment. The sole reported null finding, from the NFER Pre-School Project, may have been because it targeted only oral skills, and did not focus at all on pre-literacy skills. Also, that project and the (ineffective) non-High/Scope conditions in the Lisbon project did not involve parents. The two projects which included children under 3 suggest that interventions which begin very early can be effective – but the numbers on which this inference is based are very small. And the two projects with long-term follow-ups (Ypsilanti High/Scope, Carolina Abecedarian) suggest that benefits can be long-lasting – but here, too, the numbers are very small.

Focused intervention studies

None of the studies so far mentioned allow inferences about which particular instructional practices brought about the benefits to literacy. However, some factors can be discerned from focused intervention studies. Pre-eminent here is the well-known line of research on phonological awareness, particularly associated in Britain with Peter Bryant, Usha

Table 10.1 Pre-school intervention studies affecting literacy development

Project	Date	Reference	Samples	Outcome
Ypsilanti, Michigan (USA) High/Scope	1962–	Weikart *et al.* (1978)	50 experi-mentals, 50 controls	Project children ahead in reading at ages 9–10
NFER Nursery project (UK)	1968–73	Woodhead (1976)	100 experi-mentals, 100 controls	No significant differences at age 6
Carolina Abecedarian project (USA)	1972–	Campbell and Ramey (1995)	50 experi-mentals, 50 controls	Project children ahead in reading at ages 8, 12 & 15
Chicago Child–Parent Center (USA)	1983–93	see Karoly *et al.* (1998): 45–7	1,150 partici-pants, 389 controls	Project children ahead in reading at age 9
Parents as Teachers (USA)	late 1980s– early 1990s	National Diffusion Network (1996); see Snow *et al.* (1998: 144)	not stated in Snow *et al.* (1998)	Project children ahead in reading at age 6
Family Literacy Demonstration Programmes (UK)	1994–95	Brooks *et al.* (1996, 1997)	about 100 par-ticipants, no controls	Writing better than expected at age 6–8
Lisbon High/Scope (Portugal)	mid-1990s	see Sylva (2000: 127–31)	70 experi-mentals, 150 in other treatments, 220 controls	High/Scope children ahead of all other groups in reading and writing at age 7
REAL (Raising Early Achievement in Literacy) (UK)	1997–99	Hannon and Nutbrown (2001)	85 experi-mentals, 80 controls	Project children ahead in early literacy and letter recognition at age 5

Goswami and various colleagues. Because this work is well known and well documented, it is not necessary to go into it in detail. Briefly, over the years it has been shown that training various levels of children's phonological awareness (onset and rime, phonemic) before school benefits their literacy attainment once in school.

The Bookstart project which began in Birmingham in 1992 has been studied by Wade and Moore (1998, 2000). Out of about 300 children from the first 'cohort', they were able to trace 41 at age 5 and a different set of 41 at age 7. At both ages Bookstart 'graduates' were ahead of comparison groups in literacy – but the numbers are small and the matching of the comparison groups unconvincing. Clearer evidence from the national evaluation of Bookstart is awaited.

Parents reading to children

Other evidence on specific literacy practices mainly relates to parents sharing books with and reading to their children, which must rate as the oldest and most widespread pre-school literacy intervention, and there is very strong evidence that it benefits children's early attainment in reading. Bus *et al.* (1995) published a large meta-analysis on this topic, based on nine studies containing 2,248 children. The combined probability level was so high that they calculated (*ibid.*: 7) that 'it would take at least another 1,834 studies with null results to bring the combined probability level' back to statistical non-significance. It seems reasonable to say that here coincidence has been excluded. And contained within their analysis was another piece of good news – the effectiveness of parents reading books to their children did not vary according to SES.

It may be suspected that within the practice of parents sharing books with their children there must be variation in effectiveness according to particular approaches, but there is little research on this. However, Detemple (1995) in the USA visited 54 families when the child was 3½, 4½ and 5½ years old and studied both the quality of the mother's talk while reading to the children and the children's literacy attainment in kindergarten (age 5). She found that 'non-immediate talk' by the mothers – for example, explanations, inferences, predictions, etc. – was much rarer than 'immediate talk', such as labelling, counting and paraphrasing; but that the mothers' use of non-immediate talk when the children were 3½ was associated with higher literacy scores in kindergarten, and that the percentage of immediate talk at all three ages was negatively associated with literacy scores.

Also, Weinberger (1996) studied 42 children from age 3 to age 7 in order to extend knowledge of pre-school experiences that relate to success or lack of it in literacy learning in school. Significant factors about good readers at 7 were that at age 3 they were more likely to have had a favourite book, to have been read to a lot before 3, to have been library members, and to have been reported as knowing several nursery rhymes. Similar findings are emerging from the much larger EPPE study mentioned above.

The literature on the links between pre-school experience and early literacy development can be summed up by saying that the outlines are clear but a great deal remains to be done on the details.

Initial literacy learning

The literature here is potentially enormous: the US Education Department's National Reading Panel (NRP) reported in 1999 that approximately 100,000 research studies had been published in English alone on reading since 1966, with about another 15,000 before that time (National Reading Panel, 1999). Even if only half of these were concerned with initial literacy it would take several lifetimes to read and analyse the entire database – and by then the 'in-tray' would be many times as large. Instead, the NRP screened the set of studies for those which focused on children's reading development in the age/grade range from pre-school to grade 12 (age 17), provided comprehensive statistical data, and used an experimental or quasi-experimental design with a control group or multiple-baseline method. They boiled their list down to 417 studies, categorised as in Table 10.2.

The reason for the imbalances in the numbers of studies included or not in statistical meta-analyses was that some aspects are more unified in their methodology and focus (phonemic awareness, phonics) than others. For all other aspects (with the partial exception of oral reading), the studies varied

Table 10.2 Classification of studies used by National Reading Panel

Aspect of reading	Number of studies		
	Included in meta-analyses	Not so included	Total
phonics	38	0	38
phonemic awareness	52	0	52
fluency of oral reading	16	21	37
independent silent reading	0	14	14
vocabulary development	0	50	50
comprehension instruction	0	205	205
computers and reading	0	21	21
Total	106	311	417

Source: National Reading Panel (1999)

too much in methodology and focus to allow quantitative integration; for these aspects the panel relied instead on qualitative judgement, or 'best-evidence synthesis'.

The aspect with fewest studies, independent silent reading, produced no convincing experimental evidence that it benefits reading attainment. However, this does not mean that such benefit does not occur, only that evidence for it is so far lacking. All the other six aspects did yield evidence of benefit, massively so in the case of phonemic awareness and phonics. The large number of studies on comprehension instruction showed less massive evidence of the benefits of each of a range of strategies.

The panel entered a number of caveats about the finding on phonics. While it was true that instruction which included attention to letter–sound correspondences clearly produced better results than instruction with little or no phonics, this aspect needs to be embedded within a full and broad teaching programme. But the central importance of the phonological aspects of literacy is emphasised also in a less comprehensive British review of the evidence (Brooks, 1999).

The panel also pointed out that research on computers and reading is in its infancy, and that the finding of benefit is tentative. In particular, there was so far no research on the use of the internet as an aid to reading, on speech recognition software for writing, or on multimedia.

Though many details are lacking or under-researched, the NRP report has produced a strong picture of many aspects of initial instruction about which there should be no further overall disagreement.

Helping struggling learners

The NRP report dealt only with the teaching of 'normal' children, and specifically excluded remediation for those who struggle and all 'special' groups, including both those with Specific Learning Difficulties (SpLD)/dyslexia and those for whom English is an additional language. There seems to be no useful source summarising research on learning to read and write in languages other than the mother tongue. The International Reading Association is currently engaged in exploring this topic, but its findings will not be available until late 2002 or early 2003.

The NRP report was preceded by one from the US National Research Council (Snow *et al.*, 1998) on *Preventing Reading Difficulties*. However, precisely because its focus was on preventing difficulties arising in the first place, it had little to say on remediation or on instruction for those who struggle or have special difficulties. For these aspects I am going to rely on much less comprehensive British analyses.

Early interventions for struggling readers

The major British study of this aspect is *What Works for Slow Readers?*

(Brooks *et al.*, 1998). We analysed 20 British studies providing details of 30 interventions used with struggling but non-dyslexic children in Years 1 to 4 (ages 5 to 9). All the interventions had been the subject of a quantitative evaluation in the UK from which an impact measure could be calculated. Many other studies were omitted from the analysis because of methodological inadequacies.

The conclusions reached (none of which were surprising) were as follows:

- **Normal schooling does not enable slow readers to catch up,** thus reinforcing the case for early intervention. This conclusion was based on over 1,000 children in 'no treatment' control groups across several of the studies.
- **Work on phonological skills should be embedded within a broad approach** – most approaches which concentrated heavily on phonological aspects showed little impact. This finding extends the opinion of the National Reading Panel from 'normal' to struggling readers.
- **Children's comprehension can be improved if directly targeted.** Although this again extends one of the NRP's findings, the British research evidence for this conclusion is very small.
- **Working on children's self-esteem and reading *in parallel* has definite potential** – this is the message of a set of powerful experiments carried out in Somerset between 1970 and 1984. This finding is rare in being based on research into affective factors in literacy.
- **ICT approaches work only if they are precisely targeted** – if struggling learners are left to find their own way through computer packages this has little effect. This seems to have been the case in two large-scale ICT initiatives in Britain. This finding may not be at odds with the NRP conclusion. Conditions may be different in the USA, or the use of the technology may have improved since the British projects were conducted (in 1994–96), or it may simply reflect a difference in impact on 'normal' and struggling readers.
- **Large-scale schemes,** such as Reading Recovery and Family Literacy, though expensive, **can give good value for money.** There is some evidence from the High/Scope project in the United States that every dollar spent on early intervention saves seven dollars on social remediation later.
- Above all, **where reading partners are available and can be given appropriate training, partnership approaches can be very effective.** The partners need to be given a clear model and approach to follow, otherwise both they and their 'tutees' get confused. For example, Paired Reading (Morgan, 1976; Topping and Lindsay, 1992) gives tutors a very clear structure to follow, and nowhere are the tutee's weaknesses assaulted – in particular, trying to make the tutee use sounding-out phonics is avoided.

Children with Specific Learning Difficulties (SpLD)/dyslexia

In 1999 the British government ministry then called the Department for Education and Employment commissioned a review of the literature on *Literacy and Special Educational Needs* (Fletcher-Campbell, 2000). In addition to children with SpLD/dyslexia, the review covered children with hearing impairment, visual impairment, severe learning difficulties, communications difficulties, and mild or moderate learning difficulties. In every case there was a paucity of experimental evidence. In the case of SpLD/dyslexia, the overwhelming majority of research studies concern aetiology (origins and causes) and the cognitive processes which operate within the brain when literacy skills are being used. In an earlier and more comprehensive review and analysis of research on SpLD/dyslexia (Tansley and Panckhurst, 1981) hundreds of pages were needed to cover aetiology and cognitive processes, while just seven pages sufficed for intervention studies. Little seems to have changed in this field in twenty years, and the following conclusions (see Fletcher-Campbell, 2000: 74–5) on what might work for children with SpLD/dyslexia are based at least as much on practitioners' experience as on research, probably more so:

- Appropriate interventions need to be highly structured and targeted, with support for general learning (study skills) as well as for the lack of confidence that will arise if pupils experience repeated failure;
- There is evidence that the application of general principles of good classroom management practice (for example, time on task, guided practice, rapid feedback) is as important as particular approaches focused on elements of literacy, such as Paired Reading, though studies show that both parents and peers can be effective if trained;
- Studies also put emphasis on teachers' ability to assess comprehension by skilled questioning, so that attention is paid to meaning-making as well as to the mechanics of decoding;
- Effective programmes for pupils with SpLD/dyslexia are characterised by being structured, sequential, cumulative and thorough;
- Such pupils also benefit from phonics teaching, overlearning, and a multi-sensory approach, making the links between sound, referent and written form.

The topic of support for struggling readers is under-researched. As I have shown, there are a few convincing intervention studies on non-dyslexic or 'garden-variety' poor readers, but very few on children with SpLD/dyslexia, and virtually none on other special groups, including those with English as an additional language.

Adult literacy

There is also an imbalance in the literature in this field, in fact a more serious one: there is a wealth of information on the scale of need (derived from several national surveys), but not many reliable impact studies, and scarcely any intervention studies on adult literacy as such, though there are a few on family literacy (for much more detail on these conclusions, and on other aspects of the field, see Brooks *et al.*, 2001b). One of the major tasks of the new National Research and Development Centre on Adult Basic Skills (established in England early in 2002) will be to remedy the dearth of intervention studies. At the time of writing, a study commissioned by the University for Industry (Ufi) and conducted by the London Institute of Education on the benefit of using Information and Communication Technology (ICT) in teaching basic skills was complete but not yet reported; while an evaluation of ten Pathfinder pilot projects on basic skills was still in progress.

Given the shortage of data from intervention studies, this section will necessarily be short. I deal first with the small amount of evidence on factors associated with better progress in mainstream adult literacy, and then with the slightly larger but indirect evidence from family literacy, and conclude with a brief note on other settings.

Mainstream adult literacy

In 1993–97 the Basic Skills Agency helped to develop basic skills support for students in Further Education Colleges where 'basic skills support' was for students who needed it to help them complete another course of study which was their main objective (and where this form of support is distinct from 'dedicated' basic skills provision, in which learners work primarily on their literacy and/or numeracy). The Agency then studied the relationship between basic skills support on the one hand and drop-out and course completion/achievement on the other (Basic Skills Agency, 1997). Drop-out rates were 10 per cent for students receiving support, 30 per cent otherwise; 75 per cent of those receiving support completed their course and/or achieved a qualification, whereas only 54 per cent of those not receiving support did so. These findings can be seen as indirect indicators of factors leading to greater progress in literacy (and numeracy).

In 1998–2000 a team at the National Foundation for Educational Research carried out for the Basic Skills Agency a study of progress made in literacy by adults in basic skills provision (Brooks *et al.*, 2001a). This was a study of 'dedicated' provision in the sense just defined. Just three factors were found to relate to greater progress:

- whether tutors had qualified teacher status or not: where all the tutors in a particular provider's area had QTS, students made more progress than elsewhere;
- whether tutors had help in the classroom (from a volunteer or a paid assistant): where all or some of the tutors in a particular provider's area had such support, students made more progress than where no tutors had support. In areas where no tutors had such support students on average made no progress;
- students who had attended regularly between pre- and post-test over a period of several months had the largest subgroup gain in the entire study.

Though exiguous, the findings just mentioned are derived from statistical correlations with progress on tests of reading.

Family literacy

The Basic Skills Agency established its family literacy programmes in 1994, and to date has commissioned four evaluations of them (Brooks *et al.*, 1996, 1997, 1999; Poulson *et al.*, 1997). All produced evidence of benefit to the parents' literacy skills, and judgements on factors related to that progress. However, in no case were those judgements based on statistical correlations. Given this caveat, the principal factors identified by the researchers were: voluntary participation; clear information about goals, including progression to further study; clear focus on literacy development, with other benefits (e.g. growth in confidence) regarded as 'bonuses'; nationally recognised accreditation of learning; careful selection of staff; high quality teaching; and focusing of learners' efforts through the time-limited nature of the courses.

Other settings

There have also been studies of workplace provision (e.g. Frank and Hamilton, 1993; Basic Skills Agency, 1995) and of provision for prisoners (Prison Service, 1999). The studies of workplace provision analyse it and make judgements on factors associated with effectiveness, but provide no data on progress. It is therefore impossible to evaluate the soundness of the conclusions. The one small document on provision for prisoners gives outline information on the progress made by a small sample, but no information on factors related to the progress. In neither case can much be made of this.

Conclusions

Most obviously, the amount of research on different aspects of raising standards in literacy varies enormously. The massive amount of research on initial literacy could be seen as overkill, especially in the phonological areas. However, even within initial literacy some aspects are relatively neglected, such as the contribution of independent silent reading, and the benefits to children's learning of special programmes such as family literacy. It would be rational to move the main focus of research away from those aspects that have been massively documented and on to others.

The most under-researched of all aspects of literacy is actually writing: there are very few references to it in the analyses presented above.

The less researched groups of learners have at least two common features: they are mainly marginalised groups, and for that reason among others they are more difficult to investigate. Yet research on these groups could have great payoff. If the rise in scores in national tests at age 11 can be interpreted as reliable evidence that the National Literacy Strategy is indeed raising standards, then increasingly the pupils who are left behind should be studied. It seems unlikely that all of them will benefit from a 'slipstream' effect, and the lowest attainers deserve the chance to escape from the 'long tail of underachievement' and therefore not to join the segment of the adult population with less than functional literacy. A key concern here should be studies of prevention: what would be the best form of provision for pre-schoolers to prepare them for literacy learning in school?

In further research, both on struggling learners and on adults, individual differences should be taken into account. The main highway to literacy has now been mapped pretty convincingly, and it seems that certain broad features of instruction (see again the NRP findings) are applicable to most learners and will enable most learners to achieve good enough levels of literacy. One implication of this is that particular learning preferences or styles scarcely need to be allowed for. But it is at least plausible, some would say probable, that slower learners' learning preferences or styles may be more like blockages – if they are especially weak in one mode they or their teachers may not discover this or ways round it. A clear case in point is the hypothesis, advocated in particular by Stanovich (1988), that the central problem for people with SpLD/dyslexia is a deficit in the 'phonological core variable'. Mere repeated assault on this (at least in the form of phonics, phonics, and yet more phonics) seems not to work – good ways of circumventing it need to be found and evaluated.

The spectrum of difficulties is much wider than this, and for the full spectrum of difficulties and for the whole range of initial learners and adults with problems, differentiation and the research to support it is the next massive task.

References

Basic Skills Agency (1995) *Basic Skills Training at Work: a Study of Effectiveness*, London: Basic Skills Agency.

—— (1997) *Staying the Course: The Relationship between Basic Skills Support, Drop Out, Retention and Achievement in Further Education Colleges*, London: Basic Skills Agency.

Brooks, G. (1998) 'Trends in standards of literacy in the United Kingdom, 1948–1996', *TOPIC* 19 (Spring): item 1.

—— (1999) 'Phonemic awareness is a key factor in learning to be literate – how best should it be taught?', position paper for Ofsted Invitation Seminar on 'The Importance of Phonics in Learning to Read and Write', London, 29 March (to appear in M. Cook (in press) (ed.) *Perspectives in the Teaching and Learning of Phonics*, Royston, Herts: UK Reading Association).

—— (2000) 'The influence of pre-school experience on early literacy attainment: the research evidence', paper presented at National Literacy Trust conference on 'Early Years – Building the Foundations for Literacy', London, 6 November. Available online: http://www.literacytrust.org.uk/

Brooks, G., Schagen, I. and Nastat, P. (1997) *Trends in Reading at Eight*, Slough: NFER.

Brooks, G., Flanagan, N., Henkhuzens, Z. and Hutchison, D. (1998) *What Works for Slow Readers? The Effectiveness of Early Intervention Schemes*, Slough: NFER.

Brooks, G., Gorman, T.P., Harman, J., Hutchison, D. and Wilkin, A. (1996) *Family Literacy Works: The NFER Evaluation of the Basic Skills Agency's Family Literacy Demonstration Programmes*, London: Basic Skills Agency.

Brooks, G., Harman, J., Hutchison, D., Kendall, S. and Wilkin, A. (1999) *Family Literacy for New Groups: The National Foundation for Educational Research Evaluation of the Basic Skills Agency's Programmes for Linguistic Minorities, Year 4 and Year 7*, London: Basic Skills Agency.

Brooks, G., Davies, R., Duckett, L., Hutchison, D., Kendall, S. and Wilkin, A. (2001a) *Progress in Adult Literacy: Do Learners Learn?*, London: Basic Skills Agency.

Brooks, G., Giles, K., Harman, J., Kendall, S., Rees, F. and Whittaker, S. (2001b) *Assembling the Fragments: A Review of Research on Adult Basic Skills*, London: DfEE Research Report No. 220.

Brooks, G., Gorman, T.P., Harman, J., Hutchison, D., Kinder, K., Moor, H. and Wilkin, A. (1997) *Family Literacy Lasts: The NFER Follow-up Study of the Basic Skills Agency's Demonstration Programmes*, London: Basic Skills Agency.

Bus, A.G., van IJzendoorn, M.H. and Pellegrini, A.D. (1995) 'Joint book reading makes for success in learning: a meta-analysis on intergenerational transmission of literacy', *Review of Educational Research* 65(1): 1–21.

Campbell, F.A and Ramey, C.T. (1995) 'Cognitive and school outcomes for high-risk African American students at middle adolescence: positive effects of early intervention', *American Education Research Journal* 32(4): 743–72.

Cato, V., Fernandes, C., Gorman, T.P., Kispal, A. with White, J. (1992) *The Teaching of Initial Literacy: How Do Teachers Do It?*, Slough: NFER.

Detemple, J. (1995) 'Book reading styles of low-income mothers with pre-schoolers and children's later literacy skills', *Dissertation Abstracts International, Section A: Humanities and Social Sciences* 55(7-A): 1817.

Evangelou, M. and Sylva, K. (2001) 'New evidence: birth-to-school literacy intervention', paper presented at PEEP (Peers Early Education Partnership) conference, London, 6 July.

Fletcher-Campbell, F. (ed.) (2000) *Literacy and Special Educational Needs: a Review of the Literature*, London: DfEE Research Report No. 227.

Frank, F. and Hamilton, M. (1993) *Not Just a Number: the Role of Basic Skills Programmes in the Changing Workplace. An Account of a Leverhulme Trust Funded Research Project*, Lancaster: Lancaster University, Centre for the Study of Education and Training.

Hannon, P. and Nutbrown, C. (2001) 'Emerging findings from an experimental study of early literacy education involving parents', paper presented at UK Reading Association annual conference, Canterbury Christ Church University College, July.

House of Commons Education and Employment Committee (Education Sub-Committee) (2000) *Early Years: Minutes of Evidence, Wednesday 21 June 2000: Effective Provision of Pre-school Education (EPPE)*, London: The Stationery Office.

Karoly, L.A., Greenwood. P.W., Everingham, S.S., Houbé, J., Kilburn, M.R., Rydell, C.P., Sanders, M. and Chiesa, J. (1998) *Investing in Our Children: What We Know and Don't Know about the Costs and Benefits of Early Childhood Interventions*, Santa Monica, CA: Rand.

Mifsud, C., Milton, J., Brooks, G. and Hutchison, D. (2000a) *Literacy in Malta: The 1999 National Survey of the Attainment of Year 2 Pupils*, Slough: NFER for the University of Malta.

Mifsud, C., Milton, J., Hutchison, D. and Brooks, G. (2000b) *Do Schools Make a Difference?*, University of Malta Faculty of Education Literacy Unit Monograph Series No. 2, Msida: University of Malta.

Morgan, R.T.T. (1976) ' "Paired Reading" tuition: a preliminary report on a technique for cases of reading deficit', *Child Care, Health and Development* 2: 13–28.

National Diffusion Network (1996) *Educational Programs that Work*, 22nd edn, Longmont, CO: Sopris West.

National Reading Panel (1999) *Teaching Children to Read*, Washington, DC: US Department of Education.

Poulson, L., Macleod, F., Bennett, N. and Wray, D. (1997) *Family Literacy: Practice in Local Programmes. An Evaluative Review of 18 Programmes in the Small Grants Programme*, London: Basic Skills Agency.

Prison Service (1999) *Peer Partners*, Croydon: Prison Education Service (mimeographed).

Snow, C., Burns, M.S. and Griffin, P. (eds) (1998) *Preventing Reading Difficulties in Young Children*, Washington, DC: National Academy Press for National Research Council.

Stanovich, K.E. (1988) 'Explaining the difference between the dyslexic and the garden-variety poor readers: the phonological core model', *Journal of Learning Disabilities* 21(10): 590–604.

Sylva, K. (2000) 'Early childhood education to ensure a "fair start" for all', in T. Cox (ed.) *Combating Educational Disadvantage: Meeting the Needs of Vulnerable Children* (pp. 121–35), New York: Falmer.

Tansley, P. and Panckhurst, J. (1981) *Children with Specific Learning Difficulties: a Critical Review of Research*, Windsor: NFER-Nelson.

Topping, K.J. and Lindsay, G.A. (1992) 'Paired reading: a review of the literature', *Research Papers in Education* 7(3): 199–246.

Turner, M. (1990) *Sponsored Reading Failure: an Object Lesson*, Warlingham: Warlingham Park School, Education Unit.

Wade, B. and Moore, M. (1998) 'An early start with books: literacy and mathematical evidence from a longitudinal study', *Educational Review* 50(2): 135–45.

—— (2000) 'A sure start with books', *Early Years* 20(2): 39–46.

Weikart, D.P., Bond, J.T. and McNeil, J.T. (1978) *The Ypsilanti Perry Preschool Project: Preschool Years and Longitudinal Results through Fourth Grade*, Monographs of the High/Scope Educational Research Foundation, No. 3, Ypsilanti, MI: High/Scope Educational Research Foundation.

Weinberger, J. (1996) 'A longitudinal study of children's early literacy experiences at home and later literacy development at home and school', *Journal of Research in Reading* 19(1): 14–24.

Woodhead, M. (ed.) (1976) *An Experiment in Nursery Education*, Windsor: NFER Publishing.

Discussion

What counts as evidence?

Greg Brooks

In order to decide what counts as evidence that standards are being raised, you have to know what it is that you are trying to measure, and against what criteria, and with what instruments – and even then there are questions to be asked about the rigour of the data-gathering process. The four chapters in this section address different aspects of these questions.

In the case of any curriculum area, the first need is a description of the domain. For reading, this is supplied in England by the National Curriculum for English and the National Literacy Strategy's Framework. Both of these apply to state (publicly-funded) schools (though not to private schools), and are to that extent national, leaving little or no responsibility for defining the domain of reading to individual local education authorities, schools or teachers. Arrangements similar to the National Curriculum (but not necessarily to the National Literacy Strategy) apply in Wales and Northern Ireland, including the use of the curriculum documents as specifications for an assessment system. Scotland has a characteristically different set of guidelines.

In the United States, as Vicky Purcell-Gates mentions, there has been an attempt to provide a national definition of the domain in the form of the *Standards for the English Language Arts* produced by the National Council of Teachers of English and International Reading Association (1996). However, these appear not to have been taken up at all widely because education is so strongly a responsibility of the individual states that national guidelines would be resisted, even if endorsed or issued by the federal government. Instead, individual states issue standards, in the sense of definitions of the domain, which then become also criteria for judging achievement and/or specifications for the instruments for measuring achievement.

After considerable resistance when first introduced, the National Curriculum in England appears to have 'bedded down' and to have become almost taken for granted, as has the National Literacy Strategy. But in the United States there is considerable controversy over the standards recently introduced in some states – Purcell-Gates's chapter is an account of this movement, and a dire warning of the dangers she sees in it.

Principally, she is concerned that the model of literacy enshrined in the new sets of standards is reductionist, and therefore doomed to continue failing disadvantaged groups. While the details of this situation are specific to (parts of) the United States, the tendency to oversimplify is universal. Perhaps in all of us there is the wish that there could be a simple solution to literacy problems, the fabled magic bullet, but our rational minds know that there is no reason at all to expect the processes of reading and writing themselves, or their teaching and assessment and remediation, to be simple, and every reason to expect them to be complex. The list of research questions at the end of Purcell-Gates's chapter sketches a little of that complexity, in terms of the need to take account of the socio-cultural dimension of literacy in addition to the cognitive.

This complexity remains when we turn from considering the specifications (standards) for teaching to those for assessment. In assessing reading it is no longer good enough, as Marian Sainsbury illustrates, to rely on single-word recognition (word-naming) tests, or on multiple-choice sentence-completion tests based on single, decontextualised sentences. These were standard in Britain until at least the mid-1970s, when tests based on complete texts began to appear. It would be excellent if all tests based on out-of-date conceptualisations of reading had fallen out of use and been replaced by more authentic instruments – but it is well known, in Britain at least, that old tests, which are easy to photocopy and administer, remain in use for decades. For example, Brooks *et al.* (1998: 62) found that some intervention studies of struggling readers had used tests devised up to forty years earlier. It seems ironic that one effect of the simplification in US concepts of reading noted by Purcell-Gates might be to revive outmoded forms of reading test.

There seems no prospect of that happening in national reading tests in England, where the theory and practice of tests based on complete texts is both well developed and thoroughly embedded in the system. Sue Horner sets out an analysis of the construct of reading underlying the national tests of achievement in English for students aged 7, 11 and 14 in England. She shows how the construct is based on seven 'focuses' (these include, for example, retrieving information, making inferences, and commenting on author's style). She also shows how the balance and depth of the focuses necessarily changes according to the age of the students being tested, the texts on which the tests are based, and the questions asked.

Sainsbury goes into even more depth in discussing the validity of these same national tests. She is well placed to do so, having been in charge for several years of the team developing the tests of reading and writing for 7- and 11-year-olds in England and (originally jointly, now separately) in Wales. She also headed the team (partly the same people) who developed the English-language versions of the tests for the PIRLS (Progress in International Reading Literacy Study) survey which took place in 2001. She analyses the inevitable 'span' (others might call it the gap) between any construct and the tests devised to assess it. Most of her chapter concerns the development of more rigorous and valid methods of establishing the validity of reading assessments, and shows the care with which tests are currently developed. Given this, it is reasonable to conclude that the annual national tests of reading and writing in England and Wales are exceptionally reliable indicators of achievement.

As Sainsbury points out, the development of such methods has not occurred spontaneously or in isolation; it has gone along in parallel with changes in the conceptualisation of literacy in about the last twenty years. Also, this development has by no means come to an end; it needs to continue to reflect changes in the conceptualisation of literacy.

Sainsbury also points out that the purpose of all this is not to have better and better tests, but to have measures that reflect the domain as faithfully as possible, so that statements based on the test results are as firmly based as can be managed. An object counter-example is the evidence on trends in schoolchildren's average attainment in reading in England and Wales between 1948 and 1979 (for a summary, see Brooks, 1998). The only tests in use in that period were two multiple-choice sentence-completion tests, one containing 35 items and devised about 1938, the other containing 60 items and devised in 1955. Both were considered state-of-the-art at the time, and without them there would be no national data for England and Wales for that period. But the tests are now seen as so incomplete that the evidence they provided has to be considered as a rough indication rather than as highly reliable.

Once appropriate standards or curricula are in place, together with valid and reliable measures, the obvious question is, What do they show? Are standards (levels of achievement) rising/being raised? The part of the answer relevant to national tests of reading for 11-year-olds in England is given by Horner: there has been a steady upward trend in the percentage of pupils achieving level 4 or better in the period 1996–2000. Much more counting of the evidence is given in my own chapter. The major fact here is the vast imbalance between the massive number of studies of the initial teaching and learning of reading and the much smaller number of studies, if any, on other aspects. The US National Reading Panel (1999) has done the entire world a service by analysing the key studies on the initial teaching and learning of reading and coming to (on the whole) very clear conclusions. The clearest findings of all are that teaching phonological awareness and phonics do benefit the initial learning of reading. My inference from this is that no further studies are needed on phonological awareness or phonics *in general*, though of course there are always details to be sorted out.

But there are other aspects of initial literacy learning that have suffered massive neglect, either relative or absolute. In particular, there are far fewer studies of writing than of reading. Given that phonological awareness is not the only form of awareness that is or might be relevant to initial learning (see Layton *et al.*, 1998), it is significant that there are only a few studies of syntactic awareness, and hardly any of word or pragmatic awareness. Even within the NRP report it is clear that some areas need much more investigation: oral reading fluency, vocabulary development, comprehension, computers, and especially the contribution of independent silent reading.

Outside initial literacy, there is not a single aspect where enough evidence exists to state firm conclusions. In adult literacy the number of intervention studies can be counted on one hand; the general benefit of pre-school experience for early achievement in literacy is clear but details are almost entirely lacking; for garden-variety poor readers there are useful pointers but not yet an integrated theory or model; and for all other groups of struggling readers, especially those with Specific Learning Difficulties/dyslexia, virtually all the necessary work has yet to be done. So no one need go short of a research topic, whether on literacy learning and its assessment (the subject of this section) or on the teaching of literacy (the subject of the next section).

References

Brooks, G. (1998) 'Trends in standards of literacy in the United Kingdom, 1948–1996', *TOPIC* 19(Spring): item 1.

Brooks, G., Flanagan, N., Henkhuzens, Z. and Hutchison, D. (1998) *What Works for Slow Readers? The Effectiveness of Early Intervention Schemes*, Slough: NFER.

Layton, A., Robinson, J. and Lawson, M. (1998) 'The relationship between syntactic awareness and reading performance', *Journal of Research in Reading* 21(1): 5–23.

National Council of Teachers of English and International Reading Association (1996) *Standards for the English Language Arts*, Urbana, IL: National Council of Teachers of English.

US National Reading Panel (1999) *Teaching Children to Read*, Washington, DC: US Department of Education.

Part III

Developing teacher practice

11 Textbooks and model programmes

Reading reform in the United States

Elfrieda H. Hiebert

Efforts to reform reading education in the United States share similar goals with those in the United Kingdom. The digital age is a time when the demands of literacy have increased, for information is more copious and accessible than ever before. Judging the importance of one source over another, choosing what to remember from a source, and using this information in projects and in communication are among the critical literacy proficiencies of the digital age. In both nations, educators and policy-makers are engaged in reform efforts to ensure students' attainment of these literacy proficiencies.

Although the underlying motivation for reading reform is the same in both nations, reading reform efforts in the United States and in the United Kingdom – England in particular – have manifested themselves in different ways. In England, the National Literacy Strategy states a clear goal for 11-year-olds on a particular assessment and prescribes the Literacy Hour as a means for achieving that goal (Fisher and Singleton, 2000). In contrast, while a US goal has been and continues to be that 'every child can read by the third grade' (Bush, 2001), no tasks, texts, or assessments accompany presentations of the goal. At the individual state level, considerable time and investment has gone into establishing standards. However, none of these standards have included tasks or texts that definitively show what grade-level proficiency looks like at different levels (Stotsky, 2000). While almost every state has a statewide reading assessment, the connection between the tasks and texts of the assessments and the state standards often goes unarticulated.

While the pre-eminence of states and local educational agencies in guiding their own educational policies continues to be part of political rhetoric, two reading reform efforts can be regarded as national in scope. The origins and foci of these reforms differ, but each is likely to influence the practices of individual teachers and their students in states, counties and towns across the USA. The first reform involves the revision of reading textbooks by America's two largest states, Texas and California. These two states' policies influence the content of textbooks in less populous and less centralised states. The second reform consists of model school instructional programmes that are implemented with the help of external consultants. Over the past decade, the US Department of Education has provided funds for model programmes to states for distribution to local education agencies. Through such federal programmes, the practices of teachers and their students around the country can be influenced.

Evaluating the efficacy of reading reform efforts, which is the goal of this chapter, requires perspective on the definition of the literacy problem in the United States. Consequently, we first review the results of the National Assessment of Educational Progress (NAEP). Although US education is designated as the responsibility of states rather than the federal government, the NAEP results are presented as 'the nation's report card' (US Department of Education, 2001). With the NAEP results as a background, the content of US reading reform activities and efficacy of these efforts at attaining the goals of the reform movement are reviewed. This review points out obstacles to achieving the goal of higher literacy levels in the digital age. The third, and final, section of the chapter is devoted to proposals for removing those obstacles.

How are American students reading?

The 2000 NAEP report on fourth graders' reading achievement (Donahue *et al.*, 2001) is part of a series of congressionally mandated assessments of different subject areas at grades 4, 8 and 12 that began in 1969 and that are conducted every several years. Since 1992, fourth graders' literacy proficiency has been classified into four levels: (a) advanced, (b) proficient, (c) basic, and (d) below basic. In 2000, 37 per cent of fourth graders were below basic, 31 per cent were basic, 24 per cent were proficient and 8 per cent were advanced. The distribution has not changed substantially from 1992, when the classification system was first used.

When the NAEP results were compared across states for the first time in 1994 (Campbell *et al.*, 1996), their impact was particularly strong. Of particular interest was the performance of California's students. In 1987, California mandated that all selections in the reading textbooks of all elementary grade levels purchased with state funds needed to be 'authentic' literature (California English/Language Arts Committee, 1987) or texts sold from a trade book division, as opposed to texts written specifically for a textbook programme. California's low standing in the 1994 state-by-state comparison of the NAEP was taken to be an indictment of literature-based instruction, or whole language. While this consideration was not taken into account in subsequent interpretations of the data, California's 1994 classrooms had a higher percentage of linguistically and culturally diverse students and recent immigrants than classrooms in any other state. Many reading reform efforts, the reports of blue-ribbon panels of researchers on reading education (National Reading Panel, 2000; Snow, Burns and Griffin, 1998), changes in and emphases on reading assessments, and the debates about phonics and whole language can be traced to California's performance on the 1994 NAEP.

By the time the 1994 NAEP results were available, California schools had purchased textbooks for another seven-year cycle. However, the state of Texas, which in 1990 had enacted a mandate similar to California's for authentic literature (Texas Education Agency, 1990), moved to reverse this policy in 1997 (Texas Education Agency, 1997). Hoffman (in this volume) describes Texas's mandates regarding decodable texts for first graders. For those textbooks that will be purchased in the fall of 2002, California also has mandated decodable texts (California English/Language Arts Committee, 1999).

In the flurry of activity that followed the 1994 NAEP results, little attention was paid to a special study that examined the meaning of failure to attain a proficient level on the NAEP (Pinnell *et al.*, 1995). A subsample of fourth graders was asked to read aloud a passage that they had read and responded to silently. The findings showed the majority of students (including those who scored below basic) were accurate in their oral reading – that is, they could 'say the words'. There was no significant difference in accuracy of word recognition between those who scored 'basic' or higher and those who did not. What differentiated the students most was the rate at which they read: the students who scored below basic read significantly slower than those students who were rated basic or above.

All but a very small percentage of an American age cohort can read the words in texts (Pinnell *et al.*, 1995). For a sizeable portion, this reading is slow. Plodding reading makes sophisticated interpretations of text difficult. The kind of instruction that supports automatic word recognition and sophisticated interpretations of text is likely to be quite different from the kind of instruction that supports acquisition of the alphabetic principle. As the following descriptions of the reform efforts show, however, policy-makers have focused on the latter rather than the former.

Reading reform at the state level: textbooks

Whereas education may be the prerogative of local education agencies, national companies provide the textbooks for instruction and the tests for establishing whether instruction was successful. Furthermore, when the largest states are also the ones with centralised responsibility for education, such states wield considerable influence over textbook publishers. This is precisely the scenario that exists in the United States. Its largest two states – California and Texas – account for approximately 22 per cent or more of the nation's children and have centralised textbook selection procedures. Only one other large state – Florida – adopts textbooks centrally, but its guidelines have not been as prescriptive and its adoption of textbooks occurs concurrently with California's. While textbook publishers have long recognised the profitability of the California and Texas markets, it was not until the late 1980s that these two states began to use textbook content as their primary means of reading reform. In the 18 smaller states that adopt textbooks statewide and the 29 states where individual school districts or schools select their own textbooks, educators have little leverage that would allow them to obtain textbook programmes that are compatible with their regional policies.

What is the reform?

Textbook programmes for reading in the United States are called basal reading programmes, although their content includes writing, speaking and listening. A great many instructional schemes for reading/language arts are published in the United States such as sets of small books, typically in paperback booklets numbering 8–16 pages. However, the production of the comprehensive literacy programmes that are the focus of this chapter is limited to a small group of companies, currently six or seven. These comprehensive literacy programmes are used by approximately 85 per cent of American elementary classrooms (kindergarten through grade 5 or 6; Baumann *et al.*, 2000) and consume the lion's share of funds for educational materials.

While the market is lucrative, publishers' investment in basal reading programmes can be risky (Chall and Squire, 1991). These programmes have become so gargantuan that the initial investment is large – approximately $50 million to produce a new programme. Further, the return on the investment can be slow.

Publishers' large investments, and the consequences they suffer, have been exacerbated by California's and Texas's increased efforts to prescribe the contents of basal reading programmes. The swing to authentic literature and then to decodable text in Texas and California means that textbook publishers need to develop a new copyright every three years (the time between the California and Texas textbook adoptions) if they hope to remain competitive in these two states.

What is the evidence for the efficacy of this reform?

The textbooks are massive interventions, as policy makers have recognised. But are the efforts accomplishing the goals set out by policy makers? Have more children attained proficient reading levels in California and Texas as a result of these efforts? While states such as Texas and California have massive assessment programmes, the results of which can be viewed internationally on the World Wide Web, achievement of students in districts or schools as a function of textbook programmes has yet to be reported. When the effects of reading primarily from different kinds of texts such as those that emphasise phonically regular words and those that emphasise high-frequency words have been compared, text type has frequently been confounded with activities and form of teacher support. Insights into the effects of texts on student reading achievement come from studies of children reading passages from different textbook programmes and from summaries of the textbook programme characteristics that are associated with beginning reading acquisition.

Comparisons of textbook programmes

A major emphasis of the large-scale studies that began in the 1960s (e.g. the US Department of Education's First-Grade Studies (Bond and Dykstra, 1967)) was the examination of the effectiveness of programmes that contain different kinds of texts. But findings from these studies have been either inconsistent or inconsequential when comprehension, and not only word recognition, is measured and when student achievement is considered in subsequent grades (Lohnes and Gray, 1972). In the First-Grade Studies, particularly, variation across classrooms within a method was considerable. Further, methods often differed substantially in activities such as the amount of writing and spelling and in teacher support as well as in types of text. Recently, the problems inherent in equating a type of text with a programme are apparent in an examination of different approaches to phonics instruction by Foorman *et al.* (1998). In addition to different approaches to phonics, the three approaches examined in the Foorman *et al.* study involved different types of texts and different instructional activities that have been shown to influence students' reading achievement regardless of text type, such as writing and spelling.

It was not until Barr and Dreeben (1983) used an alternative paradigm that the influence of text on beginning reading acquisition began to be understood. Barr and Dreeben examined the relationship of student achievement to the phonic structure and number of different words that students read in their texts. Barr and Dreeben reported that what the texts covered was the variable most closely associated with first-grade learning, accounting for 83 per cent and 71 per cent of the variance in basal and phonics learning respectively and for 50 per cent of the variance in reading achievement overall. They also reported that the difficulty of the materials and the amount of time teachers devoted to reading instruction covaried. Teachers with more difficult reading programmes allocated more time to reading instruction. The number of phonics concepts covered during first grade was less responsive to the group mean aptitude than to the number of phonics concepts contained in the first-grade materials and the time allocated to phonics activities.

Juel and Roper/Schneider (1985) also examined students' reading achievement as a function of text characteristics. In this case, however, students received the same phonics lessons but they read texts from two different basal reading programmes, which differed significantly only in the characteristics of the preprimers (one with decodable words and the other with high-frequency words). The two factors that accounted for end of grade 1 reading performance were students' initial scores on the Metropolitan Readiness Text and the basal series. Students who read from decodable preprimers were more likely to learn letter–sound correspondences early and to use decoding knowledge when encountering unfamiliar words.

Both the Barr and Dreeben and Juel and Roper/Schneider studies were conducted when texts for beginning readers followed particular rules on pace and repetition. The texts have changed substantially since the early 1980s when those studies were conducted. When Hoffman and his colleagues (1994) compared the textbooks with authentic literature that were adopted in Texas in 1993 with those that had been used in the period prior to this switch, they found that the number of unique words in first-grade texts between 1987 and 1993 had increased by almost 50 per cent. Further, vocabulary control had been replaced with predictable syntactic patterns that encouraged children to use picture support, rhyme and repeated patterns and phrases to decode text. Since this shift, there have been no reports with research designs similar to those of Barr and Dreeben (1983) and of Juel and Roper/Schneider (1985) examining children's reading development as a function of textbook coverage. Further, since Hoffman *et al.*'s (1994) analysis, yet another type of textbook programme – this time, decodable texts – has been produced in response to Texas's mandate for decodable texts (Texas Education Agency, 1997). The research on the efficacy of authentic literature-based and decodable texts is limited to descriptions of children's reading of texts, in the case of the former, and to descriptions of text characteristics, in the case of the latter.

Children's reading of recent textbook programmes

As has been described, the 1993 copyrights consisted of literature, rather than the specially written stories emphasising particular vocabulary that characterised the texts of the mid-1980s. In two separate analyses of children's ability to read the literature-based texts, a sizeable percentage of end-of-year first graders were unable to read even the first levels of these texts fluently: 45 per cent in a sample in the Midwest (Hiebert *et al.*, 1995) and approximately 35 per cent in a sample in Texas (Hoffman *et al.*, 2000). In an instructional study of children's word learning in the predictable texts that served as authentic literature in the first-grade components of the past decade's textbook programmes (Hoffman *et al.*, 1994), Johnston (2000) reported that the highest readers remembered 30 of the 160 unique words in the predictable texts at the end of three weeks, the middle readers 15 and the lowest readers 6. Texts that have high numbers of unique words, as is the case with the texts in literature-based programmes, do not facilitate the reading acquisition of any but the highest students.

Analyses of the features of textbook programmes

Effects of different kinds of texts on students' reading achievement are difficult to capture when one type of text quickly replaces another kind. One technique for considering text demands in a continually changing context is to apply a task framework to texts. Task analyses describe the linguistic and conceptual knowledge needed to perform a task – in this case, to read a text independently. Hiebert (2001) has applied a task framework to the texts from Texas-adopted programmes as well as those from the textbooks of previous generations.

The texts intended for the first third or half of grade 1 have more phonically regular words, as Texas mandated. On other features, however, the texts share the characteristics of authentic literature. Specifically, the texts continue to have high numbers of unique or different words per 100 running words of text. The variables of pace (how many new words are presented in lessons) and repetition (how often words appear in instructional materials) that Barr and Dreeben (1983) identified as critical to students' reading achievement have not been part of the mandates. Comparing a cluster of the first texts from the 1980s (prior to the California mandate for literature) and the early 1990s to those of the 2000 copyright reveals that the number of unique words per 100 running words of text were 5 (1983), 29 (1993) and 21 (2000). Whereas children were asked to learn 72 new words in the first five weeks of first grade in 1983, children need to be able to read 211 different words during the same period with the 2000 books.

Millions of dollars and thousands of hours of teachers' time are devoted to obtaining and using new textbook programmes. There is no empirical evidence that the texts that have been mandated over the last fifteen years by California and Texas make it easier for children to learn to read or for teachers to teach their students to read.

Reading reform at the federal level: reform models

Beginning with the Elementary and Secondary Education Act (ESEA) in 1965, the federal government has increasingly provided states with funds for intervening or providing more intensive support for reading instruction, especially for children from low-income families. Currently, the Title I programme aimed at students who qualify as poor (based on their eligibility for free or subsidised school lunches) provides states with $8.4 billion annually. Until recently, however, there have been no mandates regarding the instructional methodology to be used with these funds. This situation is in transition, as the existence of the Comprehensive School Reform Demonstration (CSRD) programme shows.

What is the reform?

In 1998, Congress implemented the CSRD programme to permit local education agencies and schools to make better use of federal, state and local funds in low-income schools. The centrepiece of the CSRD programme is the use of 'well-researched and well-documented models for school wide change that are supported by expert trainers and facilitators' (Northwest Regional Educational Laboratory, 2001). Annually, $145 million is available to state education agencies to make grants to districts for implementation of research-based models in individual schools. Schools can select models that are not listed in the legislation with the following stipulation: '[If] a school can demonstrate that the model selected will help the school implement a comprehensive programme, it is acceptable'. The legislation specifies nine components that constitute a coherent, well-designed comprehensive school reform programme:

- Effective, research-based methods and strategies
- Comprehensive design with aligned components
- Professional development
- Measurable goals and benchmarks
- Support within the school
- Parental and community involvement
- External technical support and assistance
- Evaluation strategies, and
- Co-ordination of resources.

These model programmes are, for the most part, separate from the mainstream textbook programmes. Several of the model programmes publish their own texts to go with the programme, although in none of these programmes have the effects of the texts been analysed separately. As will become evident in the next section, there is little evidence to substantiate the effectiveness of the numerous components that are part of the schoolwide and reading-specific projects, even among those programmes offered by Congress as demonstrative of the legislation's intent.

What is the evidence for the efficacy of this reform?

In that the first component of the CSRD programme is 'well-researched and well-documented models for schoolwide change that are supported by expert trainers and facilitators', and the fourth component is the presence of 'measurable goals and benchmarks', two forms of data would be anticipated: (a) data providing the basis for a project's identification as a demonstration project, and (b) ongoing data on students' achievements from the implementation of the model funded with CSRD funds. In neither case is there a substantial amount of data. Data have been very sparse for the original models as well as those that have been subsequently added to the programme. A review of the data that programme developers provided the federal government is examined first, followed by a discussion of the nature of ongoing data.

Herman and her colleagues (1999), who summarised the evidence from the seventeen schoolwide models identified as demonstration programmes in the congressional legislation, concluded that only three had any proof that their implementation made a positive difference in student achievement. Data on schoolwide models will not be reconsidered but, instead, a closer examination is given to the reading-specific models, which are the particular focus of this chapter. The reading-specific models are presented in Table 11.1.

As the data in columns 2 and 3 of Table 11.1 indicate, convincing proof that students in economically challenged neighbourhoods leave schools with higher levels of literacy is not available for any of the reading/ language arts models.

Most of the eleven reading/language arts reform models are specific to a particular age level. Three focus on beginning reading instruction only (Breakthrough to Literacy, Literacy Collaborative and Reading Recovery), while data on another three programmes were gathered when beginning reading was their focus (Early Intervention in Reading, First Steps and Exemplary Centre for Reading Instruction). Although early interventions are effective, they require changes in the reading experiences of subsequent grades if gains in literacy are to be maintained (Hiebert and Taylor, 2000).

Neither is it clear that instructional models that foster particular literacy proficiencies in high school are transferable to the elementary school. Two of the reading/language arts reform models were originally programmes for high school or even college students: the National Writing Project and the Junior Great Books programmes. Evidence that accommodations have been made to ensure that beginning readers and progressing readers receive the kind of guidance that develops the competencies of proficient reading has not been provided.

None of the reading/language arts models provide convincing data that implementation of these efforts will be the source of changes in reading profiles of students in economically challenged schools. While particular models may enhance particular dimensions of students' reading proficiency, transformation of students' reading achievement depends on instruction that attends to different tasks at different times. An intervention that emphasises writing is unlikely to be effective in fostering the literacy fundamentals of beginning readers. Likewise, an intervention that emphasises word recognition or fluency with simple, narrative texts is unlikely to foster strategies for comprehending and remembering complex, informational texts.

If there was no initial evidence, one might still expect that evidence would accumulate as projects were funded and moved forward. But evidence for the model programmes' effectiveness has not been updated on

Table 11.1   Reading/language arts reform models

Programme	Developer data	External reviewer data
Breakthrough to Literacy (K–2)*	No published evaluations are available.	No studies are claimed.
Carbo Reading Styles Program (K–8)	Evaluations are claimed but are not available on www or in published journals.	1 dissertation, 1 description in practitioner journal, and 1 ERIC document.
CELL/ExLL (PreK–6)	Evaluations are claimed but are not available on www or in published journals.	No studies are claimed.
CORE (K–8)	No published evaluations are available.	1 evaluation is claimed but is not available on www or in published journals.
Early Intervention in Reading (K–4)	2 descriptions in practitioner journal exist (Reading Teacher).	1 evaluation is claimed but is not available on www or in published journals.
Exemplary Centre for Reading Instruction (K–12)	1 evaluation is claimed but is not available on www or in published journals.	3 descriptive articles in practitioner journals exist.
First Steps (K–10)	Evaluations are claimed but are not available on www or in published journals.	3 evaluations by Australian Council of Educational Research exist (available on www).
Junior Great Books (K–12)	1 evaluation is claimed but is not available on www or in published journals.	1 dissertation on 5th graders exists; 2 evaluations are claimed but are not available on www or in published journals.
Literacy Collaborative (K–2)	Evaluations are claimed but are not available on www or in published journals.	No studies are claimed.
National Writing Project (K–16)	1 evaluation is claimed but is not available on www or in published journals.	No studies are claimed.
Reading Recovery (1)	1 evaluation is claimed but is not available on www or in published journals; 1 book chapter.	1 study in an international journal and 2 reports (one available through US Dept. of Ed.) exist; external reviews in archival journals by, e.g. Hiebert (1994) were not cited.

Note   *Indicates grade level

the US Department of Education's designated website or on the websites of the individual models. Further, the effects of the CSRD programme as a whole have not been reported. The one evaluation that exists attends to the problems of implementing the models on a large scale (Doherty, 2000). According to this evaluation, which was conducted by US Department of Education personnel, comprehensive school reform involves more changes than any one model or strategy can address alone. As the programme completes its third year of implementation, there is no evidence that gains have been realised in student reading achievement or even that the particular models have had prior success in sustaining gains in reading achievement.

While rhetoric for research-based reading instruction has increased since the implementation of the CSRD legislation, the burden of proof has been placed on schools rather than on the developers of the intervention models. According to the personnel associated with the identification of proven models (Buehler, 2001), schools need to show how their plan is research-based. That is, rather than expecting the model developers to provide data on the effectiveness of their practices, school personnel must piece together research studies to validate the particular set of practices that they have chosen. In high-poverty schools, a high percentage of teacher turnover makes it unlikely that the programmes such schools are able to design and implement under these circumstances will be sufficient to meet the needs of the children they serve.

Yet, at the same time, findings from two recent blue-ribbon panels provide detail on the content of programmes that can support higher levels of reading achievement. The needs of students, the consistency of at least a particular set of findings related to alphabetics, fluency, and comprehension (National Reading Panel, 2000; Snow *et al.*, 1998), and the level of funding are all high. A question that is left unanswered is why the very programme developers whose efforts are promoted by federal initiatives such as the CSRD are not asked to provide data that their models produce high levels of reading achievement. At the very least, model developers should be expected to show how their programmes incorporate the practices that have been identified by the two recent panels of national reading experts as proven to support higher reading achievement.

Next steps

Interpretations of American schoolchildren's literacy levels vary. However, even the most optimistic conclusion about these literacy levels needs to be accompanied by the caveat that what was sufficient for previous generations is not sufficient for the citizens of the digital age. Both of the reform efforts recounted here have lacked clarity regarding the underlying literacy processes or goals that the efforts are promoting. The two reform efforts also lack clarity regarding the instructional paths to these higher levels of literacy.

Such clarity is needed, and care should be taken that the goals of literacy and instructional paths promoted in textbook programmes and intervention models converge. Similar goals and paths need to underlie the textbook programmes to which states devote their reform efforts and the intervention models promoted by the national government. Suggestions for a shared vision of literacy proficiency and a means for supporting attainment of this proficiency by more students follow.

Clear descriptions of critical reading goals

There are three difficulties with the current descriptions of reading within the reading reform efforts of the state frameworks that mandate textbook changes and of the federal initiatives that support the model programmes of the CSRD: (a) definitions of reading are vague – at the level of 'reading as meaning', (b) definitions are generic rather than specific to different developmental levels, and (c) the grounding of definitions in tasks and texts has been limited. These difficulties persist despite the existence of numerous projects aimed at setting standards. A federally funded programme has supported states in devising their own standards – a task that almost all fifty states have completed for reading/language arts. Further, professional organisations such as the International Reading Association and the National Council of Teachers of English (IRA/NCTE, 1996) have identified standards. But these efforts have uniformly shown little of the specificity, differentiation for different developmental levels and elucidation of the relevant tasks and texts that administrators and teachers require to work toward common and critical goals (Stotsky, 2000).

The level of information that the public – including the nation's teachers and their students – is given about reading accomplishments is typified in the following statement about fourth graders' performances on the NAEP: 'Overall, reading scale scores for the nation's fourth graders have not changed, with scores of 217 in both 1992 and 2000. ... Thirty-two percent were at or above Proficient' (Phillips, 2001). From a report such as this one, it is impossible to tell what it is that fourth graders across the nation can read and what they cannot read. There needs to be some common ground in formative assessments; we cannot rely simply on the summative assessment of the NAEP. However, as a congressionally funded activity, the NAEP does have real potential to become more focused and responsive to the needs of children and their teachers.

To illustrate the nature of descriptions that are needed if teachers are to support their students in attaining proficient reading, an analysis of the sample text and questions from the 2000 fourth-grade NAEP assessment was conducted. An excerpt from the 2000 fourth-grade NAEP illustrates the texts that are used.

Imagine shivering on a cold winter's night. The tip of your nose tingles in the frosty air. Finally, you climb into bed and find the toasty treat you have been waiting for – your very own hot brick.

(A Brick to Cuddle Up To by Barbara Cole)

A first question to consider is whether the passage is an appropriate one for fourth graders. Since the demise of readability formulas in American reading education (Anderson *et al.*, 1985), there have been no agreed-upon systems for designating text difficulty. Hiebert (in press) has developed a scheme for describing word recognition demands. The percentage of unique words that fall outside a particular curriculum of high-frequency words and phonetically decodable words is determined. The resulting figure is called the critical word factor (CWF) – the number of unique words per 100 running words that are beyond a particular curriculum. When this passage was assessed against a curriculum of the 1,000 most frequent words and all vowel patterns in single-syllable words, plus simple morphological derivatives of these two groups, the critical word factor is revealed to be 5 unique words per 100. A level of 5 critical or difficult unique words per 100 running words of text is an acceptable number for the instructional to independent level of reading.

A second issue concerns the evidence that is gathered of students' comprehension of the passage. An elaborate scheme has been developed for the question types on the NAEP. Four types of questions are used: developing an initial understanding, developing an interpretation, developing a critical stance and giving a personal reflection and response. When students' responses to seven questions on the 2000 NAEP (Donahue *et al.*, 2001) are considered, the issue appears less to be one of question type than of required response format. Many below-basic and basic students respond correctly to a critical stance question. The difficulty for 'basic' and 'below-basic' students comes in writing responses to answers. When confronted with the first written response, which requires a one- or two-sentence answer, 38 per cent of 'basic' students provided satisfactory responses. But a portion of the 'basic' and 'below-basic' group continues to perform satisfactorily, even on the last item of the test (which requires an open-ended response).

A critical new direction in the demands of responses was taken on the 1992 NAEP. Following the authentic assessment movement of the early 1990s, open-ended responses became a prominent part of the 1992 NAEP. In the 2000 NAEP, 60 per cent of the questions required written responses. In contrast to the amount of time that was spent categorising question types, little time has been devoted to developing a scheme that distinguishes between the demands of different response formats. When the demands of the response modes are considered, strategies that teachers might take to ensure greater success for their students become apparent. Considerable periods of class time should be spent writing responses to texts and integrating background knowledge into these responses.

Rather than attributing low levels of interpretation to American schoolchildren, NAEP developers need to describe and justify what makes this text an exemplar of fourth-grade reading. They must also explain that it is entirely possible and even probable, based on the findings of the NAEP special study (Pinnell *et al.*, 1995), that children can read third-grade passages or fourth-grade passages that have been designated by other means. Presentations of the NAEP data also need to indicate that it may well be that students are coming up short, not in their reading, but in their ability to write elaborated responses to questions.

Armed with information on the critical competencies, teachers could then proceed with their work. Suggestions regarding adapting the two existing reform efforts – textbooks and model instructional programmes – follow.

Clear descriptions of instructional programmes for the elementary grades

The emphasis on proven models within the congressional legislation could be a positive impetus for school change, particularly if the characteristics of these models were reinforced in the teacher guidebooks that accompany textbook programmes. Instructional programmes can provide teachers with the tools to support students. In all likelihood, the focus provided by the model instructional programmes will be better than the diffuseness of the instructional schemes promoted by textbook programmes. The use of programmes that bring in support that is external to the school is also likely to keep teachers focused and committed to working through snags as they arise. Such tools and a support network can be particularly critical in the current American context in which teachers in the most highly chal-lenged schools over the next decade are likely to be under-prepared (Darling-Hammond, 1997).

Rather than implementing a programme that attends to one grade level or one aspect of literacy, reading reform efforts need to implement the features of effective reading programmes at all grade levels. For example, Adler and Fisher (2001) report that the reading programmes in schools where potentially struggling readers are doing well share components such as a focus on student outcomes, multiple reading programmes in every classroom, shared responsibility for student success across teachers, including specialists, strong leadership at school and classroom levels, and a veteran, knowledgeable staff. Such characteristics represent a level of specificity in the goals and instructional strategies of reading that most, if not all, current models lack. Only Success for All has addressed the elementary grades in a comprehensive fashion. In other cases, models are either focused on beginning reading (e.g. Reading Recovery and Early Intervention in Reading) or they are focused on upper levels (e.g. National Writing Project, Junior Great Books). For children who come to school without conventional literacy, an early intervention alone is unlikely to be sufficient. Attention needs to be paid to literacy throughout the developmental spectrum.

Evidence that underscores the need for attention to a developmental spectrum comes from research on the 'levelling' effect of early interventions and the effects of generalising strategies designed for older students to novices (Hiebert and Taylor, 2000). Unless instruction in subsequent grades builds on students' higher literacy levels as a result of an intervention, its effects will wane over time (Hiebert and Taylor, 2000). Further, efforts to transplant effective strategies with older students in responding to literature (Junior Great Books) or in writing extended narrative and informational texts (National Writing Project) into early elementary classrooms have not produced evidence of the effectiveness of such strategies in producing independent beginning readers.

To ensure that students' reading levels improve, schools also need access to information about specific foci and tasks that are appropriate at particular developmental levels. The content of effective instruction over a child's first six years of school is clear from the recent report of the National Reading Panel (2000). In its description of these interventions, it should be emphasised that the Panel took for granted the presence of other fundamental dimensions of a literacy programme – book reading, writing, and discussions of what has been read and written. But in terms of a number of critical aspects of reading programmes, the Panel provided guidelines.

Conclusion

American reading reform efforts are massive in scope, but their efficacy is hindered by a lack of integration between state and federal efforts. The reform of textbooks by America's two largest states and funding for model programmes by the federal government are not at cross-purposes. However, by not treating textbooks as model programmes, federal efforts ignore a primary vehicle for reform. Textbook programmes are already used extensively, a part of the school lives of millions of students and their teachers. If textbook programmes were placed in the foreground rather than in the background within federal research and implementation efforts, the characteristics of these programmes could be more closely scrutinised.

Just as the vehicles for reform are available, so too are guidelines for instruction. The report of the National Reading Panel (2000) described effective practices in the primary grades. The lack of integration within states and between states and the federal government, however, means that implementation of these findings on a large scale is unlikely to occur. For example, the Panel's conclusions regarding instruction that supports fluency have not filtered down to the model reform efforts of the federal government or the teachers' guides of the large states' textbook programmes.

Without such integration, many new teachers who will teach in America's poorest schools over the next decades will struggle to bring their students to basic levels of literacy. Without integration of the vehicles for reform and the vision underlying this reform, literacy levels of those most in need in America's schools are unlikely to meet the demands of the digital age.

References

Adler, M.A. and Fisher, C.W. (2001) 'Early reading programmes in high poverty schools: A case study of beating the odds', *The Reading Teacher* 54: 616–19.

Anderson, R.C., Hiebert, E.H., Scott, J.A. and Wilkinson, I.A.G. (1985) *Becoming a Nation of Readers: The Report of the Commission on Reading*, Champaign, IL: Center for Study of Reading.

Barr, R. and Dreeben, R. (1983) *How Schools Work*, Chicago: University of Chicago Press.

Baumann, J.F., Hoffman, J.V., Duffy-Hester, A.M. and Ro, J.M. (2000) 'The first R yesterday and today: US elementary reading instruction practices reported by teachers and administrators', *Reading Research Quarterly* 35: 338–77.

Bond, G. and Dykstra, R. (1967) 'The cooperative research programme in first-grade reading instruction', *Reading Research Quarterly* 2: 5–142.

Buehler, M. (2001) personal communication with author, 8 May.

Bush, G.W. (2001) *No Child Left Behind*, Education Policy of US President, 29 January (available online: http://www.ed.gov/inits/nclb/index.html).

California English/Language Arts Committee (1987) *English-Language Arts Framework for California Public Schools (Kindergarten through Grade Twelve)*, Sacramento: California Department of Education.

—— (1999) *English-Language Arts Content Standards for California Public Schools (Kindergarten through Grade Twelve)*, Sacramento: California Department of Education.

Campbell, J.R., Donahue, P.L., Reese, C.M. and Phillips, G.W. (1996) *NAEP 1994 Reading Report Card for the Nation and the States: Findings from the National Assessment of Educational Progress and Trial State Assessments*, Washington, DC: National Centre for Education Statistics.

Chall, J.S. and Squire, J.R. (1991) 'The publishing industry and textbooks', in R. Barr, M.L. Kamil, P.B. Mosenthal and P.D. Pearson (eds) *Handbook of Reading Research*, Vol. 2 (pp. 120–46), Mahwah, NJ: Erlbaum.

Darling-Hammond, L. (1997) 'The quality of teaching matters most: what teachers know and can do makes the most difference in what children learn', *Journal of Staff Development* 18: 38–44.

Doherty, K.M. (2000) *Early implementation of the Comprehensive School Reform Demonstration (CSRD) Programme*, Washington, DC: US Department of Education.

Donahue, P.L., Finnegan, R.J., Lutkus, A.D., Allen, N.L. and Campbell, J.R. (2001) *The Nation's Report Card for Reading: Fourth grade*, Washington, DC: National Center for Education Statistics.

Fisher, R. and Singleton, C. (2000) 'Symposium: the National Literacy Strategy', *Journal of Research in Reading* 23: 242–4.

Foorman, B.R., Francis, D.J., Fletcher, J.M., Schatschneider, C. and Mehta, P. (1998) 'The role of instruction in learning to read: preventing reading failure in at-risk children', *Journal of Educational Psychology* 90: 37–55.

Herman, R., Aladjem, D., McMahon, P., Masem, E., Mulligan, I., O'Malley, A.S., Quinones, S., Reeve, A. and Woodruff, D. (1999) *An Educators' Guide to Schoolwide Reform*, Washington, DC: American Institutes for Research.

Hiebert, E.H. (1994) 'Reading recovery in the United States: what difference does it make to an age cohort?', *Educational Researcher* 23: 15–25.

—— (2001) 'Pace and repetition: The forgotten variables in the design of beginning reading programmes', paper presented as part of symposium 'Texts That Support Beginning Reading Acquisition: What We Know and How We Know It', annual meeting of American Educational Research Association, Seattle, WA, April.

—— (in press) 'Standards, assessment and text difficulty', in A.E. Farstrup and S.J. Samuels (eds) *What Research Has To Say About Reading Instruction*, 3rd edn, Newark, DE: International Reading Association.

Hiebert, E.H. and Taylor, B.M. (2000) 'Beginning reading instruction: research on early interventions', in M. Kamil, P. Mosenthal, R. Barr and P.D. Pearson (eds) *Handbook of Reading Research*, Vol. 3 (pp. 455–82), Mahwah, NJ: Erlbaum.

Hiebert, E.H., Liu, G., Levin, L. Huxley, A. and Chung, K. (1995) 'First graders reading the new first-grade readers', paper presented at annual meeting of the National Reading Conference, New Orleans, LA, November.

Hoffman, J., Roser, N., Patterson, E., Salas, R. and Pennington, J. (2000) 'Text leveling and little books in first-grade reading' (CIERA Report #1–010), Ann Arbor, MI: Center for Improvement of Early Reading Achievement.

Hoffman, J.V., McCarthey, S.J., Abbott, J., Christian, C., Corman, L., Dressman, M., Elliot, B., Matherne, D. and Stahle, D. (1994) 'So what's new in the "new" basals? A focus on first grade', *Journal of Reading Behavior* 26: 47–73.

International Reading Association (IRA) and National Council of Teachers of English (NCTE) (1996) *Standards for the English Language Arts*, Newark, DE: IRA/NCTE.

Johnston, F.R. (2000) 'Word learning in predictable text', *Journal of Educational Psychology* 92: 248–55.

Juel, C. and Roper/Schneider, D. (1985) 'The influence of basal readers on first grade reading', *Reading Research Quarterly* 20(2): 134–52.

Lohnes, P.R. and Gray, M.M. (1972) 'Intellectual development and the cooperative reading studies', *Reading Research Quarterly* 8: 52–61.

National Reading Panel (2000) *Teaching Children to Read: An Evidence-Based Assessment of the Scientific Research Literature on Reading and Its Implications for Reading Instruction*, Washington, DC: National Institute of Child Health and Human Development.

Northwest Regional Educational Laboratory (2001) 'Components of comprehensive school reform programs' (available on-line: http://www.nwrel.org).

Phillips, G.W. (2001) 'The release of the National Assessment of Educational Progress (NAEP) Fourth-grade Reading 2000 (6 April online, available: http://www.nces.ed.gov/commissioner/remarks2001/).

Pinnell, G.S., Pikulski, J.J., Wixson, K.K., Campbell, J.R., Gough, P.B. and Beatty, A.S. (1995) *Listening to Children Read Aloud: Data from NAEP's Integrated*

Reading Performance Record (IRPR) at Grade 4, Washington, DC: OERI /US Department of Education and ETS.

Snow, C.E., Burns, M.S. and Griffin, P. (eds) (1998) *Preventing Reading Difficulties in Young Children*, Washington, DC: National Academy Press.

Stotsky, S. (2000) 'The state of literary study in national and state English language arts standards: why it matters and what can be done about it', in S. Stotsky (ed.) *What's At Stake in the K–12 Standards Wars: A Primer For Educational Policy Makers* (pp. 237–57), New York: Peter Lang.

Texas Education Agency (1990) *Proclamation of the State Board of Education Advertising for Bids on Textbooks*, Austin, TX: TEA.

—— (1997) *Proclamation of the State Board of Education advertising for bids on textbooks*, Austin, TX: TEA.

US Department of Education (2001): (www.ed.gov).

12 Teacher education programmes and children's reading achievement

A report from the National Commission on Excellence in Elementary Teacher Preparation for Reading Instruction

How can we best prepare teachers to teach reading? Like many seemingly straightforward questions, this one is as difficult to answer as it is important to answer. In this chapter the National Commission (USA) on Excellence in Elementary Teacher Preparation for Reading Instruction (the Commission) will reflect on its ongoing research programme in reading teacher education and suggest possible foci for improving teacher preparation in reading. First, we will contextualise the research in the United States, the setting in which our research is conducted. Second, we will provide an overview of the Commission's research projects. And finally, we will speculate on crucial aspects of teacher preparation programmes that are both amenable to intervention and likely to influence the quality of reading instruction and children's reading achievement. Much of what we describe here is drawn from previous Commission publications (Harmon *et al.*, in press); Hoffman *et al.*, 2001; Flint *et al.*, 2001)

The current teacher preparation context in the United States

Standards-based reform dominates the education landscape in the United States as elsewhere, and reading achievement has been a major target of that reform for nearly two decades. In the US reading is most often taught in a separate teaching methods course and is supplemented by language arts methods courses that address writing, speaking and listening. Over this time period reading achievement has been relatively stable. The lack of improvement, despite the constant attention and a significant expenditure of federal dollars, has created a contentious environment and teacher education has been at the centre of the controversy and criticism.

Teacher educators have found themselves with very little data available to address these criticisms. The United States Government funded *Report of the National Reading Panel, Teaching Children to Read: an Evidence-Based Assessment of the Scientific Research Literature on Reading and its Implications for Reading Instruction* (National Reading Panel, 1999) located only eleven experimental or quasi-experimental studies of pre-service teacher education. While the eleven studies showed that pre-service education changed teacher behaviour, none of the eleven studies followed the pre-service teachers into teaching. Thus, there are no experimental or quasi-experimental data that relate teacher preparation to children's reading achievement in the United States.

There are, however, numerous correlational and descriptive studies that address this issue of the effectiveness of teacher preparation programmes. Pearson (2001) summarised much of this data. He pointed out that reviews since 1970 conclude that totally prepared and certified teachers are better rated and more successful with students in terms of promoting achievement than are teachers who either lack subject matter or teaching knowledge. A number of specific studies of reading achievement (Gomez and Grobe, 1990; Ferguson, 1991; LA County Office of Education, 1999, all as cited in Pearson, 2001) show that students taught by fully certified teachers have higher reading achievement scores. However, these studies have been virtually ignored by reformers as they continue to berate teacher educators and colleges of education.

The Commission research agenda

It was against this background that the International Reading Association (the Association) formed the National Commission on Excellence in Elementary Teacher Education for Reading Instruction (the Commission) in January 1998. It was an unusual Commission for the Association because its charge was to conduct research. The research was to describe current teacher education for reading instruction and identify programme factors that lead to excellent reading instruction and reading achievement. The purpose of the undertaking was to provide support, guidance and, hopefully, leverage for the redesign of reading teacher preparation programmes.

To identify the research sites, the Commission published a call for applications in *Reading Today* (the Association Newspaper that reaches approximately 90,000 reading educators). The application called for each site to submit descriptions of their programmes; a descriptive vignette describing actual reading instruction delivered by a programme graduate who was a first-year teacher; commentaries on the vignette by the first-year teacher, the teacher's principal, a programme professor, and a current pre-service student; and documentation of collaboration with public school systems.

These applications were reviewed by a selection committee (John T. Guthrie, University of Maryland; P. David Pearson, Michigan State University, Dorothy Strickland, Rutgers University; and Carol Santa, then president of the Association). In a first round of evaluation they identified a group of excellent teacher education programmes. In a second round they selected a group of 8 institutions that represented a range of four-year, undergraduate preparation programmes. Selection criteria included

- special attention to reading in the programme
- serves and focuses on minority populations
- history of research and development
- faculty active in teacher education research
- track record of success in preparing teachers
- commitment to field-based practices
- collaboration with schools.

No one programme was expected to meet all criteria and there was no attempt to select the eight 'best' programmes. Rather the committee selected excellent programmes that represented the diversity of four-year teacher preparation programmes. The eight commission sites are:

- Florida International University, Miami – research 1 university (i.e. research focused), serving diverse population
- Hunter College, New York – small state-owned college, serving diverse population
- Indiana University, Bloomington and Indianapolis – large research 1 institution, serving homogeneous population in one site and diverse population at another
- Norfolk State University, Norfolk, VA – state, historically black university
- University of Texas, Austin – large research 1 institution
- University of Texas, San Antonio – smaller state institution serving diverse population
- University of Nevada, Reno – state flagship university with strong clinic programme
- University of Sioux Falls – small private Christian university with 1,000 students, graduating 30 students per year.

These sites are conducting a series of three research studies over the course of four years. The three studies are: the Features of Excellence Study, the Teacher Educator Survey and the Beginning Teacher Study. These studies examine important relationships among teacher preparation programmes, beginning teachers' reading instruction, and children's reading achievement. They are briefly summarised in the following subsections.

Features of Excellence

The Features of Excellence Study examines the common and the unique features of teacher education programmes across the commission sites. The purpose is to identify those programme features that lead to excellence in beginning teachers' reading instruction. This is primarily a qualitative study. Below we provide a brief summary of the findings. The eight features of excellence are:

1   Programmes are based on clearly articulated institutional missions that reflect a sense of who they are and who they want to become (Mission).
2   Faculty has a clear vision of how the mission is instantiated in the teacher education programmes (Vision).
3   Faculty members strive to maintain the integrity and quality of the literacy programme while working within the limited resources and constraints imposed by schools, the university and the state (Autonomy).
4   Faculty and school personnel model the student centred learning they expect their students to use in teaching children (Personalised Teaching).
5   Carefully supervised apprenticeship experiences are a critical feature of these teacher preparation programmes (Apprenticeship).
6   Programmes foster the professional identity of pre-service teachers and teacher educators within and across a variety of communities (Community).
7   Based upon current research and professional standards, programmes deliver broad-based content to best meet the needs of diverse students (Content).
8   A discriminating admissions/entry/exit continuum of procedures for maintaining standards and academic accountability, both supportive of diverse candidates and aimed at producing quality reading teachers, ensures that teachers are knowledgeable, have the necessary skills, and are able to teach reading effectively (Standards).

Teacher Educator Survey

The purpose of the Teacher Educator Survey was to determine the importance teacher educators place on an array of programme components and also to rate their particular programmes for each of the components. The commission identified a population of teacher educators in the area of elementary reading. They developed a survey that consisted of three sections: a demographic section which collected information about the participants, a values section which asked teacher educators to rate the importance of programme features to producing excellent beginning reading teachers, and a section which asked teacher educators to rate their own programmes on these same features. Below we summarise briefly nine central findings of the Survey (Hoffman, Rolle, and National Commission on Excellence in Elementary Teacher Preparation for Reading Instruction, 2001).

1 Preparation programmes for teachers continue to expand in the area of reading as compared to previous decades. Respondents reported that all students are required to take approximately 6 hours per semester of reading methods courses.

2 The variety of programme structures has increased. While 84 per cent of the respondents reported having a 4-year undergraduate programme, they also had a 5-year, master's degrees and other alternative formats. Forty per cent of the respondents indicated that a specialisation in reading was available at the undergraduate level.

3 Respondents reported finding the traditional course components of a reading preparation programme both important and up to standard. Courses in reading methods, language arts methods, and children's literature and clinical experiences were ranked very high in importance and rated high in quality as well.

4 The relative importance ratings of courses in language structure, testing and measurement, and technology were lower than other courses, and respondents rated their programmes below standard in language structure. This pattern is consistent with the external criticisms and suggests that teacher educators are aware of some specific programme weaknesses.

5 Faculty who teach in these preparation programmes were reported by our respondents as appearing to be well qualified. The frequent stereotype of ill-prepared teacher educators who are professionally inactive and have never taught in elementary classrooms is simply not reflected in these data.

6 Respondents rated their programmes below standard in the areas of class size and discretionary budget. This finding suggests that programmes are underfunded. Large class sizes are a sign of institutional unwillingness to provide more classes with smaller numbers of students.

7 The emphasis on field-based experiences and the co-ordination of field experiences appears to be growing in the amount of time afforded to this level of supervision provided and articulation with coursework.

8 Our respondents, unlike many of the most vocal critics, rate their programme quality high. Only 2 per cent of the respondents ranked their programmes 'poor,' and nearly 86 per cent rated their programmes 'good' or 'outstanding.' Ratings of reading specialisation programmes were similarly high.

9 We have real concerns about the preparation of teachers of diverse backgrounds. It appears that most diverse students are prepared in large research institutions where respondents rate programme quality lower than teaching institutions. In addition, on items addressing the opportunities to work in diverse settings and on items addressing the knowledge of diversity issues, the most diverse institutions' importance and programme ratings are highest and those ratings at

predominantly white institutions are lowest. Given the changing demographics of student populations, this discovery is alarming.

In summary, the programmes described by our respondents have much to recommend them, and there are notable increases in the number of reading courses and the amount of clinical fieldwork in these preparation programmes. While we cannot say from these data that the field as a whole is making progress, we can say that there are many teacher preparation programmes around the country where pre-service teachers are receiving excellent preparation for reading instruction. We must acknowledge this excellence and look to these respondents and their programmes as we attempt to improve the level of teacher preparation for reading instruction.

Beginning Teacher Study

The purpose of the Beginning Teacher Study is to describe beginning teachers graduated from commission programmes and to compare them to beginning teachers from programmes that do not emphasise reading instruction.

The Beginning Teacher Study follows graduates of the Commission programmes into and through their first three years of teaching. In year one, the beginning teachers and some comparison beginning teachers from other programmes were interviewed at the beginning, middle and end of the year. These interviews focused primarily on reading instruction and the beginning teachers' concerns and practices for teaching reading. In year two, programme and comparison teachers were interviewed twice and observed in their classrooms. The Commission will also conduct interviews with the beginning teachers' principals and a representative sample of their students. In year three, we will observe and collect pre- and post-reading achievement data in the classrooms of 60 beginning teachers (30 programme and 30 comparison). Also during this phase we will observe a subsample of 16 teachers (eight programme and eight comparison systematically selected) for six full days evenly spaced through the academic year.

This study is in progress and will not be completed until 2003. However, we have tentatively identified ten themes from the first-year interviews. These should be viewed as tentative and the extent to which they apply varies across sites.

1   Responsive Teaching – Programme teachers describe children's reading progress in detailed language and are clearly developing instruction to meet a wide range of needs within their classrooms.
2   Hiring – Programme teachers mentioned that they were hired because of their competence in reading.

3 Community – Programme teachers participate in or build a learning community.
4 Leadership – Programme teachers take leadership roles in reading during their first year of teaching.
5 Negotiation – Programme teachers are more likely to negotiate with principals and team members to include instruction that meets children's needs.
6 Reflection – Both programme and comparison teachers are reflective.
7 Confidence – Programme teachers are confident of their ability to teach reading.
8 Attributions – Programme teachers attribute their teaching practices to their preparation programme.
9 Concerns – Programme teachers' concerns centre around the impact their instruction is having on children's learning.
10 Diversity – Programme teachers address diversity as it is present in their classrooms.

Some speculations

While the Commission has completed two of its three studies and published several articles, the real findings of the effort have yet to emerge. The power of the Commission research goes beyond the individual studies and it is the relationships among the studies that we hope will eventually inform teacher education reform efforts. While it is premature to declare these findings, after working with the participants, the programmes and the data over the last three years, we have begun to speculate about some of these important relationships. In this chapter we will write about three we think will eventually emerge and have the potential to help teacher education institutions leverage the resources they need to produce good reading teachers: content knowledge, quality apprenticeship experiences and autonomy.

Content knowledge

Content knowledge emerged as one of the strongest themes across all programmes. We initially phrased this feature of excellence as: based upon current research and professional standards, programmes deliver broad-based content to best meet the needs of diverse students. The University of Texas, San Antonio (UTSA) and Florida International University are typical of the ways the eight sites approach issues related to content. At San Antonio there is a reading specialisation that involves extended coursework and experiences in reading. At Florida International University the reading and TESOL (Teaching Reading as a Second or Other Language) content is woven through a series of courses so that all students are certified to teach reading and English as a second language when they complete their programmes.

To give a more concrete portrayal of content, we will first describe the UTSA programme. Students seeking elementary certification at UTSA major in Interdisciplinary Studies (IDS) and choose an academic specialisation within this major. Typically IDS majors choose one of four academic specialisations – reading, early childhood, bilingual education, or special education. The reading specialisation is selected by approximately 30 per cent of all students seeking elementary certification.

Like all students in the IDS programme, reading specialisation students begin their programme by enrolling in the required introductory reading courses – *Introduction to Developmental Reading* and *Introduction to Elementary Content Reading*. In addition to the required introductory reading courses, reading specialisation students take an additional 18 semester hours of reading courses. The four required specialisation courses are:

• *Introduction to Reading Problems*
• *Reading Comprehension*
• *Relationships between Reading and Writing*
• *Children's and Adolescent Literature.*

Students select two electives from the following courses:

• *Early Literacy Learning*
• *Assessment Practices in Reading*
• *Language, Literacy and Culture*
• *Oral Language and Reading*
• *Social Psychology of Literacy*
• *Reading and Studying as a Cognitive Process.*

At each commission site there is regular evaluation of course content against a variety of existing standards. The faculties regularly review courses together as a faculty to determine that all-important content is covered and that there is not unnecessary repetition. As an example of the kinds of analysis programmes do, the next section shows how the UTSA programme dealt with phonemic awareness.

Developing university student knowledge of phonemic awareness and letter–sound relationships and their role in the reading and writing process was one area that they had worked to strengthen in recent years. The Texas Essential Knowledge and Skills (TEKS) emphasise phonemic awareness in grades K-2. In response, the *Introduction to Developmental Reading* course that all education students take explains the research base for phonemic awareness and illustrates how it is fostered in young children. To ensure that pre-service teachers have both knowledge of phonemic awareness and skill in its assessment and instruction, each student assesses a young child's phonemic awareness. During class, students examine scores of books provided by the professor and determine which aspect of phonemic awareness the book reinforces. Students participate in role-play activities to teach segmentation and blending, as well as create a collection of songs and chants to enhance phonemic awareness. Students also plan and conduct a tutorial session designed to foster phonemic awareness.

This knowledge base of phonemic awareness is strengthened and reinforced in the elective *Oral Language and Reading* and in a course called *Early Literacy Learning* required for all students seeking elementary certification. As students progress through their programme and enrol in *Introduction to Reading Problems*, they have opportunities to put into practice their phonemic awareness knowledge during tutorials.

The Commission found that deeper knowledge of the content of reading is reflected in the first year teacher interviews. Comparison teachers tended to talk in generalities and about programme materials. Programme teachers talked more specifically about their actions and decisions in reading instruction being based on children's development, progress and needs. For example, comparison teachers made comments like the following:

> Some of the best experiences that I've had so far is just getting the kids excited about books.
>
> Our school got *Accelerated Reader* in February and it has been absolutely fabulous. What I did the last six weeks was I made a chart and I set up a points goal with the students and rather than them having to choose their goals, I went ahead and set the same goals for everyone.

The programme teachers' comments focused more on children's instructional needs and ways they were meeting them.

> I do mini-lessons to address anything that I see. Either one or two kids. And I'll pull them aside and give a mini lesson on something they need. If there's more than that, then I might do a whole-class mini-lesson. I try to go around the class and read individually, or listen to them read to me, take notes about what I'm hearing and the different strategies that they're using for either (tape unintelligible) for sounding out the words or context clues.
>
> Me as a teacher, I take a running record every week on every child. With their station work, I'm doing the guided reading stations, and while they're doing stations, that's when I usually do my reading with

my kids. I started out with guided reading groups, I kept track of that and kept track of their strategies that they were using.

Quality apprenticeship experiences

Carefully supervised field experiences were identified in each of the eight commission programmes as a critical feature of their teacher preparation programmes. As we studied that feature in greater depth, we discovered that it wasn't simply the presence of school-based experiences in learning and teaching that constituted excellence. The programmes exemplified components of apprenticeship in their provision of authentic experiences for pre-service teachers over extended periods of time in collaboration with master teachers. Additionally, however, throughout the diverse manifestations of the apprenticeship model within the Commission programmes, there were common characteristics that contributed to the high quality and, thus, the impact of the experiences upon the pre-service teachers' learning, teaching, and thinking about themselves as teachers.

Hunter College QUEST programme is one example of a well-implemented apprenticeship programme. They identify six factors as critical.

1   *Pairing of coursework and field experiences*: During its formation the QUEST programme made a commitment to field experiences and designed the three-credit methods and foundations courses to contain two-credit didactic, theoretical portions with one-credit field experiences. By requiring a full day each week in classrooms under the supervision of the full-time professors of their methods and foundations courses, QUEST students accumulate nearly 250 hours of classroom experience prior to student teaching.

2   *Sequential and purposeful instructional skills, strategies and techniques to guide experiences*: Not surprisingly this paired, didactic and field experience approach to coursework facilitates having the didactic portions of the QUEST courses use assignments and evaluations that are classroom-based applications of the theories and research addressed in the coursework. Thus, while QUEST students are studying a particular methodology or theory, they are practising their skills and fulfilling course requirements by applying their knowledge in real world teaching assignments.

3   *Diversity in field placements*: QUEST students take advantage of the full range of diversity that New York City schools have to offer in terms of grade levels, school philosophies, student populations, and teaching styles. A full-time Director of Clinical Field Placements co-ordinates field experiences and student teaching sites with school principals and co-operating teachers. College supervisors further diversify the experiences by ensuring that QUEST students are placed in classrooms that do not duplicate previous grade level assignments.

Through this diversity in educational settings, the students are given experience in translating their social learning experiences into effective pedagogy.

4 *Careful Supervision and Feedback*: Providing weekly opportunities to work in a diversity of classrooms is not, in itself, sufficient to produce an excellent beginning teacher. Supervision by the professors of the didactic courses is an essential component of the fieldwork. The commitment of full-time faculty members to guiding the quality of the field experience portion of the courses is an important dimension of the QUEST programme. Professors observe students three times per semester. Each observation is preceded and followed by a conference and faculty members provide written feedback. QUEST students are required to do written reflections on these observations. QUEST students receive regular feedback from their professors and ample opportunities to discuss their current teaching strengths and weaknesses.

5 *Opportunity for reflection and dialogue*: The reflective quality of field experiences is also supported by professors through in-class discussions, the use of field placement examples to illustrate theoretical concepts, opportunities for student reflection in the creation of portfolios or the use of journals, and on-going feedback provided during multiple evaluations, written evaluations and post-observation conferences. Reflection and dialogue is also built into coursework in the form of discussions, journals, and reflective entries via on-line discussions groups.

6 *Collaboration with schools and co-operating teachers*: Each semester begins with an orientation for co-operating teachers in each of the site schools and an orientation for field placements and student teaching at Hunter College for QUEST students. Often, the co-operating teachers are, themselves, graduates of Hunter College. District personnel, principals and former co-operating teachers are frequently adjunct teachers at Hunter College and/or hold administrative positions. Collaboration then is second nature to all the players.

Once again the interviews with the first-year programme teachers identify the apprenticeship experiences as an important feature in their training. When they were asked about the value of their teacher preparation programmes, programme teachers talked about their preparation and particularly their apprenticeship experiences.

But to be honest with you the fieldwork did it a lot. Being in the classroom. Because you can learn it, you can hear it, you can read it, but if you aren't experiencing it, it's not gonna be the same. It's a great reinforcement but you have to really be doing it to understand it and to really get it.

Just the time to work with kids. As far as getting to do a lot. Every class I had I was out in the schools doing stuff. That was very valuable because then you can look back and say this worked with this kid, maybe I could try it. I think that was very valuable. Just getting to work with those kids all the time and realizing that there are lots and lots of different kids out there who learn in lots of different ways.

Comparison teachers seem to attribute their effectiveness to factors other than their teacher education programmes such as a good school team, district in-service, luck, the kids' hard work and watching what other teachers did. They made comments like the following: 'I feel it [teacher preparation] didn't have too much to do with me', 'If I didn't have as good a team as I have, I don't think I would have done as well and the kids wouldn't have done as well', 'I just felt like no matter what I did, their effort didn't seem to reflect that they cared. But for my kids that tried hard ... they made strides.'

Autonomy

Another important feature that characterised faculty at commission sites was autonomy. Teachers, in today's classrooms, face a challenging task when striving to be autonomous and informed decision-makers. External mandates, accountability, standards and other such pressures often require teachers to conform to particular decisions determined by those outside of classroom practice. The decisions tend to be curricular (i.e. implementing a particular programme for reading, math, science, etc.) or structural (i.e. everyone participates in 'reading' at the same time). These actions do not take into consideration the children in the classrooms or the teachers' own belief system and pedagogical practices. As teachers work under these circumstances they become less autonomous and empowered to make decisions that are based on the needs of their students. Teachers become more like technicians and assembly line workers, where everyone is accomplishing the same thing at the same time.

Issues of autonomy impact not only teachers, but also those involved in teacher education. What decisions do the programmes have that make a difference in how pre-service teachers are prepared to teach reading at the elementary level? And more importantly, in what ways do beginning teachers from these programmes demonstrate their own autonomous actions and behaviours. Responsive to the wide variety of limitations and constraints (e.g. mandates from university, state legislatures, budgets, school districts, licensing/credentialing departments, etc.), the eight identified programmes have extended beyond the university structures to collaborate with local school and community organisations. Autonomy within the programmes to make informed decisions enables collaborations and connections to grow, which in turn contributes to providing excellence in preparing pre-service teachers to teach reading. The uniqueness of each programme (i.e. programme requirements, structures, field experiences, exit requirements, etc.) signifies how faculty members within the programmes attend to the needs of the students and design programmes that complement the context in which they exist. In the face of seemingly unlimited obstacles, faculty members must persevere, be creative and be willing to take autonomous actions in order to achieve their goals.

The autonomy in decision-making is communicated as an important value and that same autonomy is reflected in some of the beginning teacher interviews – particularly in teaching to meet the needs of children. The eight research sites have in place a variety of structures that enable pre-service teachers to have focused, intense, and meaningful interactions with children and teachers prior to graduating from the programme. These structures, whether it is the reading clinic, the cohort programme, or having the student teaching assignment under the direction of the reading/language department seem to make a difference in how the beginning teachers respond to meeting the individual needs of children.

Programme teachers commented on their abilities to make informed decisions which support autonomy and empowerment. One teacher from Florida International mentioned that even though there is a prescribed programme in place (Success for All), she is able to instruct through cross-curricular literacy projects. Two teachers from Hunter College shared how they were able to go 'against the grain' to provide more meaningful and ultimately more effective teaching,

> I must admit that I did some unorthodox [things]. For example: I was told to model, model, model! However, I tended to reintroduce content or skills if I felt they were not getting it. I did less modeling and more student engagement and interactive activities and lessons. This helped with their critical thinking skills. Stressing 'accountable' talk was time consuming, but I did it. I had to balance my instructional time carefully with subject areas like science and social studies, but I still used it and my students did well. Even though I was told not to do this, I did it anyway. [Note: teacher's reference to accountable talk refers to discussions in her classroom].
>
> Basically we have to do Success For All. And I do alter it. Once my door is closed I follow it but I add what I want to add. The last twenty minutes is supposed to be oral language. Yes oral language is important where they're communicating and playing. And that is important but I think skills are also very important too when it comes to reading. Because throughout our lesson we're talking and communicating and having fun, so I take those twenty minutes to add my own stuff. Trying to teach skills, concentrating more on writing because Success

For All really doesn't touch a lot on writing. I try to take extra time to work on that stuff.

These two teachers exemplify how they have made decisions reflective of their belief systems and that address the needs of their students. For these teachers and others graduating from our programmes, the autonomous actions we have put into place have contributed greatly to beginning teachers feeling empowered to make informed decisions.

Conclusion

As we conclude our studies and our data analyses, we hope to be able to make rigorous arguments for the relationships between features of strong teacher preparation programmes and the abilities and teaching practices of the beginning teachers who graduate from them. In addition to the more qualitative data analyses evidenced here we will have some quantitative estimates of the degree to which each of our eight sites reflects a particular feature and also some quantitative estimates of the degree to which graduates from each site teach in ways consonant with those features. Because there is variation across sites in the degree and the way features are instantiated, we expect we will find correlational evidence of relationships. We also hope to tie these analyses in with the second-year classroom observations and the third-year observations and measures of student achievement. There is much left to do, but we hope this chapter has given you a feel for what we are finding and what we may find. We think the Commission will produce valuable findings that will make a strong contribution to the improvement of reading teacher education.

References

Ferguson, R. (1991) 'Paying for public education: new evidence on how and why money matters', *Harvard Journal of Legislation* 28: 465–98.

Flint, A.S., Leland, C.H., Patterson, B., Hoffman, J.V., Sailors, M.W., Mast, M.A. and Assaf, L.C. (2001) ' "I'm still figuring out how to do this teaching thing": a cross-site analysis of reading preparation programmes on beginning teachers' instructional practices and decisions', in C.M. Roller (ed.) *Learning to Teach Reading: Setting the Research Agenda* (pp. 100–18), Newark, DE: International Reading Association.

Gomez, D.L. and Grobe, R.P. (1990) 'Three years of alternative certification in Dallas: Where are we?', paper presented at annual meeting of American Educational Research Association, Boston, MA, April.

Harmon, J., Hedrick, W., Martinez, M., Perez, B., Strecker, S., Fine, J.C., Eldridge, D., Flint, A.S., Loven, R., Assaf, L. and Sailors, M. (in press) 'Features of excellence of Reading Teacher Preparation programmes', in *National Reading Conference Yearbook, 2000*, Chicago, IL: National Reading Conference.

Hoffman, J.V., Roller, C.M. and National Commission on Excellence in Elementary Teacher Preparation for Reading Instruction (2001) 'The IRA Excellence in

Reading Teacher Preparation Commission's report: current practices in reading teacher education at the undergraduate level in the United States', in. C.M. Roller (ed.) *Learning to Teach Reading: Setting the Research Agenda* (pp. 32–79), Newark, DE: International Reading Association.

National Reading Panel (1999) *Teaching Children to Read*, Washington, DC: US Department of Education.

Pearson, P.D. (2001) 'Learning to teach reading: the status of the knowledge base', in C. Roller (ed.) *Learning to Teach Reading: Setting the Research Agenda* (pp. 4–19), Newark, DE: International Reading Association.

13 The implementation of the National Literacy Strategy in England, 1998–2001

Laura Huxford

The need for reform in the teaching of literacy

Successive governments in England from the 1970s have been concerned that standards in literacy were not sufficiently high. In comparison to other countries there was 'a long tail of underachievement'. In 1997 63 per cent of children left primary school at 11 years of age with a level 4 and above in English in the national test.[1] Reports from the government's inspectors of schools questioned the focus and quality of teaching. These indicated, for instance, that few schools used a balanced approach to the teaching of reading which included the systematic teaching of phonics and that the teaching of reading consisted of the teacher listening for variable amounts of time to children reading individually. This they described as monitoring rather than teaching in many instances (Ofsted, 1996). There was also considered to be insufficient teaching of writing (Beard, 1999; Literacy Task Force, 1997; also see Beard, this volume).

Launching a National Literacy Strategy

In 1997 a National Literacy Project was in its first year in primary schools (ages 4–11) in 14 local education authorities (LEAs) considered to be in greatest need. A project director and deputy director were running the project with literacy consultants in each LEA supported by an English inspector/advisor as local strategy manager. The consultants worked intensively with a limited number of schools in their LEAs. A *Framework* of teaching objectives, in draft form, was in use in the project schools and teaching materials were being written to support the *Framework*. Teachers were trained to teach a literacy hour comprising roughly 15 minutes of shared text work (reading or writing); 15 minutes of phonics, spelling or sentence level work, depending on the age of the children; 20 minutes with a small group doing guided reading or writing while the rest of the class worked independently of the teacher either individually, or in pairs or groups; and, to close the lesson, a plenary session.

The incoming government in May 1997 embarked on a National Literacy Strategy (NLS) to raise standards of literacy teaching in primary schools so that 80 per cent of children would leave Key Stage 2 with the skills required to achieve level 4 and above in the national tests in the year 2002; targets for individual LEAs ranged from 70 to 90 per cent. Schools were also set targets aggregating to the LEA target. In order to achieve these targets the government developed the administrative and pedagogic structures of the embryonic National Literacy Project.

The infrastructure for implementation of the National Literacy Strategy (NLS) was headed by the Standards and Effectiveness Unit within the Department for Education and Employment (DfEE, later DfES) and consisted of a team of regional directors, a strategy manager for each LEA and over 300 consultants supported by a centrally based administrative team. A National Numeracy Strategy evolved in the same way and both were administered in parallel at government and local level. Both strategies defined a progression of teaching objectives from the Reception year to Y6 and an optimum length of time for a lesson. The strategies are not statutory, but there is a clear expectation that schools will adopt the *Frameworks for teaching* and the designated literacy hour and mathematics lessons unless they were confident that their schemes of work and organisation were as good or better.

Schools were expected to audit their literacy provision in the school and, by examining test results and samples of children's work, to set qualitative targets for the school, each class and possibly for groups or individual children. In almost every school and LEA, the level of writing was pinpointed as an area for development. Schools were encouraged to 'get below the surface' to ascertain which elements of writing were letting the children down and to concentrate teaching in those areas. Each school identified a member of staff to take the role of literacy co-ordinator and between them, the head teacher and literacy co-ordinator monitored the literacy work in the school and took appropriate action to improve teaching quality where necessary.

The *Framework for teaching*

The English National Curriculum statutory programmes of study for reading and writing were the basis for the term-by-term progression of objectives in the *Framework for teaching*. The *Framework* (DfEE, 1998a) is designed to provide an outline scheme of work for the whole school and to ensure coverage of the statutory requirements for teaching literacy, high expectations appropriate to pupils' ages, a detailed progression of objectives across the primary years, the interrelationship of reading and writing and a balance of work between reading and writing and between fiction, poetry, plays and non-fiction. Specific objectives for the programme of study on speaking and listening were not included, though the use and development of these skills were indicated throughout the *Framework*. It was expected that most of the National Curriculum objectives for oral work would be covered in the course of teaching the literacy objectives. The rationale for the *Framework* was based on the assumption grounded in the National Curriculum that literate primary pupils should:

- read and write with confidence, fluency and understanding;
- be able to orchestrate a full range of reading cues (phonic, graphic, syntactic, contextual) to monitor and self-correct their own reading;
- understand the sound and spelling system and use this to read and spell accurately;
- have fluent and legible handwriting;
- have an interest in words and word meanings, and a growing vocabulary;
- know and understand a range of genres in fiction and poetry, and understand and be familiar with some of the ways that narratives are structured through basic literary ideas of setting, character and plot;
- understand and be able to use a range of non-fiction texts;
- plan, draft, revise and edit their own writing;
- have a suitable technical vocabulary through which to understand and discuss their reading and writing;
- be interested in books, read with enjoyment and evaluate and justify preferences;
- through reading and writing, develop their powers of imagination, inventiveness and critical awareness.

(DfEE, 1998a: 3)

In order to 'read and write with confidence, fluency and understanding' the *Framework* describes the knowledge and understanding of language, and the skills which children need, at the level of *word* (phonics, word recognition, graphic knowledge, spelling, vocabulary and handwriting); *sentence* (grammatical awareness, sentence construction and punctuation); and *text* (composition and comprehension: variety of text-types, purpose, organisation, structure, style, cohesion and response). A progression of objectives for each strand builds throughout the primary years; the relevant word and sentence level objectives are included to support each text level objective. For example, in Year 4 term 2, the text level objectives for reading on the subject of 'settings' and expressive, descriptive and figurative language are mirrored in the text level writing objectives:

pupils should be taught to develop use of settings in own writing, making use of work on adjectives and figurative language to describe settings effectively.

This, in turn, relates to the sentence level objective:

> pupils should be taught to revise and extend work on adjectives …
> and link to work on expressive, figurative language in stories and
> poetry: constructing adjectival phrases; examining comparative and
> superlative adjectives; comparing adjectives on a scale of intensity …
> relating them to suffixes … and adverbs which indicate degrees of
> intensity.

The related word-level objectives include:

> children should be taught to use alternative words and expressions
> which are more accurate or interesting than the common choices e.g.
> *nice, good.*

> children should be taught a range of suffixes that can be added to
> nouns and verbs to make adjectives.
>
> (DfEE, 1998a: 40, 41)

Fiction and non-fiction objectives and suggested text range are included
each term. Many of the objectives were designed to be taught using non-
fiction texts from other curriculum areas such as history, geography and
science, or a novel which the teacher and children would be reading on a
daily basis. Some objectives require the use of extracts from a number of
texts in order to make comparisons or draw conclusions about common
usage.

Teachers are encouraged to plan on a half-termly basis, choosing the
text level objectives and appropriate texts for each week and then mapping
on the appropriate sentence and word-level objectives to support children's
reading and writing development. Teachers are encouraged to construct
their class timetables to link the literacy work on non-fiction text-types
and the work in other curriculum areas in which the same text-types are
being read or written. Full integration of text and sentence level objectives
is intended so that children learn, for instance, about sentence construction
and word classes with the express intention of using that knowledge to
understand text and write effectively. It is not expected that systematic
work on phonics and learning of spelling conventions will be integrated
into work on text and sentence level but that *in the process of reading and
writing*, children will apply the skills and knowledge gained in this work
on word-level objectives.

On the whole the objectives in the *Framework* do not dictate a specific
pedagogy. They are intended to be statements of content, though in some
instances pedagogy is suggested in the verbs (e.g. 'investigate'). The introduction to the *Framework*, however, is quite clear about appropriate
pedagogy. To ensure that the objectives in the *Framework* are taught in a

coherent manner, teachers are expected to designate a clear hour for literacy teaching every day. In order to maximise the teacher's time and expertise, it is suggested that two-thirds of this time should be spent on teaching the objectives using experiences shared by the whole class: 'shared' reading and writing, systematic teaching of phonics, spelling and grammar and a plenary. The *Framework* describes successful teaching as:

- discursive – characterised by high quality oral work;
- interactive – pupils' contributions are encouraged, expected, and extended;
- well-paced – there is a sense of urgency, driven by the need to make progress and succeed;
- confident – teachers have a clear understanding of the objectives;
- ambitious – there is optimism about and high expectations of success.

(DfEE, 1998a: 8)

During the 'whole class' time there is opportunity for a number of teaching strategies allowing for many levels and forms of learning:

- direction e.g. to ensure pupils know what they should be doing, to draw attention to points, to develop key strategies in reading and writing;
- demonstration e.g. to teach letter formation and join letters, how to read punctuation using a shared text, how to use a dictionary;
- modelling e.g. discussing the features of written texts through shared reading of books, extracts, etc.;
- scaffolding e.g. providing writing frames for shared composition of non-fiction texts;
- explanation to clarify and discuss e.g. reasons in relation to the events in a story, the need for grammatical agreement when proof-reading, the way that different kinds of writing are used to serve different purposes;
- questioning: to probe pupils' understanding, to cause them to reflect on and refine their work, and to extend their ideas;
- initiating and guiding exploration e.g. to develop phonological awareness in the early stages, to explore relationships between grammar, meaning and spelling with older pupils;
- investigating ideas: e.g. to understand, expand or generalise about themes and structures in fiction and non-fiction;
- discussing and arguing: to put points of view, argue a case, justify a preference, etc.;
- listening to and responding: e.g. to stimulate and extend pupils' contributions, to discuss/evaluate their presentations.

(DfEE, 1998a: 8)

Half an hour of this interactive whole-class teaching is followed by a twenty-minute session in which the teacher works with a small group of children of similar ability on a semi-independent task. This scaffolding is a bridge between the modelling and semi-scaffolded work with the whole class and the reduced scaffolding when working independently from the teacher. While the teacher works with the small group, the rest of the children in the class are expected to work collaboratively or individually on reading or writing tasks with varying amounts of built-in scaffolding, depending on the level of ability of the children or nature of the task. The literacy hour is designed to end with a ten-minute plenary session in which the children articulate their learning and understanding of the work they have been engaged in during the hour. This model of teaching, from shared – through guided – to independent, forms the basis of teaching reading and writing.

Teaching reading

In the NLS, the teaching of reading is intended to take many forms: shared reading using enlarged texts, guided reading in small groups using individual copies of the same text, independent reading (individually or collaboratively), reading aloud by the teacher, reading to other adults, reading at home. This is supported in the early stages by the systematic teaching of phonics.

The 'interactive' model adopted by the NLS for learning to read is grounded in the National Curriculum and has its roots in the work of Rumelhart (1977) and others and expanded and illustrated by Adams (1990). This model, dubbed the 'searchlight model' (see Figure 13.1) proposed that successful reading depends on learning to use a range of strategies. The reader uses these as 'cues' to get to the meaning by recognising or decoding the whole or part of a word, predicting from the context or grammar, checking and cross-checking, identifying and correcting errors. Children are shown how these strategies are brought to bear on unfamiliar words during 'shared reading'. They are encouraged to 'orchestrate' these strategies, to bring two or more into play at once. Novice readers with limited knowledge of letter combinations may, for instance, guess the word 'bread' by reading the initial letter and looking at the picture. The teacher would encourage them to check by looking to see if other sounds that they can hear in the word 'bread', such as /d/, appear in the written word. If appropriate, the teacher could ask the class to deduce what sound in the word 'bread' is represented by the letters 'ea'. In this way children are encouraged to supplement their systematic phonics teaching with 'self-teach' (Share, 1995). In guided reading, with a small group of children at a similar reading level, the teacher checks that children can and do use all the strategies so that they can read books at an appropriate level independently.

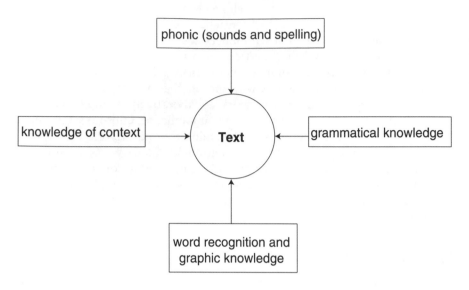

Figure 13.1   The searchlight model of the National Literacy Strategy
Source: (DfEE, 1998a: 4)

Just as shared reading is an opportunity to model the use of rudimentary strategies for beginning readers, so it can be used to demonstrate and explain more sophisticated reading behaviours such as skimming and scanning, the use of inference and deduction or the use of text marking to aid access to complex texts. Shared reading is also intended as an opportunity to deconstruct texts and examine textual features which children might then go on to deploy in their own composition.

Teaching writing

The interdependence between reading and writing is one of the cornerstones of the NLS. Nevertheless, after the first year of implementation, national tests showed that while reading scores had improved, a high proportion of children, particularly boys, left primary school with poor writing ability. A number of initiatives were explored to address this issue, the first of which was the publication of *Grammar for Writing* for KS2 teachers (DfEE, 2000a) and *Developing Early Writing* for Foundation stage: Reception and KS1 teachers (DfEE, 2001a). The National Curriculum supported by the NLS Framework emphasises the importance of the writing process: plan, draft, revise (Graves, 1983) and for the need for the writer to have a clear audience and purpose (DES, 1975). In addition, *Grammar for Writing* and *Developing Early Writing* outline a shared writing teaching sequence in which the teacher plays an important role in articulating his or her thinking while demonstrating the various processes in writing (Bereiter and Scardamalia, 1987). Teachers were encouraged to spend longer in shared writing experiences before launching the children into independent writing.

Further writing initiatives included a professional development day for trainee teachers and their class teachers on the effective use of shared writing, Web-based materials for teaching fiction and non-fiction genres and the compilation of a set of targets for writing to be used for monitoring the writing progress within a school.

Teaching phonics, spelling and grammar

School inspection reports consistently criticised schools for lack of effective phonics teaching (e.g. HMI, 1991, 1992; OFSTED, 1996). In England, as in most other countries, debate around the teaching of phonics formed a backcloth to the teaching of reading. The position taken in the National Curriculum and the NLS Framework for Teaching, as outlined in the 'searchlight model' for reading, was that phonics was an important element in the suite of strategies used in learning to read new words. The importance of phonics in early spelling, which was highlighted in the national writing project in England in the 1980s was also emphasised in the Framework. The 'word-level' module in the distance learning pack (DfEE, 1998b) for teachers included material to show the place of phonics in reading and writing and a progression in the teaching and learning of spelling. *Progression in Phonics* (DfEE, 1999a) and the *Spelling Bank* (DfEE, 1999b) provide teachers with materials for the teaching of phonics and spelling. LEA training and a training CD-ROM in phonics supported teachers in using these materials. *Progression in Phonics* is an interactive play-based approach to learning phonics which accelerates the pace of learning so that it is expected that most children with a full year in Reception would achieve the Y1 objectives.

The National Curriculum includes grammar within its programmes of study and, like phonics, the teaching of grammar was a subject of debate. The sentence level module in the distance learning materials (DfEE, 1998b) concentrated heavily on the reasons for teaching grammar and the subsequent book *Grammar for Writing* (DfEE, 2000a) provides teachers with materials for teaching. In addition, the glossary from the NLS Framework was strengthened and put onto the Web (DfEE, 2000b) and professional development was offered to teachers to support their grammatical knowledge.

Inclusion

The National Literacy Strategy was part of the government's 'inclusion' agenda. The *Framework* contains guidance to teachers on planning and teaching literacy and additional guidance for adapting their teaching for children learning English as an additional language and children with special educational needs. Government provision for children learning English as an additional language and traveller children was supported by NLS training materials. Training materials were also published to enable co-ordinators for children with special educational needs (SENCos) and teachers to accommodate children with special educational needs within the literacy hour and to support children working significantly below age-related expectations.

Professional development and initial teacher training

The teaching approaches suggested in the *Framework* and the training pack (DfEE, 1998b) were drawn from research and good practice in England and other countries, particularly Australia, New Zealand and the USA (Beard, 1999). However, for most schools some teaching approaches were new. At the outset of the National Literacy Strategy, schools were given the pack of distance learning materials and three designated days in which to use the materials. The NLS was launched with a two-day conference for every head teacher, literacy governor and literacy co-ordinator in which the principles underpinning the NLS approach to the teaching of literacy were explained with the help of video material.

The distance learning pack contained six modules, each of which was designed as a day's professional development for the whole staff. They fell neatly into three sections so could be undertaken alternatively as twilight sessions. The first module explained how the literacy hour worked and illustrated possible methods of planning. The other five modules covered word level, sentence level, shared reading and writing and non-fiction. The modules were based in research and 'good practice' giving teachers subject knowledge; research-based rationales for the inclusion of certain elements within the curriculum; approaches to pedagogy such as shared text work (Holdaway, 1979), investigations in spelling (Peters, 1985, Ramsden, 1993) and a constructivist approach to learning (Wray and Lewis, 1997).

In the following two years, further training was cascaded to schools through the LEA consultants' network. This training included modules on the management of literacy, teaching and learning, writing, phonics, spelling and grammar. These modules were accompanied by teaching materials: *Progression in phonics, the Spelling bank, Grammar for writing,* and *Developing early writing* in the form of books, videos and CD. *Progression in phonics* was also accompanied by an interacting training CD-ROM and *Grammar for Writing* by interactive Web-based instruction (DfEE 2000b).

The National Curriculum for Initial Teacher Training (TTA, 1998) outlined what new teachers needed to know and be able to do in order to teach children the National Curriculum and hence, the NLS. During the implementation of the Strategy, initial teacher training courses were adapted to incorporate all the pedagogic elements (shared and guided reading and writing; interactive whole-class word and sentence level work; plenary) and trainees were all given copies of the teaching materials.

Reception year

The *Framework* includes objectives for the Reception year but these are not divided into terms as the pattern for receiving children into Reception classes varies from one LEA to another. The guidance for Reception classes expects children to be taught the various pedagogic elements of the literacy hour (shared and guided reading and writing and phonics) although not necessarily in a single unit of time until the end of the year. It expects that children should be made aware of what they are learning and why, and that they should have the opportunity to demonstrate and articulate this learning.

Intervention programmes

The Additional Literacy Support (ALS) programme (DfEE, 1999c) was introduced near the outset of the NLS to cater for the needs of children in Y3 and Y4 who had low scores on the end of KS1 tests. The ALS programme consists of three components: phonics, reading and writing and is taught by a teaching assistant to children in small groups. There was funding for an increase in teaching assistants to be trained and use the ALS programme. The Early Literacy Support (ELS), which was piloted for a year in a number of LEAs before being launched nationally, is intended for small groups of children in Y1 who, despite the same amount of teaching as their peers, are not 'off the ground' in reading and writing (DfEE 2001b). These programmes were informed by research and successful practice in small-group teaching of literacy (Clay, 1985, 2001; Hatcher, 1994) and analysis of children's responses in the national tests.

Teaching assistants

During the implementation of the NLS, the number of teaching assistants rose through a government-funded initiative, which also provided training for them. Their role was also enhanced by the introduction of the NLS. They are integral to the intervention programmes (ALS and ELS) which were devised specifically for them. The programmes, however, were designed so that the class teacher has a cross-over role with the assistant underlying the need for communication and co-operation between teachers and their assistants. During the literacy hour, teaching assistants are expected to fulfil an active teaching role, working in tandem with the teacher.

Evaluation

The NLS is subject to external evaluation by a team from the Ontario Institute for Studies in Education (OISE) at the University of Toronto, Canada and internal evaluation by the Ofsted primary and nursery division. The object of the evaluations, which is reported annually, is to be formative as well as summative. Information on the level and nature of implementation of the strategy in schools is gleaned from LEA reporting, telephone surveys and professional organisations.

The impact of the National Literacy Strategy

Embarking on a strategy of this scale (20,000 schools, 190,000 teachers and 3 million pupils) was considered ambitious by both those involved and by observers. However, KS2 test results after two years showed a 10 percentage point increase in the number of children attaining level 4 and above (see Table 13.1).

In their first annual report, the OISE team suggested 'The NLNS[2] are among the most ambitious large-scale educational reform strategies in the world and, without question, are among the most explicit and comprehensive in their attention to what is required for successful implementation' (OISE 2000: 1). The report lists the strengths of the policies to be 'leadership, policy alignment/coherence, support and pressure, communication, resources, and responsiveness and adaptability' (*ibid.*: 38). The team point out that in order to sustain the early gains, teachers' hard work will need to continue to be rewarded, professional development will continue to be central, particularly in the area of 'assessment literacy', and schools should be seen as 'professional learning communities'. They warn against ossification and urge the Strategies to continue their 'evolving' approach through which they are open to influence from varied agencies, organisations and individuals. They link the international trend towards an increase in newly qualified teachers and stress the need to invest in initial teacher training.

Ofsted's two annual reports (Ofsted, 1999, 2000) trace the progress of the initiative in classrooms. They report 'enthusiastic' adoption by the vast majority of schools in the first year and in the second-year state 'The NLS continues to have a major impact on the teaching of English in primary schools and on the content of initial teacher training courses' (Ofsted 2000:1). In the first year they report that teachers are more confident in the teaching of reading and that insufficient attention is paid to writing. By the end of the second year they report a 'transformation' in the teaching of

Table 13.1   Percentage of children attaining level 4 and above in KS2 test

1997	1998	1999	2000
63	65	70	75

reading but serious concerns about the teaching of writing. They acknowledge the steps that were taken to give teachers more support in teaching writing, but point out that these measures had not taken effect when evidence for the report was submitted.

The two independent telephone surveys of headteachers of over 500 schools in 1999 and 2000 showed a positive take up of the NLS (BMRB, 1999, 2000, commissioned by the Centre for British Teachers (CFBT)). In both years over 95 per cent of the schools claimed to support the NLS, and by the second survey the vast majority were using the teaching materials (*Progression in Phonics* 95 per cent, *Additional Literacy Support* 94 per cent and *Grammar for Writing* 97 per cent). In the first survey 60 per cent of schools thought that the NLS would improve standards; by the second year this figure had increased to 78 per cent. In the first year 67 per cent of schools were seeing a positive effect of the NLS on the teaching of writing and that figure increased in the second year to 77 per cent.

Formal and informal evidence on the effects of the NLS is extensive. The network of regional directors, strategy managers, consultants and ITT tutors is a rich source, as are the press and surveys from professional organisations. There is a general consensus that children are reading more than before the Strategy and meet a wider range of books. On the other hand, there is some disquiet over the proliferation of published programmes which use only extracts from books and concern that children never get to read or have read to them entire novels. One of the myths related to the implementation of the NLS is that reading a class novel is no longer appropriate in teaching. However, it was stated quite clearly in the distance learning pack (DfEE, 1998b: module 5) that any good novel could be the vehicle for most text and sentence level objectives.

Over the period of the strategy many teachers admit to having raised their own level of subject knowledge. Even for those KS1 teachers who had always taught phonics, the Strategy presented a new approach based on the last decade of research. Knowledge of text types and the language forms and effects associated with each type were new to many. Those teachers who now have the content secure are able to plan lessons in which there is an integration of text and sentence level objectives, a continuity within and between literacy/language lessons and cross-fertilisation between these and lessons in other curriculum areas where appropriate. These teachers do not overlook the need for short bursts of pacy word-level skills work which they often use to get the lesson off to a dynamic start. Likewise their lessons are noteworthy for the manner in which they encourage children to apply their word-level knowledge and skill in their reading and writing.

Notes

1   Level 4 is the level that all 11 year-olds are expected to achieve in the national tests. Level 2 is the level that 7 year-olds are expected to achieve.
2   National Literacy and Numeracy Strategies.

References

Adams, M.J. (1990) *Beginning to Read: Thinking and Learning About Print.* Cambridge, Mass: MIT Press

Beard, R. (1999) *Review of Research and Other Related Evidence*, London: DfEE.

Bereiter, C. and Scardamalia, M. (1987) *The Psychology of Written Composition*, Hillsdale, NJ: Lawrence Erlbaum.

British Market Research Bureau (BMRB) Social Research International (1999, 2000) *The National Literacy Strategy: Survey of Headteachers*, London: BMRB.

Clay, M.M. (1985) *The Early Detection of Reading Difficulties*, 3rd edn, Auckland: Heinemann.

—— (2001) *Change over Time in Children's Literacy Development*, Auckland: Heinemann.

Department for Education and Employment (DfEE) (1998a) *National Literacy Strategy Framework for Teaching*, London: DfEE.

—— (1998b) *National Literacy Strategy Training Pack*, London: DfEE.

—— (1999a) *National Literacy Strategy Progression in Phonics*, London: DfEE.

—— (1999b) *National Literacy Strategy Spelling Bank*, London: DfEE.

—— (1999c) *National Literacy Strategy Additional Literacy Support modules 1–4 and Getting Started Training Booklet*, London: DfEE.

—— (2000a) *National Literacy Strategy Grammar for Writing*, London: DfEE.

—— (2000b) *The Standard's Site* (http://www.standards.dfee.gov.uk/literacy).

—— (2001a) *National Literacy Strategy Developing Early Writing*, London: DfEE.

—— (2001b) *National Literacy Strategy Early Literacy Support*, London: DfEE.

Department of Education and Science (DES) (1975) *A Language for Life* (The Bullock Report), London: HMSO.

—— (1988) *Report of the Committee of Enquiry into the Teaching of the English Language* (The Kingman Report), London: HMSO.

Graves, D.H. (1983) *Writing: Teachers and children at work*, Portsmouth, NH: Heinemann.

Hatcher, P.J. (1994) *Soundlinkage: An Integrated Programme for Overcoming Reading Difficulties*, London: Whurr Publishing.

Literacy Task Force (1997) *The Implementation of the National Literacy Strategy*, London: DfEE.

Her Majesty's Inspectorate (HMI) (1991) *The Teaching and Learning of Reading in Primary Schools, 1990: A Report by HMI*, London: DES.

—— (1992) *The Teaching and Learning of Reading in Primary Schools, 1991: A Report by HMI*, London: DES.

Holdaway, D. (1979) *The Foundations of Literacy*, Sydney: Ashton Scholastic.

Office for Standards in Education (Ofsted) (1996) *The Teaching of Reading in 45 Inner London Primary Schools: A Report by Her Majesty's Inspectors in Collaboration with the LEAs of Islington, Southwark and Tower Hamlets*, London: Ofsted.

—— (1999) *An Evaluation of the First Year of the National Literacy Strategy*, London: Ofsted.

—— (2000) *The National Literacy Strategy: The Second Year*, London: Ofsted.

Ontario Institute for Studies in Education/University of Toronto (OISE/UT) (2000) *Watching and Learning: Evaluation of the Implementation of the National Literacy and Numeracy Strategies*, London: DfEE.

Peters, M.L. (1985) *Spelling: Caught or Taught (A New Look)*, London: Routledge & Kegan Paul.

Ramsden, M. (1993) *Rescuing Spelling*, Crediton, Devon: Southgate Publishers.

Rumelhart, D.E. (1977) 'Towards an interactive model of reading', in S. Dornic (ed.) *Attention and Performance VI* (pp. 573–603), Hillsdale, NJ: Lawrence Erlbaum.

Share, D (1995) 'Phonological recoding and self-teaching: sina qua non of reading acquisition', *Cognition* 55: 151–218.

Teacher Training Agency (TTA) (1998) *Teaching: High status, High Standards: Requirements for the Courses of Initial Teacher Training*, London: DfEE.

Wray, D and Lewis, M. (1997) *Extending Literacy: Children Reading and Writing Non-Fiction*, London: Routledge.

14 Examining teaching in the literacy hour

Case studies from English classrooms

Ros Fisher and Maureen Lewis

Introduction

In September 1998, as part of the UK government's National Literacy Strategy (NLS) for England, a literacy hour was introduced into classrooms for children aged five to eleven. The place of this dedicated hour of literacy in the primary timetable is now established in the vast majority of schools, along with the use of the *'Framework for Teaching'* (DfEE, 1998) which sets out, term by term, what is to be taught at word, sentence and text level. The hour is structured around approximately fifteen minutes of whole class, shared text work; fifteen minutes of whole class, word and sentence level work; twenty minutes of independent or guided work; and ten minute plenary (see Huxford, 2002 this volume).

The introduction of the NLS into primary schools was a radical move, for it aimed to influence not only the *content* of the English curriculum but also *the way English is taught*. As well as outlining the suggested timings and groupings teachers should use, the NLS framework also suggests a range of teaching methods (including shared and guided reading and writing) and a range of teaching strategies (including, for example, direction, demonstration, modelling, scaffolding and questioning). In order to plan for and effectively teach the varied objectives within the framework, a high degree of English subject knowledge is needed by teachers. In both content and teaching, the NLS contained much that was already familiar to teachers but it also contained controversial (for some) and challenging ideas such as teaching reading through shared class and group guided reading rather than through individualised reading; a greater emphasis on the systematic teaching and use of phonics; the increased use of whole class teaching; the increased use of direct teaching and the need to plan to explicit objectives. In this chapter we will briefly examine why it was deemed necessary to change the way literacy was taught and how teachers were (and are) being encouraged to change their practices. We will then go on to examine the evidence we have of whether teachers' practices and beliefs have indeed changed, both at a surface and at a deeper level.

The background to perceived need for change

Arguments about standards of attainment have been the focus of attention for the past decade. Central to this debate is discussion about which teaching approaches are most effective in raising standards, whilst in literacy there have been heated arguments about the most effective ways to teach reading and writing. DfEE (1999) describes the research into effective teaching and the classroom practice on which the NLS is based. In its promotion of certain organisational groupings and teaching strategies, the NLS also draws on other research and on inspection evidence (see also Beard, 2002, this volume).

The NLS gives the majority of time within the hour to interactive whole class work (approximately 40 out of 60 minutes). The move to informal, individualised and group teaching that was described in the 1960s by an influential government report (Plowden Report, DES, 1967) was always challenged by some for ignoring the positive role of the teacher for fear of authoritarianism (Peters, 1969). Indeed, the picture of good practice presented by Plowden was idealised; although much was written about learning, there was little about teaching, with the teacher being seen more as a facilitator. Research studies that looked closely at pupil progress and teaching styles suggested that an individualised or group work approach could be less effective in raising academic standards than whole class teaching approaches. As early as 1976 Bennett was claiming that whole class, direct teaching achieved better results than 'informal' teaching (although he was later to rescind some of these claims in response to criticism of his methods). Similar findings came from a longitudinal study of pupils from 50 London junior schools. Mortimore *et al.* (1988: 228) claimed that, 'the amount of time the teacher spent interacting with the class (rather than individuals or groups) had a significant positive relationship with progress'. They also concluded that a larger proportion of sessions spent on a single activity (for example, everybody working on language) was related positively to pupils' progress (*ibid.*). Both of these studies highlighted the importance of effective teacher interaction which used the kind of teaching strategies now promoted by the NLS framework and training materials such as questioning, explaining, demonstrating, and so on.

In response to the growing debate about the effectiveness of different teaching approaches generated by such research and by the introduction of a National Curriculum in 1988, the government commissioned a discussion paper, *Curriculum Organisation and Classroom Practice in Primary Schools* (Alexander *et al.*, 1992), to 'Review evidence ... and make recommendations about curriculum organisation teaching methods and classroom practice' (*ibid.*: para. 1). This paper concluded that a mix of whole class, group and individual work was appropriate (*ibid.*: para. 101) and that in many schools the benefits of whole class teaching had been insufficiently exploited (*ibid.*: para. 124). It recommended that the balance of direct and indirect teaching needed to be reviewed (*ibid.*: para. 104) with more attention given to direct teaching. Opportunities for teachers to interact with pupils and use strategies such as questioning, explaining, and so on (*ibid.*: para. 105) were also re-emphasised. In a follow-up report the following year (Ofsted, 1993a) the same messages were again stressed.

With regard to the specific teaching of literacy, as early as 1981, Southgate *et al.* reported that teachers of 8- and 9-year-old children spent more time dealing with procedural matters than interacting with children about their reading or writing. Bennett *et al.* (1984) also found teachers to be spending time hearing individuals read while attending to other matters. Tizard *et al.* (1988) found that, in the classes of teachers who spent most time listening to individual children read, pupils themselves spent least time engaged in reading.

In the 1990s, there were several inspection reports (Ofsted, 1993b, 1995, 1996) which drew attention to the individualised nature of the teaching of reading. Ofsted (1995) criticised the management of the teaching of reading and argued that teachers could manage time more effectively. Whilst appropriate response and interaction with individuals is important, there clearly were difficulties for primary teachers who were trying to teach a full curriculum at the same time as working with each child individually. One report (Ofsted, 1996) that had a particular impact contrasted the characteristics of effective and ineffective practices in the teaching of reading in forty-five schools. This report concluded that 'effective direct teaching' of reading was an important feature of those schools where good practice had been observed.

Other reports commented on the difficulties some teachers had in finding a balance in the teaching of writing between 'total freedom (unsupported "emergent" writing) and total direction (remorseless copy writing)' (e.g. Ofsted, 1993b: ch. 5 para. 41). In contrast, views of teachers differed. Ofsted reported that

> 'learning by doing' was preferred to 'teaching by telling' ... Sitting pupils down and telling them things was sometimes seen as a marginal, though necessary, strategy. Consequently, the amount and quality of expository teaching received by the pupils, including giving clear explanations, asking relevant questions and responding effectively to their questions and answers was often too slight.
>
> (Ofsted, 1993a: para. 8)

Thus, while the evidence base and conclusions of these reports were often disputed, by the mid-1990s Ofsted had created a clear picture of what it regarded as good practice in the teaching of literacy. We can see that in the stress it places on the a balance between whole class and group work, on the use of interactive direct teaching and on sharply focused explicit teaching of literacy, the Strategy can be seen to be, in part, the practical outcome of the research and recommendations outlined above. Perhaps the key change in teaching required by the NLS is the importance afforded to direct instruction. The Framework for Teaching asserts,

> The literacy hour offers a structure of classroom management, designed to maximise the time teachers spend directly teaching their class. It is intended to shift the balance of teaching from individualised work, especially in the teaching of reading, towards more whole class and group teaching.
>
> (DfEE, 1998: 10)

We will now consider how a small group of teachers felt about the proposed changes and the evidence showing the extent to which the way they taught changed during the first two years of the NLS.

The research

The evidence is drawn from research that is following a small number of teachers since the introduction of the NLS. In the first year this was part of an externally funded project into the implementation of the literacy hour in small rural schools (ESRC Grant R000 22 2608). This followed twenty teachers over a year through monthly classroom observations, interviews at the beginning and end of the year and collection of children's work samples (for further details, see Fisher, Lewis and Davis, 2000 and Fisher, 2002). This continued into a second and third year with a follow-up questionnaire, interview and further observation of the classroom literacy teaching of twelve of the teachers. Although the teachers in the study taught mixed-age classes, many of the findings are of direct relevance to all teachers and reflect other studies in single age classes.

Increased focus on teaching

Before the NLS

As described above, there was some movement to more explicit and direct teaching of literacy in England in the 1980s and 1990s. However, this was set against a climate in which the whole language movement had had, at least, a partial effect. The literacy teaching practices of the teachers in our study ranged from what Donaldson (1989) describes as 'the minimal teaching movement' to others who were already some way towards including focused and direct teaching of literacy based objectives. The two teachers described below represent two ends of a continuum on which the practice of the teachers in our study lay. Before the start of the NLS in writing, teachers were likely to give some sort of introduction about the content of the writing and then move around working with groups and individuals while they wrote. Most reading was taught on an individual basis with a child reading aloud to the teacher or another adult while other children worked independently.

In July 1998 Mrs Freeman, with a class of 5–7-year-olds, would hear children read individually two or three times a week and other adults would also listen to individual children reading aloud regularly. She also described working with groups of the youngest children to introduce words and book characters and group reading with older children. She taught phonics to the youngest children by means of a television programme once a week and 'loads of sheets and work books'. She described her teaching of writing thus

TEACHER: Basically, we have a chat first and they all come in and they settle down ... Then I'll do English or Maths in the morning and it doesn't matter which way around.

INTERVIEWER: Do you do very much whole class teaching?

TEACHER: I always introduce things. Topic-wise I always introduce and we all talk together and we always come together at the end and tell each other all the detail and that sort of thing. Not for too long as they get fed up. But I suppose I do small amounts and sometimes I'll stop all of them and say, 'Look come and look at the board and look what we found out'. ... So it tends to be in small amounts not a big long session.

INTERVIEWER: What do you currently do about your planning for English?

TEACHER: I find personally that because I have been teaching for so long it happens ... I think I'm probably more general in English and I tend to use a bit of all sorts and set them off. ... I want them to learn about whatever today, or this week and then I set them off on various things and go round, but I'm not so rigid that I'm going to work with them (i.e. one particular group) today and I do pick up on things that they're confused about.

(Interview, July 1998)

Clearly a programme of pre-specified objectives with a large amount of whole class, direct teaching was going to be very different for this teacher.

On the other hand, Mrs York, a teacher in a class of 9–11-year-olds, already had a varied and effective programme of literacy teaching in which she taught whole class, groups and individuals. In July 1998, she described her practice in teaching reading as,

We have some things that run throughout the school. For example, the children give a book presentation and talk about a book that they've read. We have reading partners whereby the oldest children have a reading partner who is younger than them and they work together, read books and share the books. But in terms of things we do in the class, the group reading is quite a strong part of it. We also do reading that is related to other work that we do and at the moment non-fiction skills are being developed through other on-going work.

In writing, her practice was already very similar to that proposed by the NLS – moving from reading into writing – but with less sharp focus than is suggested by the NLS guidance.

> We'd look at some piece of text first because it would have a focus; it might be, say, if we were writing a story, it might be something about a character and talk about them and I try to draw out from the children what were the features of that piece of writing that – maybe gave you a clear idea of what the character was like, what they looked like, how they spoke, what their personality was like. Then talk about how they were going to plan but other times devise their own plans or we devise them together, and they would tend to maybe write a bit of it on their own, and then we'd come back and look at it and say 'What do you like about this … ?' and I would be very involved in, I suppose, supporting those who would find it hard.

For this teacher, working with the whole class was unlikely to be anything new and she welcomed the initiative saying she liked new things and it largely reflected the way they worked already.

After a year of the NLS

In the interviews at the end of the first year of the NLS, nine of the twenty teachers mentioned an increased amount of whole class teaching as a feature of how their practice had changed. These interviews were semi-structured with open questions. For instance teachers were asked how they felt their teaching had changed rather than a specific question about the amount of whole class teaching. Therefore, the fact that eleven teachers did not mention whole class teaching does not mean that this had not increased, just that it was not the main feature that came to mind.

Mrs York commented,

> I think I'm doing certainly more class work than I would have done, whole class teaching, yes, than I would have done given that … each class has two year groups and we have a very wide ability range. I mean that's a really strong feature of the school. So there's more class teaching than there would have been.

Mrs Freeman really felt her teaching had changed from her practice a year earlier. In the interview at the end of the first year, in response to a question as to whether she thought her teaching had changed, she said,

> Yes. Yes I do. Just from the point of view of a whole class. It definitely makes you think more about specific things. Certain parts of the language, the grammar and the spelling. It really gets you down to the nitty gritty. Whereas perhaps you might have only – if you're around the classroom – might have imparted that bit of information as necessary, when perhaps they were reading to you, or when you were with a group writing, or something like that. Whereas now you are doing it all together.

After the first year of the NLS, thirteen teachers made some reference to the way their teaching had become more focused and explicit and that there was more direct teaching than before. Five of these teachers felt this was a positive feature of the NLS. Mrs Harman explained how she used to be 'sort of knowing intuitively what I was going to do rather than thinking about it in more detail'. Mr Leonard felt that during the year he had learned 'to simplify things by having less objectives each week so you can really work at something'. However, seven teachers (including three who had referred to the positive features of more direct teaching) expressed some concern about how much was being taught without children having the chance to really learn. The sort of comments that were made include: 'too much to cover', 'trying to cram too much in', and 'a whistle-stop tour, they've needed more input and support'.

After two years

Two years on, interviews with those teachers who were still in the same post as the previous year showed that the problem of catering for individual difference was perceived as less acute. Most of the twelve talked about the way in which familiarity with the framework made them better able to plan to meet the needs of their own particular group of children. For some teachers, this gave less of a sense of cramming or 'drilling the phonics into them'. Most teachers seemed satisfied with the way their teaching had developed and pleased with the results.

Mrs Harman, an experienced teacher of the youngest children, had been very concerned before the start of the NLS by how she would be able to plan from objectives rather than taking a book and following the way the children's interest took her. After two years she said she felt her teaching was now more varied and focused. She described the way she felt she had learned to 'teach skills as opposed to knowledge'. By this she meant she now felt she was teaching children *how to use* the skills she taught them. These views are echoed by other teachers who also expressed the belief that their teaching was more focused and explicit than before the NLS. However, one or two still were concerned about it being boring or mechanistic. 'I feel I am reading a script rather than getting involved with language and the use of language' (Ellis interview, July 2000). It is interesting to reflect that Mr Ellis was a teacher who was very enthusiastic about the NLS in the beginning saying, 'What I like about it is that I feel I am teaching children something all the time, all the time ... I think it has legitimised large group teaching' (Ellis interview, September 1998).

Teaching two years on

Thus the teachers we followed reported that they had made key changes to their teaching since the introduction of the NLS, in particular:

- an increase in explicit, direct teaching of reading and writing, much of which was to the whole class
- a literacy curriculum with clearly focused literacy objectives.

Although the sample here is too small to draw conclusions there is some evidence that changes in teachers' teaching style may be more in their own mind than in actual fact.

Mrs Quick is a teacher who initially had mixed feelings about the NLS. Although, after one year in which life in her school was particularly pressurised she was very unhappy with the work children were doing, at the end of the second year she was clearly much happier. She had said at the end of the first year that she was very dissatisfied with the scrappy bits of work children produced in the literacy hour. When asked to reflect on this twelve months on, she explained that she had learned to be 'far more conscious of building a piece of work over a number of days'. Now she felt that she was able to ensure children had both the skills and the time to write a longer and more meaningful piece of written work than those they were producing in the first year. She also felt she had changed her teaching in some way by the much clearer expectations she set for writing and in her use of focused objectives. She seemed pleased that the result was improved standards in the national assessments. However, although she emphasised how much more structured and focused her teaching had become with her use of the framework of objectives, the observer notes

> The lesson today reflected ... teacher composed objectives. However, it wasn't clear in the lesson what she was getting at. She used closed questions a lot to get children to come up with bits of information and they did compare poems but teacher didn't really explain why they were doing that.
>
> (Field notes, July 2000)

Although there is insufficient evidence to draw any conclusions here, there is a sense in which this teacher's improvement in her teaching, as she sees it, may be more in her own mind than in reality. Perhaps this gives some insight into the way that although teachers may be given a framework to work from, if they do not either understand or subscribe to that model of teaching, the practice is unlikely to be effective.

Another example from a literacy hour with a class of children aged 5 to 7 years, observed after two years of implementation, shows how teachers, although teaching a literacy hour in terms of the time division of the lesson, may still not have changed their practice in any fundamental way. Mrs Freeman, a description of whose practice is cited earlier, felt after two years that her teaching was much more focused, but the example below belies this impression. In the lesson observed here, Mrs Freeman was addressing a text level objective 'to discuss meanings of words and phrases that create humour, and sound effects in poetry, e.g. nonsense poems, tongue twisters' (DfEE, 1998: Year 2 Term 3 Text 8).

The lesson started with the teacher showing a large picture of a sandwich; she discussed with children what was in the sandwich in the picture and what sort of sandwiches they enjoyed. In this she was perfectly justifiably linking the 'text' with children's own experiences. Children joined in enthusiastically sharing their likes and dislikes of sandwiches. However, when the teacher then introduced a tongue twister about a sandwich, they were engaged and interested in the contents of the sandwich rather than the words the poet used to gain effect. The observer wrote

> what actually happened was they heard several tongue twisters, joined in a bit and talked about the definition of a tongue twister. The teacher announced they were doing tongue twisters today but she didn't say what they were doing with them or why they were doing them or what they were meant to be learning from the lesson.
>
> (Mrs Freeman, follow-up visit June 2000, field notes)

Had this teacher linked more successfully her knowledge of gaining children's interest with an understanding of the language objective of the lesson, more children may have gained an understanding of language than was evident in the observed lesson.

Discussion

The NLS set out to increase the amount of direct teaching that teachers use in their literacy teaching and to maximise the impact of this. This has involved increasing considerably the amount of whole class and group teaching and reducing the time teachers spend with individuals. From the evidence of the schools in our project, this has certainly happened. Teachers readily took on shared reading and increasingly used shared writing. The range of aspects of literacy that is taught seems to have increased, as has the amount of subject specific vocabulary used. Contrary to the expectations of some teachers, the children in this study enjoy the literacy hour. They have found the increased range of texts interesting and enjoyed the big books. The game-like approach to phonics proposed by *Progression in Phonics* has been well received, as have some of the investigative techniques used in grammar and vocabulary work. Also contrary to expectations, less able children seem to have benefited from the experience of 'reading' and 'writing' more challenging texts and being included in whole class parts of the literacy hour.

Nearly all the teachers after one and two years of the NLS said they felt their teaching had become more structured and focused. Certainly their planning contained more specific objectives and covered a wider range of aspects of literacy. However, we have tried to show that the way these teachers went about teaching in the literacy hour varied. Either some teachers' enthusiasm for the text or their concern to involve all children made them cover a whole range of ideas and thoughts. Although they felt their teaching was focused, this focus was not always clear to the observer or, maybe, the children. Other teachers tended to take the product as the focus of the lesson as opposed to the learning. For example, the *production* of a particular type of text rather than examining how different forms of language affect the meaning or the impact of a text.

There are questions about the extent to which all teachers were able to implement the recommended style of teaching, and, when they did, whether there were still important elements of successful teaching that were missing. The NLS describes a model of good teaching as 'discursive – characterised by high quality oral work' and 'interactive – pupils' contributions are encouraged, expected and extended' (DfEE, 1998: 8). Such teaching is difficult to achieve and there is evidence that some teachers have not yet changed their practice to fit the NLS ideal. Mroz *et al.* (2000), in an analysis of the classroom discourse of ten literacy hours, found that both whole class and guided work sessions were essentially teacher-dominated.

> Because of the teachers' claim to prior knowledge of the subject content and right to control the pacing and sequencing of its transmission, pupils rarely managed to impose their own relevance outside the teachers' frame of reference. ... In all 10 lessons the teacher was predominantly seen to be retaining control over the direction and pace of the lesson and the lines of knowledge which were to be pursued.
>
> (Mroz *et al.*, 2001: 82)

Similar concerns were raised by Moyles *et al.* (2000) in an early report of the SPRINT project examining how primary teachers conceptualise and utilise interactive teaching. Interviews with teachers showed that they were

15 The literacy block in primary school classrooms, Victoria, Australia

Bridie Raban and Gillian Essex

Australian context

In Australia, the debate surrounding literacy has been similar to that around the world. In 1991 the Australian government called for greater proficiency in English literacy for all Australians (DEET, 1991). However, the amount of funding allocated to early literacy was relatively small (de Lemos and Harvey-Beavis, 1995). In 1993, The Literacy Challenge, a report from the House of Representatives Standing Committee on Employment (1993), recognised and emphasised again the importance of early literacy intervention.

More recently, the National Schools English Literacy Survey of Australian school students (Masters and Forster, 1997) was conducted during 1996 and a subsequent report (Masters, 1997) identified the increasing gap between Year 3 and Year 5 students, as well as pointing to particular groups of students who had not achieved a satisfactory standard in reading and writing. These groups included:

- students from language backgrounds other than English
- boys
- students from families categorised as low socio-economic
- indigenous students.

In response to these findings, the Australian government outlined the National Literacy Plan (DEETYA, 1998), agreed to by all jurisdictions in every state and territory. This document also emphasised the importance of the early years of schooling, 'It is in the first years of school that all children can be helped to acquire the foundation skills that will set them on the path to success in reading and writing' (*ibid.*: 8).

The National Literacy Plan included a requirement that education authorities throughout the country specify a plan for ensuring students reach minimum acceptable literacy standards (*ibid.*: 9) and use assessment data to monitor outcomes for the most disadvantaged students. Individual states and territories and the different systems of schooling within these jurisdictions (Catholic, independent and government schools) responded to this imperative in a variety of ways. This chapter describes the responses made by the government school system in the State of Victoria.

The Victorian context

The State of Victoria is one of the smaller states in Australia geographically; however, it is approximately similar in size to England, Scotland and Wales together, and has a population of some 4.8 million people. With respect to education policy, the 1990s in Victoria was a period of increasing flexibility for government schools in regard to their own budgets. With devolution of decision-making, came the need for advice rather than control from the centre. In particular, the need for expert advice on the cost effectiveness of budgetary decisions in relation to improved student outcomes was recognised.

In 1996, the Early Years Literacy Research Project (ELRP) was established within this local context and the more global context of increasing international recognition of the importance of the first three years of schooling, especially in regard to the development of literacy skills. The purpose of this three-year project, a joint venture of the Victorian Department of Education, Employment and Training and the University of Melbourne, was to identify, at a whole school level, the design elements that would be critical for achieving improvement in student literacy standards.

Over 300 schools applied to be in the initial group of 25 trial schools, selected from amongst the most disadvantaged in the state, and as the project became established it generated increasing interest from other schools. The Early Years Literacy Program (DEET:Vic, 1997, 1998, 1999) was developed alongside the ELRP. The materials were designed to assist all schools in making the type of whole school improvement required to achieve the increase in student literacy levels demonstrated by the trial schools. They drew heavily on the work of Crévola and Hill (1998) and the experiences of the trial schools in the project. However, the programme also drew on other research (Slavin *et al.*, 1996), the experiences of other systems (e.g. New Zealand), and those of the 100 schools that were asked to trial the programme during its development stage. Broad consultation took place for each component of the programme.

The interest generated by the ELRP meant that schools saw a real need for training and materials that would assist them in participating in a similar process to the trial schools, and the majority chose to access the training and implement the programme as soon as they could. The trial schools also benefited from the formalisation of the process as a written programme and the fact that the materials evolved beyond what was originally presented to them.

Whole school approach

The Early Years Literacy Program rests on the premise that effective teaching and learning are strategies and processes that are clearly located in classrooms where teachers and students transact the business of education. However, these strategies and teaching approaches themselves are outcomes of a hierarchy of beliefs and understandings embedded in schooling and the systems within which classrooms are located. Classrooms are not isolated sets of social and educational circumstances. They are embedded in a network of policy and practice imperatives that more or less overtly influence the quality of education experienced by individual students. This network has been more sharply defined through the work of school effectiveness theorists and researchers, including Slavin and colleagues in the USA (1996), Hill in Australia (1995), Barber and Sebba (1999) and Reynolds and colleagues (1994) in England, and Fullan (2000) in Canada. These studies together identify nine general design features for a whole school approach to student improvement and are summarised by Hill and Crévola (1998). These are outlined below:

- **Beliefs and understandings.** There is a belief that all students can succeed given sufficient time and support, and that teachers are a key element in making a difference to student learning outcomes.
- **Standards and targets.** Realistic challenges are in place for all students and there is a commitment at all stages to supporting those students who are underachieving.
- **Monitoring and assessment.** Regular monitoring of student achievement and progress informs further teaching and creates records of performance that are maintained for each student.
- **Classroom teaching strategies.** Teachers use a range of teaching approaches adapted to meet the individual needs of students.
- **Professional learning teams.** Groups of teachers engage in learning experiences designed to have a high impact on their classroom practices.
- **School and class organisation.** Effective teaching and learning is best achieved through flexible use of time, resources, staff and additional assistance.
- **Intervention and special assistance.** Early support for underachieving students is an integral part of school provision.
- **Home, school and community partnerships.** Effective relationships are built and maintained with parents, communities and pre-school settings to support students' learning.
- **Leadership and co-ordination.** Strong and committed leadership supports the professional learning teams of teachers, working together to achieve enhanced student outcomes.

These design elements strongly accord with those recommended by the Snow Report (Snow *et al.*, 1998).

Early Years Literacy Program

The first stage of the Early Years Literacy Program (reading) was released in mid-1997 and by 1998 over 1,000 of Victoria's government schools (approximately 1,300) had begun to implement the programme, including some special schools. The developers of the programme had been practising teachers prior to engagement in writing the programme. The development of subsequent parts of the programme has drawn directly on the particular expertise of academics in collaboration with the programme developers.

The programme formed part of a comprehensive strategy designed to support schools through an effective change process. Schools were assisted by the provision of training for school-based co-ordinators provided by approximately 40 state-wide trainers trained centrally by the programme developers, and on-going support from 9 region-based project officers, appointed for this purpose. Initially, trainers were drawn from the ranks of Reading Recovery tutors or curriculum consultants, but many school-based trainers have now been recruited, and by early 2001 the state-wide team of trainers had expanded to 186.

School-based co-ordinators were given the responsibility of training and providing on-going support for their own teams of early years teachers. Support included modelling and mentoring, but also, most importantly, the development of a team approach within a climate of shared reflection on practice and commitment to continuous improvement – the school-based professional learning team.

One of the critical success factors of the Early Years Literacy Program was that it and other components of the Early Years strategy were provided on an 'opt in' basis . However, receipt of additional funding to support implementation of the Early Years Literacy Program was made dependent on the development of an individual School Early Literacy Plan that detailed all the elements contained within the Hill and Crévola model and committed to Statewide Minimum Standards developed from student data obtained as part of the Hill and Crévola research. The funding targeted specific elements, literacy co-ordination and one-to-one intervention at Year 1, that were difficult to fund from existing budgets. Schools could choose not to access this extra funding, but those that did – ultimately all mainstream schools and most special settings – were required to participate in a statewide data collection process designed to monitor the effectiveness of the funding strategy. In the year prior to the introduction of funding, schools were asked to volunteer to be involved in establishment of baseline data (and trial of the data collection process), and more than half did so.

Through the development of the Early Years Literacy Program, and the infrastructure that supported it, 'the system' has been seen by primary school personnel to be responsive to their needs, as indicated by surveys.

School personnel have, in turn, been responsive to system needs by being overwhelmingly willing to participate in trialling and development of new materials and supportive of statewide data collection. As well as the additional funding, schools were supported by increased teacher recognition, training and ongoing support, conferences, the development of supplementary materials and systemic support for emphasising literacy (and numeracy) within the curriculum.

Literacy teaching and learning

Approaches to the teaching of reading have been a focus for debate throughout the twentieth century and possibly before (Huey, 1908). Top-down approaches have been compared with bottom-up approaches and each has attracted advocates, theorists and researchers. In reviewing the literature, it is possible to detect a clear distinction between bottom-up, or phonics-based approaches (Adams, 1990), and top-down or whole language approaches (Weaver, 1990). However, observations of practice reveal a more 'balanced' approach to the teaching of reading (Cato *et al.*, 1992; Raban *et al.*, 1994). Crévola and Hill (1998) have indicated from their review of the literature that these teaching approaches include the following:

Oral language	Modelled writing
Reading to children	Shared writing
Language experience	Interactive writing
Shared book reading	Guided writing
Guided reading	Independent writing
Independent reading	Language experience (for writing)

Indeed, in the US report reviewing more recent studies, Snow, Burns and Griffin (1998) strongly recommend attention in every early years classroom to the full array of early reading strategies. This 'balanced' approach is also recommended by Beard (1993) in the UK and by Freebody and Luke (1990) in Australia, who argue that effective literacy teaching involves teaching students how to break the code, develop the capacity to understand meaning from text, use texts functionally and analyse texts critically.

The Snow Report stresses that children at risk of school failure require early intervention, and this also accords with Australian research (Ainley and Fleming 2000). This is because waiting for children to fail reduces self-esteem, rarely sees this group catching up to their age-related peers and creates a strain on finite resources. In addition, this report strongly suggests rich language and literacy environments in pre-school settings, and this recommendation is supported by the Australian work of Raban (2000a).

Recommendations in the Snow Report include the critical importance of teachers and their knowledge base, and that this is developed over time, not only during the pre-service years. Language minority students are seen as being particularly at risk. The report concludes that to be effective, schools will need manageable class sizes during the early years of schooling, generous student–teacher ratios, high quality instructional materials in sufficient quantity, good school libraries, pleasant physical surroundings and a well-designed classroom reading programme delivered by experienced and competent teachers. The report adds that 'achieving and sustaining radical gains is often difficult' (Snow *et al.*: 11) when changes are made on a classroom-by-classroom basis. Changes for improvement and effectiveness will need to be conducted on a whole school basis and include parents and other relevant parties as indicated by Cairney and colleagues (1995).

The two-hour literacy block

A key element of the Early Years Literacy Program is the implementation of a daily uninterrupted, highly focused and structured two-hour literacy block. The system support for this reversed the trend towards depleted time for focused literacy teaching under the pressure of an increasing variety of curricular demands on schools. Such had been this pressure that the notion of the two-hour literacy block was greeted with initial disbelief by the teachers involved in the research, but this gave way to relief as they realised that they were being given systemic support to focus on the core business of teaching literacy. The implementation of the two-hour block required whole school support in terms of timetabling, allocation of resources and smaller classes in the early years classrooms, but this was supported by the recognition of the value of receiving more literate students into middle years classes. Indeed the implementation of the early years programme has been a key driver for middle years reform.

The purpose of the literacy block is to enable teachers to meet the needs of their students, school and the local community. The classroom programme outline of the Early Years Literacy Program (displayed in Figures 15.1, 15.2 and 15.3) adds the overlay of speaking and listening on the approaches used for teaching reading and teaching writing. Within the two-hour literacy block, students spend most of the time working in small groups, either with their teacher or in learning centres.

1.   *Whole class focus on reading*
Reading with students: shared reading

2.   *Small group focus on reading*

Teaching groups   *Learning centres*
either   writing centre, listening post,
Beginning/emergent readers   computer centre, library corner,
                                            big book area, word games centre,
            Reading to students   alphabet centre, poem box
            Language experience
            Shared reading

or

Emergent/early/fluent readers
Guided reading   *Book box*
                                            Familiar texts
                                            Easy unfamiliar texts

3.   *Whole class reading share time*
Reflecting on and celebrating students' learning

Figure 15.1   Early Years Literacy Program Literacy Block: teaching readers
Source: (DEET:Vic, 1997)

Teaching approaches used in the two-hour block

Whole class focus

Reading to

This approach provides an opportunity for teachers to demonstrate their enjoyment in reading and allows students to see a purpose in learning to read.

Shared reading

Whole class shared reading provides opportunities for the teacher and students to work together using an enlarged text to gain meaning from text and examine the reading process. Initially, the teacher may do much of the reading. However, as students become more familiar with the text the teacher gradually allows the students to assume more control and contribute more to the reading process. The teacher's role at this stage is to provide support when necessary.

---

4. Whole class focus on writing
Modelled writing or shared writing

5. Small group focus on writing
Teaching group either   Students engaged in
                                                independent writing tasks

Beginning/emergent readers
        Shared writing
        Language experience   Teachers conducting
        Interactive writing   roving conferences
        Guided writing
or

Emergent/early/fluent readers   Students working on various
        Shared writing   aspects of writing process:
        Interactive writing   planning, composing,
        Language experience   recording, revising,
        Guided writing   publishing

6. Whole class writing share time
Reflecting on, sharing and celebrating students' writing.

Figure 15.2   Early Years Literacy Program Literacy Block: teaching writers
Source: (DEET:Vic, 1998)

Using the **SAID** framework:
                    Stimulate
                    Articulate
                    Integrate
                    Demonstrate
within all of the teaching approaches.

Figure 15.3   Early Years Literacy Program Literacy Block: teaching speakers and
        listeners
Source: (DEET:Vic, 1999)

Modelled writing

Modelled writing involves the teacher writing on a large piece of paper, whiteboard, overhead projector, or as displayed on a large computer monitor, making explicit the considerations and thinking behind the piece of text as well as articulating the process.

Shared writing

Shared writing involves the teacher (as scribe) and students collaboratively composing a piece of writing. Meaning, topics, ideas and choices of words are discussed, negotiated and decided by the teacher and students. This approach enables the students to participate in writing experiences that result in writing that is much richer than students would be able to write for themselves. Students can focus on composing and thinking without being encumbered by the complexities of the recording aspects of the writing process.

Whole class share time

This is an opportunity for the whole class to come together to reflect on, celebrate and share their learning. This process is facilitated by the teacher.

Small group focus

Language experience

The language experience approach helps students to develop and extend their oral language competencies through experiences that lead to reading and writing. The sequence is as follows: experience – spoken language – written language – reading – rereading. Experiences that can be used include common school experiences, classroom events, outings and visitors and students' personal experiences, or they may arise out of something the students have drawn, painted or made. The teacher's role is to model the language that can be used to describe the experience and to provide a stimulating and supportive environment in which the students are encouraged to explore their own ideas and express these ideas in their own way. The student talk elicited in this way is valued by accurate recording of what the students' actually say. Texts can also be used as the stimulus for language experience. Students can innovate on book language, retelling a story in a new form, or by keeping the original structures but inserting new vocabulary.

Shared reading

Through hearing and joining in with texts, students become familiar with the structure and form of written language, sometimes memorising repetitive parts of the text. Through shared reading students extend their understanding of how texts work and how print is used consistently to convey a message. It provides a positive interactive environment for students to read at their own level of expertise, joining in as the text becomes more familiar. Shared reading enables the teacher to model fluent, expressive reading and demonstrate the use and integration of all cue sources.

Guided reading

Guided reading helps students develop greater control over the reading process by providing opportunities for them to interact with the teacher and the text. Guided reading is an approach that assists students in developing appropriate strategies to construct meaning and allows them to further explore the structures and features of language. It encourages students to talk, read and think their way through a text while enabling the teacher to observe how each student in the group recreates meaning from text.

- During tuning in, the teacher initiates discussion in the tense of the text.
- In the book introduction phase, the teacher shows the students how to use the text to find answers to the questions posed.
- During independent reading, the teacher provides prompts that retain the message of the text and encourages students.

Shared writing

This approach is described above as a whole class teaching approach. When using this approach with a small group, teachers focus on the particular needs of the teaching group in relation to aspects of the writing process.

Interactive writing

Interactive writing involves the teacher and small groups of students jointly composing a large print text on a subject of interest to the students, sharing responsibility for the recording at various points in the writing. Teachers quickly record those words that students know how to write and engage students in problem solving and recording those words to provide challenges and opportunities for new learning.

Guided writing

Guided writing involves the teacher guiding a small group of students in their attempts to create individual written texts, responding to students' attempts and extending their thinking during the process. Teachers help students to discover what they want to write and how to write it. Guided writing happens after students have had many opportunities to see writing demonstrated and the process articulated in shared contexts. The students now incorporate aspects of the writing process that have been demonstrated by the teacher.

Roving conference

During independent writing, students use the knowledge and skills gained from demonstration and engagement in the writing process to write their own texts. This includes adding to and revising pieces begun at an earlier time. The student takes responsibility for problem solving the challenges within the writing process. Teachers may support the writing task by giving students quite specific direction at the conclusion of the whole class focus on writing.

Teaching matched to student needs

A key component of the Early Years Literacy Program is flexible and fluid grouping of students according to their learning needs. Developmental stages are outlined and suggestions are made as to appropriate teaching strategies to be used with students in each case. Within the reading block, the text level at which a student can read for instructional purposes (90 to 95 per cent accuracy), as determined by Running Records (Clay, 1993), is used as an indicator of student learning need. Students are monitored to determine the strategies that they use to problem-solve on text and these observations also inform the grouping of students for instruction. Similarly, students' writing abilities are monitored and these observations provide a basis for formation of specific teaching groups within the writing block. In addition, observations of students' speaking and listening influence the formation of teaching groups within both the reading and writing blocks.

Flexible groups are formed on a needs basis. The formation of the groups changes as the needs of the students change. Formation of the groups is also dependent on the particular aspects of the reading process or writing process being addressed at the time. The teaching approaches are designed to match the needs of the students in the group. As the teacher works with the teaching group, other students are involved in working independently at learning centres in the first three years of schooling and at learning tasks during the fourth and fifth years of schooling.

Speaking and listening

Teaching speaking and listening in the Early Years Literacy Program does not require time in addition to the two-hour block. This is because teachers and students are speaking and listening throughout this time. What this programme (DEET:Vic, 1999) specifies is that teachers deliberately and intentionally use talk to support the teaching approaches described above. The SAID framework, Stimulate, Articulate, Integrate and Demonstrate, designed specifically for this programme by Raban (2000b) gives talk a purpose that directly addresses the students' learning needs (see Figure 15.3, p. 223).

Targets and outcomes

Through their School Early Literacy Plans, schools commit to Statewide Minimum Standards in reading for the first two years of schooling. Additional support procedures are put in place for schools that do not reach these minimum standards. The standards were determined on the basis of the Early Literacy Research Project and approximate the standards achieved by the trial schools (some of Victoria's most disadvantaged schools) after three years in the project (Crévola and Hill, 1998). Students who do not reach the minimum of Text Level 5 by the end of their second year of schooling are considered to be 'at risk'.

The minimum standard for the end of the first year of schooling is 80 per cent of students at Text Level 1. The remaining 20 per cent of students generally receive daily one-to-one intervention in their second year. Statewide, funding has been provided for 20 per cent of the cohort of students in their second year at school to access Reading Recovery or other one-to-one intervention programmes. The actual proportion of students who accessed Reading Recovery in 2000 was 22.37 per cent as schools supplement funding for this programme from within their own budgets. The total proportion of students receiving daily one-to-one intervention during this year (2001) would be higher still.

Schools also set school-based targets that in most cases are significantly higher than the minimum standards. To assist them in setting appropriate targets schools are provided with information about their performance in relation to like schools. (There are nine groupings of schools for this purpose based on factors relating to socio-economic and language background.)

The Statewide Minimum Standards for reading are:

- 80 per cent of students reading unseen texts with 90 per cent accuracy at or above Text Level 1 by the end of their first year of schooling
- 100 per cent of students reading unseen texts with 90 per cent accuracy at or above Text Level 5 by the end of their second year of schooling (Text Levels are based on Reading Recovery text levelling).

The reading ability of students has improved for each of the last two years (1999 and 2000) for all three year levels (Prep, Year 1 and Year 2) particularly at the higher Text Levels beyond the minimum; for example:

- the number of students at the end of their first year of schooling, reading Text Level 5 with at least 90 per cent accuracy increased from 62.4 per cent in 1998 to 66.2 per cent in 1999, to 70.6 per cent in 2000 (a total increase of 8.2 percentage points);

- the number of students at the end of their second year of schooling reading Text Level 15 with at least 90 per cent accuracy increased from 71 per cent in 1998 to 76.4 per cent in 1999, to 79.9 per cent in 2000 (a total increase of 8.9 percentage points);
- the number of students at the end of their third year of schooling reading Text Level 20 with at least 90 per cent accuracy increased from 85.5 per cent in 1998 to 90.3 per cent in 1999, to 92.9 per cent in 2000 (a total increase of 7.4 percentage points);
- the number of students reading at less than 50 per cent accuracy at these Text Levels has also shown a significant improvement (i.e. it has declined) over the two years that data have been collected.

A crucial element of the success of the Early Years Literacy Program has been the raising of the status of teachers as professionals. A comprehensive central and regional conference programme in high quality venues has been introduced using a mix of presenters: teachers, principals, academics and consultants. First-time presenters are provided with advice and support. At school level, the professional learning team is highly valued with time set aside for planning, sharing and reviewing teaching practice. Expectations of teachers are high and, in general, teachers have responded to this with enthusiasm and commitment. Anecdotal evidence suggests that the principal plays a crucial role as curriculum leader rather than just business manager in the most successful schools. Similarly the Early Years co-ordinator is an important member of the school leadership team. This notion is reinforced at annual early years leadership conferences focusing on curriculum leadership issues relating to early years literacy.

The shift towards statewide testing has been a fairly rapid cultural change over the last few years but one that has been accepted by schools. Extension of the scope of this assessment will be driven as much by schools' need for more information as by system accountability requirements. It will be important to balance demands at both system and school level for more information with the need to minimise additional workload and to ensure that the focus remains on teaching rather than measuring.

With the success of the Early Years initiative, attention has now moved to the middle years of schooling. Whilst it is acknowledged that the issues in the middle years of schooling are more complex, particularly in relation to student well-being and engagement, similar structures can and are being provided to support schools in addressing these issues. Programs aimed at improving student literacy are being developed on the basis of collaborative research. A 'train-the-trainer' model will be used to deliver these programmes to schools, and school funding is dependent on the development of a school-based action plan in which schools commit to specific targets in relation to literacy and attendance and retention of 'at risk' students.

References

Adams, M.J. (1990) *Beginning to Read: Thinking and Learning About Print*, Cambridge, MA: MIT Press.

Ainley, J. and Fleming, M. (2000) *Learning to Read in the Early Primary Years*, report from Literacy Advance Research Project to Catholic Education Commission of Victoria, Australia.

Barber, M. and Sebba, J. (1999) 'Reflections on a world-class education system', *Cambridge Journal of Education* 29: 183–93.

Beard, R. (1993) *Teaching Literacy: Balancing Perspectives*, London: Hodder & Stoughton.

Cairney, T., Ruge, J., Buchanan, J., Lowe, K. and Munsie, L. (1995) *Developing Partnerships: The Home, School and Community Interface*, Canberra: DEET, Commonwealth of Australia.

Cato, V., Fernandes, C., Gorman, T. and Kispal, A. (1992) *The Teaching of Initial Literacy: How Do Teachers Do It?*, Slough: NFER.

Clay, M.M. (1993) *An Observation Survey of Early Literacy Achievement*, Auckland: Heinemann.

Crévola, C. and Hill, P. (1998) 'Initiation evaluation of a whole school approach to prevention and intervention in early literacy', *Journal of Education for Students Placed at Risk* 3(2): 133–57.

De Lemos, M. and Harvey-Beavis, A. (1995) 'The development and assessment of literacy: background papers for the National School Literacy Survey', unpublished Paper, Melbourne: ACER.

Department of Employment, Education and Training (DEET) (1991) *Australia's Language: The Australian Language and Literacy Policy*, Canberra: AGPS, Commonwealth of Australia.

Department of Employment, Education and Training: Victoria (DEET:Vic) (1997) *Teaching Readers in the Classroom Early Years Literacy Program Stage 1*, S. Melbourne: Addison Wesley Longman

—— (1998) *Teaching Writers in the Classroom Early Years Literacy Program Stage 2*, S. Melbourne: Addison Wesley Longman.

—— (1999) *Teaching Speakers and Listeners in the Classroom Early Years Literacy Program Stage 3*, S. Melbourne: Addison Wesley Longman.

Department of Employment, Education, Training and Youth Affairs (DEETYA) (1998) *Literacy for All: The Challenge for Australian Schools*, Canberra: AGPS, Commonwealth of Australia.

Freebody, P. and Luke, A. (1990) 'Literacy programs: debates and demands', *Cultural Context. Prospect* 5: 7–16.

Fullan, M. (2000) 'The return of large-scale reform', *Journal of Educational Change* 1: 5–28.

Hill, P. (1995) 'School effectiveness and improvement: present realities and future possibilities', Inaugural Professorial Lecture in Dean's Lecture Series, Faculty of Education, Parkville, Victoria: University of Melbourne.

Hill, P. and Crévola, C. (1998) 'Developing and testing a whole-school design approach to improvement in early literacy', paper presented at 11th International Congress for School Effectiveness and Improvement, Manchester, UK.

House of Representatives Standing Committee on Employment (1993) *The Literacy Challenge: A Report on Strategies for Early Intervention for Literacy and Learning for Australian Children*, Canberra: AGPS, Commonwealth of Australia.

Huey, E.B. (1908) *The Psychology and Pedagogy of Reading*, New York: Macmillan.

Masters, G. (1997) *Literacy Standards in Australia*, Canberra: AGPS, Commonwealth of Australia.

Masters, G. and Forster, M. (1997) *Mapping Literacy Achievement: Results of the 1996 National School English Literacy Survey*, Canberra: DEETYA, Commonwealth of Australia.

Raban, B. (2000a) *Just the Beginning ... : DETYA Research Fellowship Report No.1*, Canberra, ACT: Commonwealth of Australia.

—— (2000b) 'Talking to think, learn and teach: the SAID classroom framework', in P. Smith (ed.) *Talking Classrooms*, Newark, DE: International Reading Association.

Raban, B., Clark, U. and McIntyre, J. (1994) *Evaluation of the Implementation of English in the National Curriculum at Key Stages 1, 2 and 3 (1991–1993)*, London: School Curriculum and Assessment Authority.

Reynolds, D., Creemers, B.P.M., Nesselrodt, P.P., Schaffer, E.C., Stringfield, S. and Tedlig, C. (eds) (1994) *Advances in School Effectiveness Research and Practice*, Oxford: Pergamon.

Slavin, R,E., Madden, N.A., Dolan, L.J., Wasik, B.A., Ross, S., Smith, L. and Dianda, M. (1996) 'Success for all: a summary of research', *Journal of Education for Students Placed at Risk* 1: 41–76.

Snow, C., Burns, M. and Griffin, P. (eds) (1998) *Preventing Reading Difficulties in Young Children*, Washington, DC: National Academy Press.

Weaver, C. (1990) *Understanding Whole Language: From Principles to Practice*, Portsmouth, NH: Heinemann.

16 Globalisation, literacy, curriculum practice

Allan Luke and Victoria Carrington

Introduction

What is the relationship between economic and cultural globalisation and everyday literacy practices for teachers and students in that most stolid of twentieth-century institutions, the state primary school? What happens when the very institution that was designed for the propagation of print literacy, for the transmission of encyclopedic knowledge, for the inculcation of industrial behaviours, for the development of the post-war citizen, for the domestication of diversity into monocultural identity – the technology of the modern state par excellence – faces the borderless flows and 'scapes' of information and image, bodies and capital? And, no less important, what might happen if we engage in a momentary suspension of belief in current policy-driven preoccupations with pedagogical method, with decoding and basic skills – and ask a larger curriculum question: within the existing walls and wires, capillaries and conventions of the school, how might we construct a literacy education that addresses new economic and cultural formations?

From the prototypical work of economist Harold A. Innis in the 1940s to the work of Marshall McLuhan and the educational psychology of David R. Olson, the legacy of Canadian communications theory is an undertaking that dominant modes of information – from speech to script to print to digital image – have distinctive and identifiable 'biases'. By this Innis (1951) did not mean simple 'prejudice' or 'predisposition'. He and McLuhan, who joined the University of Toronto in the decade after Innis's death, both believed that communications media enabled blended and new conventions and aesthetics of expression, and that communications media powerfully influenced social organisation, spatial and demographic formation, intellectual practice and cognitive habits, and, importantly, the exchange of economic and political power. In work that anticipated current theories of global networks and scapes, Innis (1950) argued that communications technologies had been the agents of 'empire': creating what he called 'knowledge monopolies', reorganising space–time relations between metropolis and hinterland through the use of technology, and thereby shaping and controlling the contours of social identity at the margins in the interests of an imperial centre.

Half a century later, it is an axiom of the 'new literacy studies' (Barton, Hamilton and Ivanic, 2000) that how literacy is shaped as a social practice is linked to larger social structures. How those linkages are established is in part an ethnographic and in part a discourse analytic question: pursued through local analyses of the power relations, knowledges and identities built through literacy education and everyday life. The oft-repeated lesson from the history of literacy is that what people do with technologies of writing and inscription – and, from an educational perspective, what we normatively teach kids to do with these technologies – is shaped in relation to the contexts of work, of consumption and leisure, of citizenship and national ideology, and of varied projects of 'selfhood' and cultural identity. As literacy educators, we can pursue these links between literacy and social formation either by default, by a science that neglects or denies such links, or through a broader understanding of literacy not just as 'social practice', but literacy as curriculum practice.

For educationally acquired social practices with texts and discourses are both 'shaped' by dominant and alternative economic and social relations, and they are potentially 'shaping' of these relations. Following the work of sociologist Pierre Bourdieu (1998), we believe that literacy education involves:

- the teaching and learning of textual *disposition* – that is, the curricular and pedagogic construction of the literate habitus of embodied skills, knowledges and competences;
- the structural *positioning* by schools and teachers of the aspiring literate in relation to social systems and structures – that is, the production and reproduction of relationships to dominant modes of information and means of production;
- the development of the capacities to use literate practice to *position take* in the social and institutional fields of exchange that require literacy – that is, the construction of habits of agency and a sense of and capacity with the relative power of text and discourse in any particular social field.[1]

Literacy – and by association literacy education – are both historically constructed and historically constructive, normative enterprises. In current conditions, they are about the shaping of patterns and practices of participation in text-based societies and semiotic economies.

These conditions raise alien issues for many teachers and teacher educators: How might literacy and literacy education respond to the challenges of new world cultures and economies and, indeed, forms of governance and citizenship? Without falling prey to the traps of taking globalisation as either universal evil or civilising force – the 'mother of all metanarratives'

(C. Luke, 2001) – we wish to raise a series of open-ended questions about how to reshape what Richard Hoggart (1956) termed 'uses of literacy' almost a half century ago. Our focus is not on narrowing debates over literacy, basic skills and accountability – debates driven as much by the policy imperatives of funding and restructuring a creaky post-war state schooling infrastructure as by a 'science' of literacy education per se (Luke and Luke, 2001). Instead our concern is with the potential of literacy education as a curriculum practice for the generation of 'student' dispositions, positions and position-takings for viable and powerful life pathways through new cultures and economies, pathways that wind through globalised and local, virtual and material social fields.

This is an introductory view for literacy educators and researchers of these changes, their impact upon local communities and their potential for the transformation of how we see and 'do' literacy education in what remain relatively conventional classroom settings of state primary schools. We use the metaphors of globalised 'flows' to explain the impact of new media, new cultures and new economies on children's identities and developments. We then describe the force of these flows on a regional, small Australian township – Harlow (pop. 1,300) [2] – its school and teachers and how they teach literacy. We document the experience of spatialised poverty – the deleterious community-specific effects of economic flows on families' and children's life pathways. Our proposed response is an amended curriculum agenda for critical literacy for these children: one that distinguishes a 'glocal', cosmopolitan focus from what we define as 'parochial' and 'fantasy' approaches to literacy education. Our aim, then, is to move yet again away from limiting debates over basic skills and commodified methods into a much broader debate about literacy education as a sustainable and powerful curriculum practice.

The industrial school meets new times

What we call it – 'liquid' modernity (Bauman, 1998), postfordist economy and postmodern culture (Harvey, 1988; Cvetkovich and Kellner, 1997; Burbules and Torres, 2000), 'networked' societies (Castells, 1996) – is for those of us who work in classrooms and teacher training not very important. What seems certain is that many of the patterns and practices of everyday life are shifting and oscillating, albeit unevenly and at different rates, in relation to powerful economic and technological forces that at the least appear beyond immediate local control and, for many communities, belief and comprehension. The effects and consequences of economic globalisation are both spatialised, local and site-specific – with primary resource and manufacturing economies sitting alongside infotech in some communities, with emergent nation states supporting and sustaining peasant economies alongside industrial parks. Any sense that we have hit some kind of decisive millennial shift ignores the non-synchronous character of contemporary change. In most nations and regions, disparate economies and lifeworlds sit in various states of emergence and decay, like radioactive isotopes with persistent half-lives.

The common characteristic seems to be the speed and durability, flexibility and mutability of networks and flows: as bodies and capital, information and image move across increasingly permeable political borders and geographic barriers. The result in the post-industrial West and North is the creation and transformation of cultural and economic 'scapes' (Appadurai, 1996) in local communities. These are sites for the changes in everyday experiences and uses of space and time, the emergence of new practices of work, leisure and consumption, and the writing of blended, hybridised forms of human expression, artefact and identity. Whether in Bangkok or Brisbane, a particular new species and social class of 'world kids' play and learn in shopping malls and basketball courts, on the internet and in schools.

Societies of the North and West are based on complex and blended economies – where means of production entail an increasing majority of working people engaging directly with dominant *modes of information* – concentrated in culture and creative industries, public and private sector, service sector work, and those fast growth sectors involved in the management and movement of imaginary capital, property and consumer goods. Even in strongly resource-driven economies like Australia's, the percentage of workers engaged in the direct exploitation of the natural and biological world through manual or industrial techniques is in slow but steady decline. In these so-called knowledge economies, human beings' dispositions and position takings occur in those social fields constituted by and regulating regional, national and multinational flows of ideas and information, capital and bodies, material and discourse artefacts alike. One's capacities to sign and to engage in a universe of signs have principal exchange value in these fields. The institutional and occupational fields themselves shift quickly and, as the citizens of Harlow have discovered, erode traditional life pathways, patterns of work, consumption and leisure.

The pattern of flows moves capital, information and bodies increasingly towards the cosmopolitan centres of world cities, creating culture scapes where the lifeworlds of Sydney and Brisbane are more likely to resemble those of Los Angeles or London than those of their kin in rural and remote communities – in some cases, indigenous and Anglo-Australian communities less than a hundred kilometres away in the bush. In this way, capital and labour is deterritorialised away from rural and edge city communities[3] – at the same time that new forms of information, image and representation are directed through electronic and digital networks to communities at the margins. The irony is that while citizens in these new diaspora increasingly lose their productive capacity and force in key aspects of economic and semiotic production – they are repositioned as global, generic consumers and 'end-users' of goods, government and social services. These same world kids, desiring subjects who form a growth market for textual and material products created by Pokemon, Nike and Virgin, may at the same time be distantiated from the metropolitan and cosmopolitan sites of production of these and other culture industries.

Yet there are few uniform effects on these new diasporas: global flows are mediated and refracted by local variation and response, constituting a push–pull 'glocalisation' effect (Robertson, 1992). Local communities like Harlow become the sites for the playing out of global and local forces, between cosmopolitan heterogeneity and local homogeneity. Yet while mobility, the global flow of bodies across borders – political refugees, migrants, business migrants, guest workers, transnational knowledge workers – is one of the key factors of glocalisation – many areas of poverty are sites of increasing immobility. The underside of shifting capital and employment is that many families are quite literally stuck in locations from which they cannot shift. Others are caught up in a mythic transit between edge cities looking for work and cheap housing.

While in some urban areas the industrial-era phenomena of inner city poverty remains a persistent problem – in Australia, poverty has begun to shift to the hinterlands. These include both traditional farming and rural areas, and, increasingly, suburban edge cities characterised by inexpensive land and housing, often lacking in significant social capital and infrastructure. This phenomenon of spatialised poverty is focused on regional location, where inequality in incomes and local identity reflects a complex interaction of cost of housing, local employment and jobs infrastructure, and the available cultural capital of the population. In such situations, there is little evidence that an educational system in and of itself – without the co-ordination of the availability of other kinds of social, economic and even ecological capital – can alter life pathways on a large scale.

But, as we will see – a key problem is the inability of the educational system to provide the cognitive and textual tools and discourse resources to explicate these changes for the citizens of communities like Harlow, who remain positioned in the flows and fields of globalised economies without capital, without mobility and, indeed, without an analysis. In fact, across Australia, schools and state departments have been slow to make economic and cultural globalisation a key problematic in curriculum and instruction.

To understand the significance of these shifts and the implications they might have for our work as literacy educators, we need to reappraise the genealogy of current approaches to schooling and our approaches to the teaching of print literacy. Earlier generations grew up in an Australian society arranged around an industrial, Fordist model of work, identity and politics. In this society-past, the productive worker (predominantly white and male) could depend on government to provide a basic level of social and economic capital (here defined as equitable and ready availability of non-discriminatory social infrastructure, institutions and networks), including education, health care, psychic and physical protection, and a relatively secure and stable job market. The nation protected its citizens and guaranteed a better future by warding off migration and diversity, while protecting industries with high tariffs.

In exchange, citizen-workers demonstrated loyalty to both employer and government, paying taxes, with a highly motivated will to capital and maintaining levels of consumption. In the idealised social model underpinning this economic order, males engaged in paid employment while females reconciled themselves to acceptance of the role of child-bearing and rearing and maintenance of the nuclear family home (Carrington, in press). In such a lifeworld, transience was a kind of deficit, a risk to encased concepts of community, family and neighbourhood and counterproductive to the expansion of capital.

The industrial school, then, aimed to develop the dispositions to position workers within a particular economy and lifeworld, streaming students into a bifurcated pathway that led, variously, towards university-based and vocational training. In this inter- and post-war schema, literacy – neutral, secular and non-ideological, print-based skills available to all – was defined in relation to the decoding of print-based text, and meaning making around canonical texts that entailed moral and ethical models for secular, industrial society. If, indeed, the education of empire had prepared one to be a colonial subject, the modernist education system that we presently work with prepares and constructs the dispositions of the industrial subject: behaviourally skilled, ideologically and economically patient, and motivated by a will to capital and the maintenance of stable community and nuclear family. That vision is captured and frozen in the cultural and social scapes of the modern basal reading series.

But the social facts of new times weigh heavily on this version of the world. The Australian economic and employment landscape has undergone significant upheaval in the course of one generation: gone is the 'job-for-life' and the promise of a state-funded retirement, gone is the certainty of learning one set of job-related skills sufficient for a life-time's employment; gone is the security of a delineated, hierarchical work order; vanishing is the job market for non-tertiary educated youth; vanished is the job market for the under-qualified and the elderly (Carrington, in press). In their place are new uncertainties, new flexibilities and new citizen-workers. Prognoses suggest that job and mid-life career shift will increasingly become the norm, rather than the exception.

At the same time, the shift out of a Fordist economy and social order has made cultural and linguistic diversity a focal policy issue. In states like Queensland that might have conceived of themselves and their systems as stable and homogeneous, governments and education systems are contending with the realisation that almost one in five children is of indigenous or migrant backgrounds. New capitalism has created the conditions for the deployment of new and hybridised identities and the emergence of new literate practices, even and perhaps especially in the new hinterlands of edge cities. The fragmentation of the normative model of identity, community and nation that underpinned the older economic system has placed on educators' tables issues of identity, culture, sexuality or race – whether through presence or absence. Many citizens of Harlow would tell us that the problems they face are due to, variously, Asian migrants who work too hard and cheaply, Aborigines and Torres Strait Islanders who don't work hard and cheaply enough, urban women who should raise families but choose to work, and, indeed, corrupt urban politicians who aid and abet the capital drain on their communities.

Teachers working in 'at risk' communities face a surface set of problems that appear amenable to longstanding approaches. According to the teachers in Harlow, the problems include: an apparent decline in main-stream cultural and linguistic resources required for school success among school-aged children; increasing impatience with conventional pedagogy and curricular approaches; increasing rates of ascertained 'attention deficit disorder' and other symptomologies; and affiliated forms of 'unruliness' and behaviour management problems. In consultations undertaken on behalf of the state government in Queensland in 2000, these phenomena were attributed by teachers to: deficit parenting with a specific focus on failure to read to children at home, absentee parents, overexposure to tele-vision, deterioration of the family structure and increased transience, video games and popular culture in all its forms, oral language deficit, and behavioural disorders (Luke, Freebody and Land, 2000). In other words, the response of many teachers is to see what might well be manifestations of the impacts of new economies and cultures as signs of conventional 'lack' in those cultural and discourse resources that we took for granted in monocultural, middle-class communities in the post-war print era.

There is some belated discussion of what these trends might mean for education and schooling systems. The policy responses of Western and Northern educational bureaucracies focus variously on:

- the consequences of information technology for classroom infrastruc-ture and pedagogy, under the assumption somehow that digitalisation will both update and revive pedagogical and curricular systems led by an ageing teaching force;
- the further deployment of a range of compensatory 'pull out' program-mes that attempt to address the ostensive needs of culturally heterogeneous and increasingly mobile student populations (e.g. early intervention, learning support, ESL specialist interventions);
- compensatory funding responses to educational exclusion and failure in particular spatial 'zones' hit hardest by economic changes; and, in some states;
- an early debate on the putative human capital demands of new economies.

From a sociological viewpoint, what has been interesting has been how debates over literacy have focused on early intervention and basic skills, especially in the US and UK, with the assumption that testing and account-ability systems are the most effective response to the problems of populations and communities displaced, variegated and replaced by new economies. Policy debates over literacy frequently are steeped in deficit terminology, and are struggling to speak to the phenomena of world kids, new family configurations and the diasporic communities that have been adversely hit by these economies. In the face of major economic shift, these debates seem to be at once retro and nostalgic, and attempting to restore or main-tain an educational equilibrium around traditionally transmitted and measured print-skill levels among students and schools.

Roughly half of the Australian and North American teaching force is over fifty. For a generation of teachers raised on debates over Cold War ideologies in the curriculum, over deschooling and progressivism, still caught up in the great debate over phonics and word recognition, the issues we have raised here may seem at best medium to long term and, at worst, an irrelevance to the everyday challenges of work intensification in classrooms and staffrooms. Yet the irony is that such changes, and the consequential effects on students' dispositions and social positions, are unlikely to go away, and are proving particularly resistant to the regimes of treatment past (e.g. use of high stakes testing, expansion of specialised early intervention programmes, the roping in of teacher behaviour through standardised and commodified curricula, single-method instruction). And they will continue to remain invisible to an explanatory schema that is still searching out and naming educational problems and human subjects which have morphed into new forms.

Literacy teaching and learning in the new white diaspora

Harlow is a edge-city community caught in the headlights of economic globalisation. It straddles the semi-rural zone between two major high-ways, each leading to the outermost western fringe of the state's southeastern corner. It sits at the edges of an urban area – about 75 kilo-metres from the state capital. In its heyday over fifty years ago, it acted as an intermediary service terminus between the city and its outlying grazier and farming communities. But with the decade-long downturn in the adjoining rural communities – exacerbated by drought and deregulation – and with the improvement of direct transportation, communication and just-in-time shipping links between the bush and city, its historical moment, if it had one, has passed. It is caught in a nether world: it is neither a traditional bush community with a longstanding sense of identity and bloodlines, nor is it close enough to the urban centre to participate viably in the service economy. Over the last two decades, Harlow's popula-tion has shifted from a long-term base to a significant annual turnover, with families and youth coming to the community for affordable housing, at once finding themselves 'locked in' by mortgages yet compelled to commute or leave in search of work. Harlow's population is relatively homogeneous, comprised of Anglo-Australian families with a few Asian migrants. Harlow is a white diaspora at the edge of the global economy.

Levels of unemployment are high. The official government data puts the unemployment rate around 16 per cent, double the state average, but the actual level of unemployment, including adults not actively seeking work and drop-outs not on the dole would be much higher. Many employed adults work in service (e.g. retail) and trades work (e.g. construction) in suburban communities an hour away. The real levels of unemployment among youths aged 16–25 is set at 24 per cent but it probably hovers around 50 per cent. The percentage of people on welfare is double the state norm, with the few jobs in transport and construction unable to offer the many who complete or leave high school sustainable employment.

Yet while several townspeople complained to us about unruly youth – the actual social environment of the community is quite remarkable, with high levels of community participation in sports, low levels of local crime, a strong sense that Harlow is a safe and stable place to raise children, and, in one of its prime attractions, affordable housing. Kids play on the streets and in fields after school with negligible risk or fear. In the last state and federal elections, it has supported right wing candidates who oppose immigration, call for reimposition of protective tariff barriers, and oppose formal reconciliation and treaty with Australian Aboriginal and Torres Strait Islander peoples.

We are university researchers and teacher educators. We work closely both with the state educational bureaucracies on literacy policy and with local teachers developing school and classroom level interventions. In the last year, we were asked to assist Harlow primary school in developing a 'whole school literacy plan'. The school had been working on its literacy programme for several years, with a relatively stable teaching population. Yet, despite its best efforts, Harlow state school's scores on the statewide year 3 and year 5 standardised reading achievement tests have stalled slightly below the state norms for 'like schools' of similar socio-economic and community profiles. A core of 25 per cent of the children struggled with basic reading problems across the years. And while most could functionally decode by the completion of their studies, there were persistent reading comprehension problems, resistances to reading and struggles to write in syntactically and intellectually complex ways.

Despite strong administrative commitment, focused remedial work, parental support programmes, purchase and implementation of a popular phonics-based curriculum package, teachers and students were unable to raise reading outcomes. Those identified as 'the usual suspects' – working-class white boys, children of the unemployed, mobile families whose children had interrupted schooling – were continuing to perform relatively poorly according to standard measures of literacy. Reading Recovery programmes and special education support generated some short- and medium-term gains but had no visible effect on raising the overall performance profile of the school. The teachers wanted to improve not just baseline reading skills and performance but overall school achievement as well. In their words, they wanted to know what they were doing 'wrong', but they also wanted to know 'what was wrong with these children'. Why weren't they responding to the remedial programmes? Why weren't their reading test scores improving proportionate to the effort of staff?

The teachers – all women ranging from mid-thirties through to retirement age, along with two male staff: the principal and special education teacher – are a stable and experienced staff. They are dedicated to their work and, for the most part, seem to have avoided the industrial alienation and culture of complaint that has become more common in Australian schools. They would view themselves as progressives, as 'child centred' and behind the state system's commitment of equity and social justice. There is none of the high teacher turnover that characterises bush and indigenous community schools. Though many have long histories at Harlow, none of them live in the district, commuting from either of the two larger suburbs 50–60 minutes away. The mismatch of teachers' and students' cultural and economic locations and world views went unremarked in their comments to us.

The teachers' comments reflected these differences in standpoint. We were told that there are few community role models, that welfare parents don't provide supportive print environments, that families move about too much, and that the students' expectations of their futures seem either wildly exaggerated or limited. Clearly, student transience is one of the key difficulties – between Year 1 and 6 the school has a 60 per cent turnover of students. This limits the effectiveness of blanket early intervention programmes. Additionally, the teachers felt that this made its curriculum 'integrity' difficult: 'one step forward and two backwards'. Additionally, they stated, there was 'apathy' in parental commitment. A dedicated and progressive staff, they were worried that kids would end up 'stuck' in the area, on welfare and with limited futures. Over 30 per cent of the children attending Harlow are from single parent families and even more are from welfare families. Taken together, the teachers' comments painted an overwhelming picture of student 'deficit' and 'lack', set against a backdrop of genuine concern, commitment and professionalism.

The other side of the coin emerged in our 'audit' of what the children of Harlow were fluent with. While perhaps not matching the expectations of the teachers, the children in this community have a number of strengths. These include strong social networks in the community, in-depth local knowledge about the geography, demography and culture of their own community, knowledge and skill in handling their allowance and earned money, interest in sports, knowing how to 'make the best' of difficult family and financial situations. When prompted, the teachers acknowledged that the students had extensive knowledge of video movies and cable television programmes, vast knowledge of popular music, fashion and youth culture, and took readily to computer and video games, internet surfing and the new technologies. Additionally, the teachers reported, these children often carry more of the emotional work of their families than do more affluent, middle-class kids and yet are extremely accepting of difference. They are generally well behaved and eager to learn. Reportedly, as a whole the children appear to enjoy school, like their teachers and want to do well.

We worked with the teachers for several days to audit and develop their classroom strategies. Like many other Australian primary schools, Harlow has instituted a 'literacy block' – one and a half hours each day dedicated solely to literacy activities (see Raban and Essex, this volume). In this session, basic skills development and consolidation are the focus. Across the school, students engage in sound-letter recognition activities, the development of dictionary and other research skills, decoding strategies, big book reading and activities, cloze activities and some, albeit highly variable, work with functional grammar. In this regard, there was nothing particularly remarkable or unremarkable about the existing practices. These core strategies are part and parcel of the Australian literacy teachers' repertoire for dealing with print literacy. At the same time, the teachers found that there had been poor communication about who was doing what – particularly between lower primary and upper grades teachers – and that they, as a school staff, lacked a shared descriptive metalanguage for (a) describing their practice; and (b) talking about language.

After two days of working with the teachers, the pieces of the puzzle began to fit together for them and for us. If we tracked the children's dispositions and trajectories through the school, across varying patterns of participation and achievement, onto the local high school and out into the world of work, a clear pattern began to emerge. The kids of Harlow were relatively patient and willing to participate in their schooling through and across primary school. This was established in no small part by the school's child-centred environment, the anti-bullying and behaviour management programme and the visible emotional investment in the children by the teachers. Yet that participation was momentary, almost stoic, in the face of larger forces: by the time children hit high school, achievement plateaued or declined, behaviour problems increased, particularly among the boys, and retention rates fell off. The local state high school had one of the highest expulsion rates in the state. Many of the same students who had been average achievers in secondary school, after leaving school would commute to hang out at the shopping malls an hour away, all the while maintaining strong personal commitments to popular culture and Australian team sports.

In our view, students were patiently 'doing time' in a primary literacy programme which was:

- focused on delimited sets of skills and knowledge and was narrow in its focus on now traditional approaches to decoding;
- squarely modernist, pre-digital and anti-popular culture in the form and content of its approach to reading comprehension;
- escapist and irrelevant in its approach to teaching literature.

This programme more or less was 'free-standing' as part of the literacy block study in the morning. When we asked when the kids were taught about the changes in the communities around them – we were told that this wasn't part of the literacy programme but sat in the varied project work and traditional key learning area studies that were part of the 'integrated studies' kids undertook in the late morning and afternoon. Hence, the literacy programme also tended to be:

- disconnected both temporally and thematically from any substantive 'reading of the world' based on specific discourse and field-specific knowledges.

This offered us a possible explanation to the 'rise and stall' scenario of the school's test scores. Put simply, the baseline skills that teachers were attempting to instil in their students were more or less being achieved through a focused and delimited literacy programme, despite high student turnover. Both teachers and students were pursuing this programme in good faith and effectively. That programme had become disconnected and decontextualised on at least three levels. The literacy programme was:

- temporally and programmatically partitioned from the rest of the school curriculum;
- disconnected from the background knowledges, skills and life experiences that the students brought to the classroom; and
- its traditional print format and discourse content were disconnected from a broader analysis of community, of environment, of the experiences and practices of glocalisation.

The biggest difficulty faced by the teachers of Harlow was not simply a question of method. There is no doubt that their whole school plan will focus and co-ordinate their pedagogic efforts, bring them together into a stronger shared vocabulary, and add a few notches to their test scores and affiliated league tables kept in central office. But the teachers and the programme were in some ways caught in their own implicit assumptions about what constitutes 'literacy' and how it should be taught in school. For all their good intentions and hard work, they hadn't hardwired what counted as 'literacy' in the school with the lives of the children and their families – nor were they adept at anticipating and teaching to the kinds of 'literate futures' their students would face as adolescents and young adults.

Critical literacy as a technology for remediating globalisation

We have here provided a shorthand account of how students and teachers in one Australian edge community have experienced economic and cultural scapes of New Times. Is there a simple and happy ending to Harlow's story? Perhaps that the teachers had found the 'right' pedagogy or method, that test scores had risen, that this had set in place the foundations for overall improvements in student achievement, that the communities' and students' life trajectories had shifted as a result. These are the narrative chains underlying current policy interventions in many OECD educational systems. Yet there are competing claims that we need to consider: that basic skills acquisition is necessary, but not sufficient, to turn around the overall educational achievement of the most at-risk students, that higher order thinking, depth of intellectual engagement (Newmann, King and Ringdon, 1997), critical literacy and 'connectedness to the world' (Lingard *et al.*, 2001) have the best chance of 'redesign[ing] social futures' (New London Group, 1996) and altering these kids' dispositions, positions and position-takings.

The story is unfinished. We are continuing to work with Harlow to develop school literacy programmes that bring together a richer, more intellectually demanding and 'contemporary' analysis of these kids' identities and competences, a more cogent understanding of the overlapping and multiple communities that these children inhabit with a balanced focus on code breaking, meaning making, using texts in everyday life and critical literacy. In so doing, we are working within the parameters of a state literacy policy that has an eye equally on basic skills of reading and, as importantly, the emergent multiliteracies required in the cultural landscapes and workplaces of new economies (Luke, Freebody and Land, 2000).

Harlow's dilemma suggests some very different lessons for us: about the inability of education systems and literacy education per se to change life pathways without other kinds of flows of capital and culture across borders and institutions; about the difficulties teachers, researchers and curriculum developers face in understanding both the new knowledges, experiences and skills kids bring to classrooms and the new knowledges, experiences and skills they will need to 'navigate' and 'surf' emergent culture scapes. We conclude with a barely modest proposal for what a critical literacy might entail in conditions of 'glocalisation'.

It was Marx and Engels' contention that the dominant ideas of an age were those that served the interests of particular forms of social organisation, of production and manufacture, and, indeed, of social class. It was Kuhn's contention that scientific paradigms reached crisis points where lifeworlds presented and generated hosts of problems and anomalies that could not be addressed by the redeployment of existing theories and methodologies. Regardless of which of these or other analytic tacts we might take to explain the new blends of literate practices, texts and discourses, skills and developmental patterns at hand, virtually all social science analyses of contemporary social and economic conditions lead us to a similar transit: that education, literacy practices and childhood itself have reached an historical juncture of transition and change, of residual discourses and text forms coexisting and blending with the new, of persistent old inequalities and new ones, of century-old educational practices sitting alongside of ones that have never been seen in classrooms before.

We are of the opinion that while the new communications technologies are a catalyst for economic change and potentially for pedagogic change, they are neither the core problem nor the main answer for teachers and students in what is increasingly resembling a transitional period in the history of schooling. One of the first themes that arose in our discussions with the teachers of Harlow was the assumption that if they just switched to new technologies – that if they just brought in the wires and boxes and went on line – that 'empowerment', engagement with the new economy and so forth would magically occur. While we struggle empirically with the question of which blends of print and virtual skills and knowledges might 'count' for the kids of Harlow, we are painfully aware that it is some time away, perhaps years, before we will have answers about which blends of communications technologies – oral and written, digital and visual, performed and virtual – are optimal for accommodating and articulating some of the new forms of social practice, representation and cognition.

In the meantime, a teaching force with an average age of 47 struggles with a curious cocktail of effects from cultural and economic flows. Answers are at hand. But how we deal with and reshape the kids' use of the old technology of print is as important, though not mutually exclusive, from their engagement with the new. And in this context the explanatory discourses from conferences, publishers and software peddlers, and professional development experts available to the teachers of Harlow have tended to operate in binary opposition: high tech online facilities and pedagogy will solve the problem and/or low tech, phonics-based programmes will solve the problem. Neither is adequate.

A key lesson that we take away from this case study is that many of the current debates over reading and literacy – the 'available discourses' for talking about literacy education and schooling more generally in new times – are developed and primed to deal with the entry and traverse of children into another universe: a print-based, industrially and economically stable community within which the achievement of rudimentary print literacy was a necessary and, for many, sufficient condition to 'becoming somebody'. The teachers in Harlow were doing their mighty best to describe and contend with the manifestations of a new socio-economic milieu. Yet at the same time they were struggling to recognise, understand and even 'name' it. While they might not have seen it in such terms, in practice they were putting the weight of their efforts into trying to contain and ameliorate the effects of globalised culture and trying to counter the effects of truncated and static life pathways. They were, in many ways, swimming upstream against deteriorating community economic conditions.

Their professional vocabulary for dealing with this – that of 'recovery', of skills versus whole language, of learning disability and oral language deficit, of behaviour management and deficit parenting – led them down a road to simplistic answers, answers that were more about the micro-management of lessons and plans, to belief in packaged programmes and commodities, rather than towards a re-envisioning of the curriculum, of the students' needs and life pathways, and, indeed, of the kinds of literate dispositions that might effectively vie for position in the social fields of globalised capital. Intervention was more rearguard or, to paraphrase Marshall McLuhan (1966), 'rear view mirror' action. Our view is that neither the available discourses around 'methods' for teaching reading, or about cultural, linguistic and intellectual 'deficits' of children can begin to address the complexity of problems faced by schools and teachers. And while a floor of basic skills has been established, the question of 'preparedness' for this particular construction of adolescence, for school-leaving, for an environment of flight from and to structural unemployment across and between edge communities was still moot.

What might be the shape of critical literacy as curriculum practice – fitted for the analysis, critique and engagement with the lifeworlds of new, globalised and 'glocal' economies and cultures? The points of disconnection between literacy and glocal 'communitas', between old literacy and world cultures are the very nodal points where a rebuilding of the curriculum could begin. We want to argue for a kind of critical literacy that envisions literacy as a tool for remediating one's relation to the global flows of capital and information, bodies and images.

David Olson (1986) described the cognitive effects of the technology of print as the construction of 'possible worlds'. Following Innis, McLuhan and Goody, he argued that the 'bias' of writing was its capacity to take human subjects to other worlds, to traverse the constraints of place and time. Whether in its highly amplified digital form or in its traditional static form, one of the communicative effects of the technology of writing is its capacity to represent in a portable and replicable format times and places that are otherwise inaccessible to place-bound readers. It is this capacity of reading – both traditional and digital – that can provide the basis of a reconceptualisation of literacy as a technology for mediating one's position within globalised flows. As literature teachers have always known, literacy pedagogy can displace and disrupt space, place and time, taking one out of one's immediate synchronicity – cutting across different spaces and times, and engaging, both virtually and psychically, with specific social fields and markets that otherwise aren't available to, in this case, the children of Harlow. The simultaneous universe envisioned by McLuhan, and before him Innis and Mumford, becomes accessible through one's capacity to read, whether online or off.

That capacity can equally be used – as it was in literature study in Harlow – as a kind of sublimation from engagement with the texts and contexts of glocalisation, a deliberate suspension of the local and pursuit of texts and discourses 'other' to immediate experience. That is, literature study can be enlisted to disengage readers from a 'reading of the world' of globalised scapes and flows. In Table 16.1 we term this a *fantasy literacy* that aims for a suspension of position in the social fields and scapes of globalisation and a psychic disengagement with flows. While this might have therapeutic purpose, it acts as a pedagogy of disengagement and estrangement from the glocal.

At the same time, the teachers of Harlow used many archetypal strategies, from language experience and 'show and tell', journal writing and project work to make their teaching more 'relevant' to kids' local experiences. These ranged from studies of local wildlife to a regular discussion focus on local sporting events and community activities. Teachers argued that this focus on local texts and discourses increased levels of interest, was important for raising student 'self-esteem'. But it appeared that much of this work did not seem to intellectually or textually 'go anywhere': there was often limited articulation into a broader conversation about how local contexts, experiences and issues 'fit' with the parallel worlds, cultural and economic scapes outside of Harlow. In Table 16.1, we refer to this as *parochial literacy*, local in scope and focus and reproductive of kids' local discourses, dispositions and positions.

Table 16.1 Uses of literacy in globalised conditions

Mode	Curriculum practice	Positioning
Parochial literacy	Engagement with local texts and discourses, knowledges and experiences	Material reproduction of position through valorisation of local experience.
Fantasy literacy	Disengagement by taking the reader and writer out of local place, space and time	De-positioning or suspension of position; introduction of 'other' discourses; disengagement with flows.
Glocalised literacy	Engagement with relationship of local to other textual possible worlds	Material repositioning; critical analysis and repositioning of flows; reflexive analysis of other and local texts.

Parochial literacy and *fantasy literacy* are two curriculum approaches with long and distinguished pedigrees, both of which would purport to address the alienation from schooling experienced by at-risk kids such as those of the new white diaspora. These are, respectively: the argument that 'relevance' of curriculum and activity will effectively suture the home–school mismatch and transition problem and the argument that a rich, imaginative literary focus will build self-esteem, expand psychological horizons and world views, and create a 'love of literature'.

Our argument here is that texts – both print and virtual, canonical and popular – and engagement with reading and writing can form a kind of 'trialectical' moment (Soja, 1999) in each learner's life that bridges the 'push–pull' effects of glocalisation. The focus here would be on a 'reading of the local' that connects this with those of other possible worlds, a curriculum approach that focuses students' work with texts on the analysis of the flows of effects between this time–space locality and others.

In Harlow, such an approach to critical literacy curriculum could take multiple forms: using the internet to audit and analyse the global flows of work, goods and discourse that are leading to changes in Harlow, whether by studying the history and economics of the rural sector, the origin of local environmental issues, or patterns of population movement between communities like Harlow (Comber and Simpson, 2001). It could entail using writing and online communication to participate with virtual communities around 'fandom' and popular culture (Alvermann, Moon and Hagood, 1999). Or it could involve reading multiple literary texts that generate or engage intercultural and contrastive historical perspectives on new times, those of economies, cultures and places past, present and future. In these ways, the aim would be to engage children critically in the borderless flows of data, information and image that characterise information economies – using both digital and print media. It would entail working intertextually across various cultural and historical texts and discourses. What this kind of literacy might enable is the modelling of 'position-takings' that actively remediate one's position – both in terms of the capital flows that make forms of work possible and available, but as well to manage the information flows of images, representation and texts that constitute identity and ideology, and, finally, to engage with other cultures and bodies across time and space.

Our aim in this discussion is to move forcefully not just beyond a great debate over method – that should go without saying – but, as we debate between approaches to content and method (from language exp ence to process writing) that focus on the local, the parochial, the hand', and those approaches that stress the 'wonder', the 'mystery' 'going elsewhere' through the experience of literature. Both are power tools, but, if we are looking for a refashioning of literacy as a normat preparation for a critical engagement with glocalised economies, we wou need to begin talking about literacy as a means for building cosmopolit world views and identity: of enhancing, in Bourdieu's terms, historical memories and contemporary understandings of how these economies of flows actually structurally position (and perhaps exclude) one, how differing dispositions will have different effects in the various fields of flows, and how to actively engage with those fields in agentive and trans- formative ways. As idealistic as such models might sound, there are viable prototypes in the field drawn from the extensive literature on the teaching of critical literacy and critical language awareness (e.g. Fairclough, 1992; Muspratt, Luke and Freebody, 1997; Comber and Simpson, 2001; Knobel and Healey, 1998). Such models do not discard basic knowledge of print codes, syntactic metalanguage, enhanced automaticity of skill, or metalin- guistic awareness, but they ensure that they are lodged within broader curriculum contexts that are not anachronistic, disconnected, dated, or simply intellectually infantile.

Will such approaches to literacy alleviate the patterns and consequences for the children of Harlow and like communities across North America, the UK, New Zealand and Australia? Not in and of themselves. The picture of change and risk here shows that schools and education systems can make a difference, but that that difference is contingent on the avail- ability and flows of other kinds of capital and power as well. At the same time, though, cases like Harlow tell us with some certainty that the answer lies as much in re-envisioning literacy education as curriculum practice as it does fetishising the teaching of basic print skills.

Notes

1   Describing human subjects' traverse across social fields, Bourdieu explains that one brings acquired cultural capital (a 'habitus' of embodied practices and knowledges of all sorts) to particular social fields such as workplaces, schools and families. Each social field, in turn, operates according to objective regulari- ties and patterns that 'position' one in relative relations for the exchange of capital. At the same time, each individual has the capacity to engage in agentive 'position taking' in relation to social fields. For a shorthand version of Bourdieu on literate capital, see Carrington and Luke (1997).

2   Harlow is an anonymised composite of four schools in Queensland and Tasmania that we have undertaken professional development with over the past three years. We thank these teachers for sharing their work, problems and strategies with us.

3   The term 'edge city' refers to the new suburban satellite cities that have arisen in many post-industrial nations. Many of these are sites where the new working- and under-classes can source low cost housing, often without the social capital of community infrastructure, services and networks. The prevailing assumption of inter- and post-war urban sociology was that poverty tended to be centred in the urban core, with minorities radiating outwards towards secure, affluent white suburbs. Australia is the site for the new 'spatialisation' of poverty (Soja, 1999).

References

Alvermann, D.E., Moon, J.S. and Hagood, M.C. (1999) *Popular Culture in the Classroom*, Newark, DE: International Reading Association.

Appadurai, A. (1996) *Modernity at Large: Cultural Dimensions of Globalisation*, Minneapolis: University of Minnesota Press.

Barton, D., Hamilton, M. and Ivanic, R. (eds) (2000) *Situated Literacies*, London: Routledge.

Bauman, Z. (1998) *Globalization: The Human Consequences*, London: Polity Press.

Bourdieu, P. (1998) *Practical Reason: On the Theory of Action*, London: Polity.

Burbules, N. and Torres, C. (eds) (2000) *Globalisation and Education: Critical Perspectives*, New York: Routledge.

Carrington, V. (in press) *Landscaping the Family in New Times*, Amsterdam: Kluwer.

Carrington, V. and Luke, A. (1997) 'Literacy and Bourdieu's sociological theory: a reframing', *Language and Education* 11(2): 96–112.

Castells, M. (1996) *Rise of the Network Society*, Oxford: Blackwell.

Cvetkovich, A. and Kellner, D. (eds) (1997) *Articulating the Global and the Local*, Boulder, CO: Westview Press.

Comber, B. and Simpson, A. (eds) (2001) *Negotiating Critical Literacies in the Classroom*, Malwah, NJ: Lawrence Erlbaum.

Fairclough, N. (Ed.) (1992) *Critical Language Awareness*, London: Longman.

Harvey, D. (1988) *The Condition of Postmodernity*, Cambridge: Polity Press.

Hoggart, Richard (1956) *The Uses of Literacy*, Harmondsworth: Penguin.

Innis, H.A. (1950) *Empire and Communications*, Oxford: Oxford University Press.

—— (1951) *The Bias of Communications*, Toronto: University of Toronto Press.

Knobel, M. and Healey, A. (eds) (1998) *Critical Literacies in the Primary Classroom*, Rozelle, NSW: Primary English Teachers Association.

Lingard, R., Ladwig, J., Mills, M., Christie, P., Hayes, D., Gore, J. and Luke, A. (2001) *Queensland School Longitudinal Restructuring Study: Final Report*, Brisbane: Education Queensland.

Luke, A. and Luke, C. (2001) 'Adolescence lost, childhood regained: on early intervention and the emergence of the techno-subject', *Journal of Early Childhood Literacy* 1(1): 91–120.

Luke, A., Freebody, P. and Land, R. (2000) *Literate Futures: The Queensland State Literacy Strategy*, Brisbane: Education Queensland.

Luke, C. (2001) *Globalisation and Women in Academia: North/South/East/West*, Malwah, NJ: Lawrence Erlbaum.

McLuhan, M. (1966) *War and Peace in the Global Village*, New York: Random House.

Muspratt, S., Luke, A. and Freebody, P. (eds) (1997) *Constructing Critical Literacies*, Creskill, NJ: Hampton Press.

Newmann, F., King, M.B. and Ringdon, M. (1997) 'Accountability and school performance: implications for restructuring schools', *Harvard Educational Review* 67 (1): 41–69.

New London Group (1996) 'A pedagogy of multiliteracies', *Harvard Educational Review* 66(1): 60–92.

Olson, D.R. (1986) 'Learning to mean what you say: towards a psychology of literacy', in S. DeCastell, A. Luke and K. Egan (eds) *Literacy, Society and Schooling* (pp. 145–58), Cambridge: Cambridge University Press.

Robertson, R. (1992) *Globalization: Social Theory and Global Culture*, London: Sage.

Soja, E. (1999) *Thirdspace*, London: Verso.

Discussion
Developing practice

Ros Fisher

This section, indeed the whole book, reflects a commitment from all concerned to ensure the highest possible literacy standards for all children. A key factor in any move to raise literacy standards must be the teacher. How teachers are prepared for their work in the classroom and how they are helped in the development of their practice over the time of their career must be central concerns. The research described in the first section provides clear indications of what we know about how children learn to read and write. However, the shift from research monograph to teacher manual is a tricky one. Classrooms are messy places full of individuals with different beliefs, experiences, worries and enthusiasms. The task of the policy maker, whether at national, local or school level, is to ensure the best of our understandings from research are used effectively in the classroom.

The authors in this section examine initiatives in the USA, England and Australia to raise standards of literacy. All involve, to a greater or smaller extent, changes to the way teachers teach. Questions are raised as to how possible it is to mandate teaching programmes that are relevant to every context and every teacher. Yet research must be able to help teachers, who may teach for 30 to 40 years after their initial training, to gain new understanding and learn new strategies. More than this, policy makers and teachers must be sensitive to the current, if not future, needs of literacy learners. It is not enough to fine-tune the teaching of those skills that were sufficient thirty years ago. We need teachers who have the vision and knowledge to prepare their pupils for life in the twenty-first century.

It is clear that the two descriptions of ambitious large-scale initiatives to achieve this arise from teachers' experience and are grounded in research evidence. It is unarguable that those who describe their content are enthusiastic and believe in their success. However, it is equally clear that such initiatives can only be part of the solution. Elfrieda Hiebert, as Greg Brooks earlier in this volume, reminds us that literacy attainment is also dependent on economic factors. Allan Luke and Victoria Carrington argue strongly that literacy teaching needs to engage the needs and interests of today's children rather than appearing to hark back to a different era.

The lack of centralisation and greater autonomy within and between school districts in the USA results in there being many approaches to raising literacy standards there. Hiebert contends that these are not based on untainted research evidence and argues that there should be a co-ordinated approach to gathering evidence about their efficacy. It is particularly important that programmes work with those groups of children who are not achieving high standards already. However, she also reminds us that it is not only the content and delivery of the teaching that counts but social and economic factors have a part to play. She also argues that 'what was sufficient for previous generations is not sufficient for the citizens of the digital age' (p. 167). She fears that reform efforts widely used in USA lack clarity both about the underlying literacy processes and about how to achieve higher levels of literacy. Like Luke and Carrington, she accuses reformers of harking back to previous standards and previous methods that were barely sufficient with different children leading different lives.

The report from the National Commission on Excellence in Elementary Teacher Preparation for Reading Instruction (NCEETPRI) reviews how the best teacher preparation programmes in the USA give students more courses about reading instruction and more opportunities to try out their teaching in the classroom. The commission has found that first-year teachers trained on these programmes are much better equipped to relate the programmes used in their schools to the needs of the children, and have more confidence in recognising those needs and in adapting approaches. Here the key seems to be ensuring beginning teachers have enough subject and pedagogical knowledge and experience to deliver the programmes, but also the confidence and autonomy to translate a blueprint into something that fits the beliefs of the teachers and the needs of the children. The commission found that where beginning teachers had graduated from programmes that encouraged autonomy, they felt empowered to make informed decisions rather than becoming 'more like technicians and assembly line workers, where everyone is accomplishing the same thing at the same time' (p. 186).

The different approaches adopted in schools and teacher education programmes in the USA are in contrast to the large-scale initiatives described in the three chapters following. The National Literacy Strategy (NLS) in England and the Early Years Literacy Program (EYLP) in Victoria, Australia are large-scale initiatives to improve the teaching of literacy and thereby raise standards. In these programmes, the content and format of the literacy programme are prescribed and have been taken on by the vast majority of schools. Both are based on research into literacy and early test results show evidence of some success. In both the United Kingdom and Australia, the impact of these initiatives has gone beyond England and Victoria and they are being adopted in largely similar forms in other parts of these countries.

The NLS has aroused considerable interest worldwide with its ambitious aim to 'change for the better teaching approaches across the entire education service' (DfEE, 1997: para 27). Laura Huxford outlines how the NLS has gone about achieving this aim through an impressive array of training and support materials for teachers. Her enthusiasm and commitment are obvious and she claims formal and informal evidence of its success. Teachers report that the framework has helped them (as well as children) to increase their subject knowledge and the range of texts they use with children. Huxford also raises the worrying outcome that some teachers resort to reliance on published materials that use only extracts from books, resulting in children never getting to enjoy the whole novel or a text for the pleasure of the text.

My and Maureen Lewis's research which followed twenty teachers over the first two years of the NLS show the reality of large-scale reform in an individual context. We found that there had certainly been changes in the content and organisation of literacy teaching. Particularly, we found that the amount of whole class teaching and the range of literacy covered had increased. However, we also raise questions about the extent to which teachers are able to make fundamental changes to their teaching when their beliefs and understandings vary. The use of focused objectives in teaching is an aspect that most of the teachers in the study thought had changed how they went about literacy lessons. However, transcripts and observations of lessons show that not all teachers were able to implement this teaching as clearly as intended.

NCEETPRI's concern about teachers being like technicians or assembly line workers comes to mind here. In the first year of their study, Fisher and Lewis found that some teachers were worried that their teaching had become 'boring or mechanistic'. Others were concerned that the array of objectives meant that they were trying to cram too much in or were on a 'whistle stop tour'. However, after two years most teachers had begun to be able to adapt the objectives and the literacy hour to the needs of their particular classes.

These two chapters seem to point to the NLS having considerable success in raising test scores, particularly for reading, although, as the external evaluation team point out (Earl *et al.*, 2000), it is too soon to tell whether the trend of rising scores will continue. Indeed, 2001 national test results show no further increase in the number of 11-year-olds gaining level 4 in English. Similar positive trends are evidenced by the Early Years Literacy Program in Victoria, which shares many similarities with the NLS. It draws on a similar 'balanced' approach involving teaching children how to 'break the code, to develop the capacity to understand meaning from text, to use texts functionally, and to analyse texts critically'. It also adopts a similar system of pressure and support to ensure schools implement the programme. Bridie Raban and Gillian Essex describe what the literacy block entails and how this has been implemented. They report that Victorian teachers have responded mostly with enthusiasm and commitment and welcome the increased amount of time afforded to literacy teaching after a period where other curriculum areas had taken time away from this.

The main differences between the two approaches seem to be in the greater amount of time allocated to literacy in the Victorian programme and also the more overt recognition of the importance of speaking and listening in EYLP. Raban and Essex report a similar pattern of raised test scores for reading. Although, the teaching of writing occupies half of the two-hour literacy block, no results are given for improvement in writing. As Brooks (this volume) points out, writing is a neglected area in literacy research. Evidence from national tests in England show that the increases in scores for English reported by Huxford conceals the fact that scores for writing have been slower to change.

Alongside their enthusiasm, Raban and Essex warn of the dangers of the focus on targets and raising test scores. They argue that it is important that demands at both school and system level are manageable in order to 'ensure that the focus remains on teaching rather than measuring'. Huxford reflects this concern in her reference from the external evaluation report to 'assessment literacy' (Earl *et al.*, 2000). They argue that the public and teachers need to become more assessment literate to be able to understand the numerical data used to describe the impact of educational reform. They conclude that teachers need to 'become less susceptible to naive conclusions based on numbers and more likely to use sound data as a basis for improvement planning' (*ibid.*: 40).

Notwithstanding the successes claimed by Raban and Essex, and by Huxford, Luke and Carrington question responses to the need to raise literacy standards that seem to do little more than provide more literacy and more training. They argue that what can be described as a 'focused and delimited literacy programme' enables students to achieve baseline skills, but that such programmes can become disconnected and decontextualised from the rest of the curriculum, from children's lives and from the literacy demands of the twenty-first century. Their concerns that teachers in Harlow had become beguiled by simplistic answers which were more about management and reliance on pre-packaged materials reflect concerns raised in other chapters here. They argue that teachers and policy makers should be thinking more about 'a re-envisioning of the curriculum, of students' needs and life pathways and, indeed, of the kinds of literate dispositions that might effectively vie for position in the social fields of globalised capital' (p. 245). Like Hiebert, they call for a literacy curriculum that meets the different demands of young people today. They go beyond Hiebert's call for support for the 'acquisition of sophisticated interpretations' to a 'curriculum approach that focuses students' work with texts on the analysis of the flows of effects between this time–space locality and others'. They argue that literacy should be taught as a means of building cosmopolitan worldviews and identities (p. 247).

Raising standards of literacy raises all kinds of questions about how literacy is envisioned, how it is taught and how it is assessed. All of these questions are essentially interrelated. This section has examined specifically how teachers teach reading and writing and how research findings and policy can influence – indeed, dictate – what is taught and how it is taught. Those involved in the implementation of policy believe strongly in the efficacy of what they are doing. Initial results seem to support these beliefs. However, the message from this section seems to be a warning that we should not be satisfied with simple solutions – this includes both those teachers or schools who rely naively on prepackaged materials or programmes, and those policy makers who are prepared to implement programmes without any valid evidence that they will make a difference with their children in their schools. Teachers clearly need the knowledge, the support, the resources to teach effectively, but there also seems to be another dimension to teaching that cannot be scripted. Studies of school and teacher effectiveness are described by Willinsky (1990: 162) as a 'pedagogy of proficiency'. In fact, classrooms and teachers do not always operate proficiently – not because of any clear deficiency in themselves but because of the nature of the task itself. The more control we exert on the content and format of literacy teaching, the more danger there is that teachers will rely on simple solutions and lose the ability that those beginning teachers in excellent programmes described in the NCEETPRI report had to adapt to meet the needs of the individual children in individual schools.

Having said this, we must also be alert to another form of simple solution: that of blaming someone else. Luke and Carrington describe how Harlow teachers were inclined to blame the children, the parents and indeed themselves for their pupils' lack of achievement. Programmes such as the NLS demand high expectations. They do not accept excuses that children cannot achieve high standards and they have found success through this. Let us also have high expectations of teachers that, given the knowledge, the support and the resources, they can have the autonomy to exercise their professional skill in the choices they make.

References

Department for Education and Employment (DfEE) (1997) *The Implementation of the National Literacy Strategy*, London: DfEE.

Earl. L., Fullan, M., Leithwood, K. and Watson, N. (2000) *Watching and Learning: First Annual Report of OISE/UT Evaluation of the Implementation of the National Literacy and Numeracy Strategies*, Ontario Institute for Studies in Education, University of Toronto, January.

Willinsky, J. (1990) *The New Literacy: Redefining Reading and Writing in Schools*, London: Routledge.

Index